UNVEILING
THE END TIMES
IN OUR TIME

UNVEILING THE END TIMES IN OUR TIME

*The Triumph of
the Lamb in*
REVELATION

ADRIAN ROGERS

BROADMAN
&HOLMAN
PUBLISHERS

Nashville, Tennessee

0–8054–2691–4

Published by Broadman & Holman Publishers,
Nashville, Tennessee

Dewey Decimal Classification: 236.9
Subject Heading: BIBLE. N.T. REVELATION \ BIBLE
PROPHECIES \ ESCHATOLOGY

1 2 3 4 5 6 7 8 9 10   10 09 08 07 06 05 04

*D*edication

This book is dedicated with deep appreciation and gratitude to three wonderful friends and co-laborers—Mark Dougharty, Bob Sorrell, and Elmer Bailey. These men have served with me as associate pastors in my ministry. They are gifted administrators and personal friends. Many times they have "propped me up on my leaning side." I love you gentlemen.

Contents

Preface

A young seminary student asked his wise, old professor what he knew about the second coming of Jesus Christ. The professor replied, "Not as much as I used to." I can personally resonate with that.

In my younger years I had more certainty of some details of prophecy than I now have, but I have greater and stronger faith in the ultimate triumph of the Lamb than I have ever had.

The Book of Revelation is a great treasure. However, it can be a source of fanaticism and foolishness to the careless or carnal reader. The book was not given to engender fanaticism or foolishness but faith. The misuse and abuse of this wonderful book has caused many to shy away from it altogether. When they do that, they miss incredible encouragement and penetrating insight, not only into the future but for today. How sad that is. We will see that God has promised a very special blessing for those who read and heed this closing book of the Bible.

Having said all of that—I must say that one should read and study Revelation with an extra measure of humility. I am convinced pretribulation premillennialist. I will explain more about that later. However, many who hold that same view with me and come from that same basic approach will still disagree with me and with others at various points. In heaven we will have a Bible conference with the apostle John and let him teach us all.

I have endeavored to bring these studies from a devotional point of view. The chapters of this book are outlines so as to be adapted by the Bible teacher, preacher in ordinary everyday ministry. For those who are looking for a detailed and critical study, I recommend that they go elsewhere.

I am convinced that there are some things in the book of the Revelation that will not be known until they are unfolded. Some prophecies await fulfillment for understanding. The bottom line is this: Jesus is coming, and I am certain of that and very, very glad. I have resigned from the program committee, and have moved over to the welcoming committee. Even so, come Lord Jesus!

Acknowledgments

I want to give profound thanks to those who have helped to make this volume possible.

First of all, I want to thank my son Steve, who was an editorial assistant and co-laborer in this effort. Steve, you are the greatest. Thanks for your help.

Also, I want to thank my personal assistant Linda Glance, who has helped me through the years and has been a valuable aid in getting these materials done.

Also, my thanks go to Len Goss, John Landers, and all of the staff at Broadman & Holman for their guidance and patience with me in this process.

Next, I wish to acknowledge the saints of Bellevue Baptist Church who first heard these studies and encouraged their publication.

Last and certainly not least, I give thanks, praise and glory to Jesus Christ who is the hero of this book. He is coming again, and I can hardly wait.

The Future Is Here

◄o►

CHAPTER 1

◄o►

R evelation is a book of prophecy.

Only God can prophesy, and I am glad. I really don't want to know my day-to-day future in intimate detail. That would take all of the romance and adventure out of my life.

A part of the thrill of living is the principles of surprise and discovery. Who knows—or for that matter wants to know—what each day will bring before it happens? At the best, it would bring long periods of boredom.

Not only would boredom fill part of our lives, but stark terror would fill the other. The thrill would be gone, and dread would take its place. Would you want to go on a vacation with the certain knowledge in your heart that in six weeks on a Tuesday afternoon at 3:46 p.m. your grandchild would be killed crossing the street on his way home from school? What dread the knowledge of that accident would bring to your mind in the ensuing time.

"Remember the former things of old: for I am God, and there is none else; I am God, and there is none like me, Declaring the end from the beginning, and from ancient times the things that are not yet done, saying, My counsel shall stand, and I will do all my pleasure" (Isaiah 46:9–10 KJV).

Have you ever wondered why the psychics who peddle their gifts on cable television never win the lottery? And even the weatherman can only make an educated guess concerning the weather. I heard of a weatherman who moved away from his former location to another city because the weather didn't agree with him in the old place. A prophet of God is right 100 percent of the time.

This is not to say that we live an aimless life because we don't know tomorrow's details. Not at all. God's plan for us is not a roadmap but a relationship. He knows the future, and we know Him, and that's enough. It is our lack of knowledge of day-by-day detail that keeps us closer.

Foolish people spend time and money poring over horoscopes and consulting so-called psychics trying to see the dark unknown. How much better to walk through life holding the hand of One who knows the way and cares for us!

Having said that, there is a sense in which I do want to know future. I want to know that God has an ultimate plan for the universe and all that is in it. I want assurance that from heaven's viewpoint all is planned, under control, and on schedule. The Book of the Revelation tells me that the future is in God's hands, and the best is yet to come. Of that we can be certain!

While we have this assurance through the Book of the Revelation, there is someone who hates the books. His name is Satan. In fact, there are two books in the Bible that Satan especially hates—Genesis and Revelation, the first and last books of God's Word.

Why does Satan hate these two books? In the Book of Genesis, Satan's doom is prophesied. In the Book of Revelation, Satan's doom is realized. There is no devil in the first two chapters of God's Word or in the last two chapters of God's Word. For every child of God, these are books that tie the gospel message together.

In Genesis we see the creation of the heavens and the earth. In Revelation we see the creation of the new heavens and new earth. In Genesis we see the first Adam reigning on earth. In Revelation we see Jesus, the last Adam, reigning in glory. In Genesis we see an earthly bride brought to the first Adam. In Revelation we see a heavenly bride brought to the Lord Jesus Christ, the last Adam.

In Genesis we see the beginning of death and the curse. In Revelation the Savior brings us to a state where there is no more death and no more curse. In the Book of Genesis man is driven from God's face in sin. In the Book of Revelation we see God's face in glory. In Genesis, Satan appears for the first time. In Revelation he appears on earth for the last time. The Book of Revelation is the golden clasp that seals God's Word in holy, divine perfection.

Now, let's begin our study of Revelation with four simple truths that I want to lay on your heart.

The Central Person of Revelation

I find Jesus wherever I look in the Bible. He is the heart of the entire Bible. He is the Rose of Sharon. He is the Lily Fair. If you read the Bible and you don't see Jesus, you need to reread it. Indeed, Jesus is the hero of the Bible and especially in the Book of Revelation. Revelation 1:1–2 tells us that the central person of the book is Jesus, and the testimony of this book is Jesus: "The *revelation of Jesus Christ* that God gave Him to show His slaves what must quickly take place. He sent it and signified it through His angel to His slave John, who testified to God's word and to the testimony about Jesus Christ, in all he saw."

When the world begins to wind down, we will not be looking for something to happen; we will be looking for someone to come. And His name is Jesus. Sometimes people call this book "Revelations." It is not Revelations. It is Revelation, singular. It is the revelation of One—the spotless, glorified Lamb, Jesus Christ.

The English word *revelation* translates the Greek word *apokalupsis*. It is the word from which we get our English word *apocalypse*. It literally means "an unveiling." Have you ever seen the unveiling of a work of art? It is an important occasion where dignitaries are present; someone pulls a drawstring, and the artwork is publicly seen for the first time as the artist intended. That is exactly what this word means.

I saw a headline in my newspaper one day that caught my eye: "Elder Bushes Unveil Sculpture with Pride." The article said, "With parental pride, former President George Bush and First Lady Barbara Bush unveil [apocalypse] a sixteen-foot concrete sculpture of their first son, the nation's current leader." Just before former President Bush unveiled the statue, he said, "This means a lot to a very proud mother and father." Can you imagine the heartbeat of God the Father when His Son is unveiled in all His glory to the world?" Here is the unveiling of My dear Son who is not the president of the United States, but who is the King of kings and Lord of lords!"

The second coming of Jesus will be so different from His first coming when His glory was veiled. He came the first time to a crucifixion; He is coming again to a coronation. He came the first time in shame; He is coming again in splendor. He came the first time to a tree; He is coming again to a throne. He came the first time and stood before Pilate; He is coming again, and Pilate will stand before Him to be judged. He came the first time as a servant; He is coming again as a sovereign.

Today, Jesus is abused, misused, neglected, and scorned. He does not have His rightful place in society. After the tragedy of September 11, 2001, President George W. Bush called for a day of prayer at the National Cathedral in Washington, D.C. Thousands watched it on television. If you may recall, they sang Martin Luther's hymn (which may be my favorite hymn), "A Mighty Fortress Is Our God." What you may not remember is that they left out the following verse:

> Did we in our strength confide, our striving would be losing;
> Were not the right Man on our side,
>   the Man of God's own choosing:
> Dost ask who that may be? Christ Jesus, it is He;
> Lord Sabaoth, His Name, from age to age the same,
> And He must win the battle.

During this ceremony, Billy Graham preached about the cross of Jesus Christ, and yet National Public Radio omitted part of his message. When asked about this, NPR responded, "We were changing the tape." You be the judge. When Jesus returns, not one word will be omitted. We will behold His unveiled glory, not as He was, but as He is—the King of kings and Lord of lords.

The Clear Purpose of Revelation

Revelation 1:1–2 says, "The Revelation of Jesus Christ, which God gave unto him, *to show unto his servants things which must shortly come to pass;* and he sent and signified it by his angel unto his servant John: Who bare record of the word of God, and of the testimony of Jesus Christ, and of all things that he saw" (KJV).

Only God knows the future, and the clear purpose of Revelation was for His Son Jesus to show His servants the future. This word *servant* in verse 1 is the Greek word *doulos,* which means "bondslave"—those who willingly become the slaves of the Lord Jesus Christ. These are the ones who have understood what Paul talked about in 1 Corinthians 6:19–20: "Do you not know that your body is a sanctuary of the Holy Spirit who is in you, whom you have from God? You are not your own, for you were bought at a price; therefore glorify God in your body."

Are you a slave of Jesus Christ? Have you bowed your knee to Him? Have you crowned Him Lord of your life? If so, the Holy Spirit who resides within you will give you a rightful understanding of this book. If you are not a child of God, then you do not have the Holy Spirit to give you understanding of this book. The Bible is a closed book to those who have never bowed their knee to Jesus Christ.

The great historian, H. G. Wells, wrote a book entitled *The Fate of Man* in which he said, "Who, except cranks and lunatics, reads the Book of Revelation?" I must disagree. God has given us divine insight into the future and a message in the Book of Revelation that He is in control. Ephesians 1:11 says that God "works out everything in agreement with the decision of His will." God is not wringing His hands in heaven and wondering what He is going to do. The holy Trinity never meets in emergency session. God is in control, and His will most certainly will come to pass.

Don't get the idea that some people have—that the devil knows the future. The devil does not know the future. If the devil knew the future, he would know that he will never be exalted above the stars of God. Put it down big, plain, and straight—Satan is a knucklehead! He is brilliantly stupid and hideously beautiful. One of these days he is going to hell. He is not in hell yet, but he is destined for hell. And when he gets there, he will not reign in hell.

Where do people get the idea that Satan knows everything? I believe it comes from what I call "round-robin" theology. Many are teaching doctrines that are not from the Word of God. We need to get our theology from the Word of God, not from the hearsay of others.

Every morning about 11:30, the telephone operator in a small Nevada town would receive a call. The man on the other end would ask, "What time is it?" The telephone operator would give him the time. This happened day after day until one day, she got up enough nerve to ask the man, "Why do you call every morning at this time and ask what time it is?"

"Well," he said, "I'm the foreman at the local sawmill, and I blow the whistle at 12:00 noon for lunch break. I want to make certain that I blow the whistle at the exact time, so I call you." She laughed out loud and said, "Sir, I set my clock when you blow the whistle." Friend, we need to trust in the Word from above, the Word from Almighty God.

Why do we have the Book of Revelation? *To show us things to come.* The things that are spoken of in the Book of Revelation have not already been fulfilled in the first century, as some theologians teach. And Revelation is not an outline of history, beginning in the first century and continuing to the present day. The book is also not a spiritual allegory, comparing the battle of evil and good.

Revelation deals with the consummation of the age to come. When you're certain of your future, you can concentrate on your present.

The Comforting Promise of Revelation

There is a blessing in the Book of Revelation: "Blessed is the one who reads and blessed are those who hear the words of this prophecy and keep what is written in it, because the time is near!" (Revelation 1:3).

Read it. Revelation is a blessing book if you will read it and keep it. It brings a special blessing. Do you want to be blessed? Then read the Book of Revelation.

Hear it. It is one thing to read the Book of Revelation; it is another thing to hear it. Jesus said, "If any man have an ear, let him hear" (Rev. 13:9 KJV). Did you know that you can read this book and still not "hear" it? Do you remember your parents or teachers ever saying to you, "Do you hear me?" They were not asking if you heard them with your eardrums; they wanted to know if you understood what they were saying. Did it sink in?

Keep it. Many people are curious about the future. But God wants more than just a curious mind when you read the Book of Revelation. There are commands in this book for you to obey. For instance, one command is for you to bring souls to Jesus. Revelation 22:17 says, "Both the Spirit and the bride say, 'Come!' Anyone who hears should say, 'Come!' And the one who is thirsty should come. Whoever desires should take the living water as a gift."

You are to get your head out of the clouds of prophecy and put your feet on the pavement of soul winning. If you really believe that the end of all things may be close at hand, you will not be casual about sharing Christ with your unsaved family, friends, neighbors, or coworkers.

We are to read it, hear it, and keep it; then we will be blessed. The Bible is the only book I know of that is God-guaranteed to bless. You can study books on science and technology, but they will never bless you. Albert Einstein said, "All our lauded technological progress—our very civilization—is like the axe in the hand of the pathological criminal." Vance Havner, evangelist and preacher, said, "Civilization is like a chimpanzee with a blowtorch in a room full of dynamite." Scientists and programmers may have made the world a neighborhood, but they have not made it a *brotherhood*.

Books on sociology are not the answer. Sociologists are just repainting and redecorating the *Titanic*, trying to make the world a better place to go to hell from. Books on politics are not the answer either. We win wars and lose the peace. The circle seems never-ending.

Let's look at three blessings you will receive by studying the Book of Revelation.

It Will Unlock the Mystery of History

In Eastern religions, history just goes in a cycle. That is why adherents of these religions believe in reincarnation. Religious followers keep coming back until they get it right. But Bible history is not cyclical; it is linear. Christians are moving toward a goal.

What are you trying to do when you play checkers? Move your man into king's row and say, "Crown him." That is just what God is doing. He will move His Son, the Lord Jesus, into king's row and say, "Crown Him." Revelation 11:15 says, "The kingdom of the world has become the kingdom of our Lord and of His Messiah, and He will reign forever and ever!"

The world is in such a mess today because things are out of place. The King (Jesus) belongs on His throne. The bride (the church) belongs with the groom. The criminal (Satan) belongs in prison. One of these days, when the King is on the throne, the bride is with her groom, and the criminal is in prison, we will understand the way things are meant to be. Revelation unlocks the mystery of history.

It Will Bring Sense to Our Suffering

What do you say to a Christian brother or sister who is suffering such unbearable pain that even the strongest medicine cannot take it away? What do you say when you stand beside a husband at the graveside of his darling bride and he holds the hand of their only child? What do you say to a mother when her little baby is carried away by the angels to heaven and her arms are empty?

I will tell you one thing you can say—"This is not God's final plan." Revelation 21:4 says: "He [God] will wipe away every tear from their eyes. Death will exist no longer; grief, crying, and pain will exist no longer, because the previous things have passed away."

It Will Bring Stability in Chaotic Times

Have you listened to the news lately? The days in which we are living are absolutely incredible. And yet, the Lord Jesus Christ said, "'I am the Alpha and the Omega,' . . . 'the One who is, who was, and who is coming, the Almighty'" (Revelation 1:8). Hebrews 13:8 says, "Jesus Christ is the same yesterday, today, and forever." Someone gave me a little plaque that reads: "Adrian, trust Me. I have everything under control. Jesus." He is the Almighty.

It doesn't take a college degree to understand that knowing God brings stability in chaotic times. The simple can understand it. The learned can understand it. All it takes is the Almighty to give us that understanding.

One day a man who loved the Book of Revelation and had no theological training was criticized and ridiculed by much "wiser" theologians. They said, "You don't understand that book. It's an enigma—a puzzle. Nobody can understand it." He said, "I understand it." They said, "Oh yeah? Then, what does it mean?" He said, "It means we win!"

Jean François Gravelet, the Great Blondin, was a master tightrope walker. In fact, on June 30, 1859, he was the first man to cross the gorge of the Niagara River on a tightrope. Someone once asked him, "How do you manage to do that without falling?" He said, "Go and look on the other side in the direction in which I am walking. Do you see that silver star? I placed it there. I never take my eyes off of it. I put my eyes on that star, and I walk toward it. That's what gives me stability."

The second coming of Jesus Christ, our Bright and Morning Star, can give you stability if you look forward to His coming. The Book of Revelation is a blessing, because it is a stabilizing hope in these days in which we live.

The Certain Prophecy of Revelation

The time is at hand. Revelation 1:3 says, "Blessed is he that readeth, and they that hear the words of this prophecy, and keep those things which are written therein: *for the time is at hand*" (KJV). What does John mean that "the time is at hand"?

It does not mean that the time is immediate. It means that it is imminent. Jesus Christ can come at any moment. We are not waiting for some event to take place before Jesus can return; He can come whenever He chooses. We are always living on the edge of eternity. And we are to be living on "ready." Jesus may come this afternoon. Read what these men inspired by God wrote more than two thousand years ago:

> Now the end of all things is near; therefore, be clear-headed and disciplined for prayer (1 Peter 4:7).
>
> Now these things happened to them as examples, and they were written as a warning to us, on whom the ends of the ages have come (1 Corinthians 10:11).
>
> Let your graciousness be known to everyone. The Lord is near (Philippians 4:5).
>
> You also must be patient. Strengthen your hearts, because the Lord's coming is near (James 5:8).
>
> Children, it is the last hour. And as you have heard, "Antichrist is coming," even now many antichrists have come. We know from this that it is the last hour (1 John 2:18).

"Now wait a minute," you may be saying. "These men are saying that Jesus' return is at hand. Were they wrong?" No! They were right. We have been living in the last days for more than two thousand years. The apostle Paul expected Jesus Christ in his lifetime. He was not wrong to believe that way; he was right. Every Christian should be living in the light of the imminent coming of the Lord Jesus Christ.

As we study Revelation, we will see that there are some who say that Christians will go through the Great Tribulation before Jesus can come. But I disagree. Christians are not waiting for the seven vials of wrath or the mystery of Babylon to be unfolded—we are waiting for Jesus! At any moment He will give the shout and burst through the blue skies. And we need to be ready.

His imminent return does not mean that there are not signs of His coming. Revelation tells us that some horrific things will happen, such as a one-world government and an amalgamation of all the world's religions headed up by Satan's superman, the Antichrist. There will also be an incredible increase in knowledge. The world will be systematized as every person will be given a mark, a number, and they will not be able to buy or sell without that. We are seeing pieces of these prophecies happening today.

Richard Swenson was on James Dobson's program, *Focus on the Family*. He was discussing how history is coming to a climax. He spoke of a principle called exponentiality, which means that our civilization is moving faster and faster. Things are coming at us so quickly that our minds are numbed with the speed of these changes. Swenson believes they are coming so fast we are unable to reverse them. For example, we cannot undiscover things that have been invented, such as television, the Internet, genetic engineering, robotics—they are all quickly filing into the memory bank.

Swenson shared the following illustration. If you were to take a sheet of paper and fold it one time, then fold that fold another time and fold it like that forty times, how high do you think it would be? If you folded this sheet one hundred times, Swenson said that the folded paper would reach past the Milky Way to the far recesses of the universe!

Here is another illustration of the principle of exponentiality. The Pacific Ocean is sixty-four million square miles and has an average depth of fourteen thousand feet. If you put all of the continents on earth in the Pacific Ocean, you would still have room for another Asia.

Furthermore, Swenson explained that if you drained the Pacific Ocean, then began adding water, starting with just one drop, but doubling the amount each time, in just eighty times you would refill the entire Pacific Ocean. On the seventieth drop it would only be less than one tenth of one percent full. On the seventy-ninth drop it would be one-half full. On the eightieth drop it would be full. On the eighty-first drop you'd have two Pacific oceans. That's the principle of exponentiality, and that is what is happening in our society.

If we drew a line of technological advancement of knowledge from zero to 1975, that line would be relatively flat. But from 1975 to the present day, the line would go straight up. One scientist said that in the next one hundred years science will have progressed as much as it has in the last twenty thousand years.

We are living in a day that is quickly coming to a climax. Think how the world changed following the tragedies of September 11, 2001. One day we went to work, the sun was shining, and everything was normal. Then everything changed—just like that. The security of every man, woman, and child on American soil became threatened. Airports became fortified with countless security portals. Access to any large event became more strictly regulated.

Someone asked Ernest Hemingway, "How do you go into bankruptcy?" He said, "At first, slowly, and then quickly." That is the same way our world is escalating today. But you may ask, "Aren't all the advancements in medicine, communication, and technology for our good?" Well, it depends. We are living in an era when weapons of mass destruction can fall into the hands of a relatively few people. This is an unprecedented moment in the world's history.

The archangel Michael said in the Book of Daniel, "Many shall run to and fro, and knowledge shall be increased" (Daniel 12:4 KJV). The Bible also says, "In fact, all those who want to live a godly life in Christ Jesus will be persecuted. Evil people and imposters will become worse, deceiving and being deceived" (2 Timothy 3:12–13).

Someone has said, "When little men cast long shadows you know the sun is about to set." As the end draws near, we will witness more and more degradation and sin. We must ask ourselves, How long can the world as we know it exist before it implodes from evil? Am I being pessimistic? No, I am a glowing optimist because I know that the kingdoms of this world will be the kingdom of our Lord and His Christ (see Revelation 11:15). I also know that all of the things prophesied in God's Word will come to pass. How grateful I am that God gave us His Word to give us comfort, guidance, and assurance of His sovereign plan!

Years ago the filmmakers of Hollywood produced many Western movies. One of the singers in the background music of these Westerns was a talented cowboy singer/songwriter named Stuart Hamblin. Stuart even appeared in a few of the movies, but he was probably more notoriously known for his hard living.

One day God changed all that. Stuart learned about God's salvation through His Son Jesus Christ. A young actor named John Wayne noticed a change in Stuart's life and asked him, "Stuart, what is your secret?" His answer became a beloved hymn performed by thousands and translated into several languages. He said, "It is no secret what God can do." The chorus of this song says it all:

> It is no secret what God can do.
> What He's done for others, He'll do for you.
> With arms wide open, He'll pardon you.
> It is no secret what God can do.

Do you want to be ready when Christ returns? The only way to do that is to receive the One who came and died on a cruel cross for the forgiveness of your sin and the salvation of your soul. Indeed, it is no secret what God can do. What He's done for me, He'll do for you.

Making Numbers Count

◄o►

CHAPTER 2

◄o►

The Book of Revelation is full of symbols, signs, analogies, hyperboles, figures of speech, and cryptic numbers. Many people have asked: Do we interpret Revelation *literally* or *symbolically?* The answer is yes! We interpret it literally *and* symbolically.

For example, further in this book we will discuss the symbolism of Satan as a great red dragon. Satan is not literally a dragon. And he doesn't literally sweep a third of the stars from heaven with his tail. That is symbolism.

But don't make the mistake of saying that there is no devil simply because he is symbolized as a red dragon. There is a literal devil who is cruel, ferocious, powerful, and malevolent. Symbolism does not do away with literal interpretation. You have to understand symbolism in order to understand the Book of Revelation. Find out what the symbol stands for; then you can literally believe it.

Cracking the Code

Before we discuss the symbolism of numbers, we need to learn about the word *sign,* a variation of which is first used in Revelation 1:1: "The Revelation of Jesus Christ, which God gave unto him, to show unto his servants things which must shortly come to pass; and he sent and *signified* it by his angel unto his servant John" (KJV).

There is significance in the word *signified,* which in the Greek is *semainō.* The first four letters in the word are S-I-G-N, which in the

Greek is *sēma*. There are symbols and signs in Revelation, and if you don't understand them, you cannot crack the code. Think of some of the symbolism:

In the Book of Revelation, we learn that John speaks like a *zoologist*. He draws the symbolism of Jesus as a lamb and as a lion. Further into the Book of Revelation, we find beasts around the throne of God called *zōē* in the Greek. One has the face of a lion; one has the face of an ox or calf; one has the face of an eagle; and another the face of a man. This is highly symbolic. Another symbol is a wicked, grotesque beast that comes out of the sea, which is the Antichrist, and another beast that comes out of the land, which is a false prophet.

Sometimes John will speak like an *astronomer*. In the first chapter of Revelation, we learn that Jesus Christ holds seven stars in His right hand. We also learn in Revelation 12 that there is a great red dragon (Satan), which sweeps a third of the stars from heaven with its tail. Today we symbolically use the word *star* to talk about movie stars or rock stars.

Other times John will use the symbols of an *artist*, as he paints on the canvas of our minds with his colors. For example, John uses the color white as a symbol of purity over and over again. There are people in white robes, people riding white horses, the bride of Christ is dressed in a white wedding gown, the Lord Jesus Christ sits upon a great white throne. John also uses the color green, which is the symbol of life on his canvas. Green is around the throne of heaven. We will learn about horsemen who ride horses of different colors. The black horse speaks of famine, the gray horse speaks of death, and the red horse speaks of war. We will also learn about a woman dressed in purple, which is the color of richness and royalty.

John has also spoken like a *geographer*. For instance, we learn that there is a woman who sits upon seven mountains that most likely speak of the city of Rome. There is also a heaving, restless sea, which speaks of peoples, nations, and languages. And there is a crystal river flowing from the throne of God. This speaks of the beneficence and blessings of God.

Finally, we see that John speaks like a *mathematician*. For example, the key number in Revelation is seven. Revelation 1:4 says, "John: To the *seven* churches in the province of Asia." Revelation 1:20 says, "The secret of the *seven* stars you saw in My right hand, and of the *seven* gold lampstands, is this: the *seven* stars are the angels of the *seven* churches, and the *seven* lampstands are the *seven* churches." And there are many more sevens—seven seals, seven trumpets, seven vials of judgment, seven new things, and seven persons.

The Scientific Matter of Numbers

Sometimes people talk about the laws of nature. There are no laws of nature; there are only God's laws that nature obeys. God is a God of order and design, and because of that He has created the laws of numbers in the universe.

The laws of numbers help astronomers explain what happened in the heavenly realms in the past and predict what will happen in the future. The laws of numbers also help scientists, doctors, and chemists. Have you ever had to memorize the Periodic Table of Elements in chemistry class? Have you ever studied biology, anatomy, physiology, or zoology? There is a mathematical arrangement in everything. All flowers have a certain number of petals. Every cell in your body has a certain number of chromosomes.

All mathematical precision originated in the mind of God. God loves numbers. As a matter of fact, He has a book in the Bible called Numbers. The philosopher Aristotle said, "Numbers are the principle of all things." I'm not good at numbers, but I know that God is. I am more like the guy who said, "There are three kinds of people in the world: those who can count and those who can't."

The Symbolic Meaning of Numbers

Numbers were more than a scientific matter to the writers of the Bible; they had symbolic meaning. And I believe that the study of the symbolic meaning of numbers provides one of our greatest confirmations of the inspiration and thematic symphony of the Word of God.

The Number One

To begin our study of numbers, what better place to begin than with the number one. For obvious reasons, one is the number of unity. It is, therefore, the number that portrays the nature of God. There is one God; His name is Jehovah. He is the one and only. Here are a few Scriptures that illustrate the symbolic meaning of the number one:

> Hear, O Israel: The LORD our God is one LORD
> (Deuteronomy 6:4 KJV).

And the LORD shall be king over all the earth: in that day shall there be one LORD, and his name one (Zechariah 14:9 KJV).

There is one body, and one Spirit, even as ye are called in one hope of your calling; one Lord, one faith, one baptism, one God and Father of all, who is above all, and through all, and in you all (Ephesians 4:4–6 KJV).

The Number Two

The number two is the number of witness. The Old Testament taught that no one could bring an accusation without a witness to confirm (see Deuteronomy 19:15). Jesus said, "Even in your law it is written that the witness of two men is valid" (John 8:17).

We see the policy of a witness carried out in today's society. If you are in a business meeting and a motion needs approval, another person says, "I second the motion." In other words, the person is saying that he bears witness to that which is true.

The Bible itself is a testimony of witnesses. We have two testaments that bear witness of the Lord Jesus Christ—the Old Testament and the New Testament. Jesus Christ is the witness as the second person in the Trinity. There is God the Father, God the Son, and God the Holy Spirit. Revelation 1:5 says that Jesus is "the faithful witness." Revelation 11:3 also speaks of two witnesses with extraordinary power. In Mark 6:7 we read that Jesus sent out His disciples two-by-two to share the gospel. Two is the number of witness.

The Number Three

Three is the divine number of God in His tri-unity. God is not only one, but He is also three in one. Revelation 1:8 says, "I am Alpha and Omega, the beginning and the ending, saith the Lord, which is [one], and which was [two], and which is to come [three], the Almighty" (KJV, explanatory notes added by the author).

Matthew 28:19 says, "Go, therefore, and make disciples of all nations, baptizing them in the name of the Father and of the Son and of the Holy Spirit." When Isaiah saw the Lord upon the throne, he saw angels worshiping the Lord and crying out, "Holy, holy, holy, is the LORD of hosts" (Isaiah 6:3 KJV). Holy is the Father. Holy is the Son. Holy is the Spirit.

Three is the simplest compound unity. Three is also the simplest compound figure as seen in an equal-sided triangle. Man, who is made in the image of God, has a triune nature of body, soul, and spirit. First Thessalonians 5:23 says, "Now may the God of peace Himself sanctify you completely. And may your spirit, soul, and body be kept sound and blameless for the coming of our Lord Jesus Christ." Jesus also rose from the dead on the third day.

Everything that God made in this world is a reflection of His triune nature—that is, time, space, matter, and energy. Time is triune—past, present, and future. Space is triune—height, width, and depth. Matter is triune—energy, motion, and phenomena. Energy is made up of three different wavelengths or light types: ultraviolet radiation, visible radiation, and near-infrared radiation.

The Number Four

In the Book of Revelation, four is the earth number. It deals with creation. The earth has four distinct seasons—spring, summer, fall, and winter. There have only been four world empires in all of history. The Bible speaks of the four corners of the earth:

> And he shall set up an ensign for the nations, and shall assemble the outcasts of Israel, and gather together the dispersed of Judah from the four corners of the earth (Isaiah 11:12 KJV).

> Also, thou son of man, thus saith the Lord GOD unto the land of Israel; an end, the end is come upon the four corners of the land (Ezekiel 7:2 KJV).

> And after these things I saw four angels standing on the four corners of the earth, holding the four winds of the earth, that the wind should not blow on the earth, nor on the sea, nor on any tree (Revelation 7:1 KJV).

What does "the four corners" mean? The four points of a compass: north, south, east, and west. This is the very nature of things as they are.

The number four is also significant in Revelation 4:6–7, where the four beasts represent all of creation around the throne: "Also before the throne was something like a sea of glass, similar to crystal. In the middle and around the throne were four living creatures covered with eyes in front and in back. The first living creature was like a lion; the second living creature was like a calf; the third living creature had a face like a man; and the fourth living creature was like a flying eagle."

If you take four and multiply it by ten, you get forty. The Bible uses the number forty in testing and trial. It rained for forty days and forty nights when the flood came over all the earth (see Genesis 7:12). The Israelites were in the wilderness for forty years (see Exodus 16:35). When Moses climbed Mount Sinai, he was there for forty days and forty nights (see Exodus 24:18). When Jonah entered the city of Nineveh, he cried, "Yet forty days, and Nineveh shall be overthrown" (Jonah 3:4 KJV).

The greatest temptation ever recorded was in the Gospels with our Lord Jesus. "Then Jesus was led up by the Spirit into the wilderness to be tempted by the Devil. And after He had fasted 40 days and 40 nights, He was hungry" (Matthew 4:1–2).

Four is the earth number. Why? Because earth is the place where we have our testing and trials.

The Numbers Five and Ten

Five and ten speak of completeness. We have five fingers, five toes, and five senses (sight, smell, hearing, taste, touch). God gave us Ten Commandments, which is "the whole duty of man" (Ecclesiastes 12:13 KJV).

In the time when the Antichrist will take over, he will have full power. John writes in Revelation 13:1: "And I saw a beast coming up out of the sea. He had 10 horns and seven heads. On his horns were 10 diadems, and on his heads were blasphemous names." Satan will ensconce his man of sin (the Antichrist) upon the throne of this earth, and he will have ten horns with ten crowns.

The number ten speaks of fullness. When God judged Egypt, He sent ten plagues:

1. Blood (Exodus 7:14–24)
2. Frogs (Exodus 8:1–15)
3. Lice (Exodus 8:16–19)
4. Flies (Exodus 8:20–32)
5. Pestilence (Exodus 9:1–7)
6. Boils (Exodus 9:8–12)
7. Hail (Exodus 9:13–35)
8. Locusts (Exodus 10:1–20)
9. Darkness (Exodus 10:21–29)
10. Death of the firstborn (Exodus 11:1–10)

According to Revelation 2:10, the number ten has a special significance when the church will be persecuted fully: "Don't be afraid of what you are about to suffer. Look, the Devil is about to throw some of you into prison to test you, and you will have tribulation for 10 days. Be faithful until death, and I will give you the crown of life."

John is not referring literally to ten days of tribulation. Instead, he is explaining that God will allow a full and complete tribulation.

The Number Six

The number six is probably the most famous number when people discuss the symbolic usage of numbers in God's Word. Six is the number of man: "Here is wisdom: The one who has understanding must calculate the number of the beast, because it is the number of a man. His number is 666" (Revelation 13:18). The beast is the Antichrist who will come to rule the world.

Man also was created on the sixth day. By the beast identifying himself as 666, he is pretending to be God. Three is the number of God, and six is the number of man. The Antichrist will sit in the temple of God promoting himself as God.

The Number Seven

Seven is the number of perfection. Natural man will never be a seven, apart from grace, because every man, woman, and child is a sinner in need of salvation.

God has written the number seven through everything. For example, how many days are in a week? Seven. How many notes are in a musical scale? Seven. When Joshua came against Jericho, how many times did he march around the city? Seven (see Joshua 6:12–16). How many parables of the kingdom in Matthew 13? There are seven:

1. Parable of the Seed and the Sower (Matthew 13:1–23)
2. Parable of the Wheat and the Tares (Matthew 13:24–30, 36–43)
3. Parable of the Mustard Seed (Matthew 13:31–32)
4. Parable of the Leaven (Matthew 13:33)
5. Parable of the Buried Treasure (Matthew 13:44)
6. Parable of the Precious Pearl (Matthew 13:45–46)
7. Parable of the Fishing Net (Matthew 13:47–50)

There are multiples of seven that have significance, just like multiples of four and five. For example, Jesus sent out seventy to preach the gospel (see Luke 10:1). There are seventy weeks [of years] in the Book of Daniel that speak of God's dealing with all of time (see Daniel 9:2, 24). Psalm 90:10 tells us that the human life span is seventy years: "The days of our years are threescore years and ten; and if by reason of strength they be fourscore years, yet is their strength labour and sorrow; for it is soon cut off, and we fly away" (KJV). A score is twenty; threescore is sixty; ten added to threescore makes seventy.

Not only does God create symbols from the *multiples* of numbers, but also from the *division* of numbers. For example, half of seven is three and one-half. When you find seven cut in half in God's Word, you will find violence done to the seven (this speaks of danger, division, and foreboding).

When Elijah preached and prophesied, how long did he shut up heaven? Three and one-half years (see Luke 4:25; James 5:17). The Antichrist will make a covenant with Israel for seven years—then in the midst of those seven years, he will break that covenant.

> And he shall speak great words against the most High, and shall wear out the saints of the most High, and think to change times and laws: and they shall be given into his hand until a time [*one year*] and times [*two years*] and the dividing of time [*six months*] (Daniel 7:25 KJV, explanatory notes added by the author).
>
> And there was given unto him a mouth speaking great things and blasphemies; and power was given unto him to continue forty and two months [*three and one-half years*] (Revelation 13:5 KJV, explanatory note added by the author).

Revelation 4:5 says, "And out of the throne proceeded lightnings and thunderings and voices: and there were seven lamps of fire burning before the throne, which are the seven Spirits of God" (KJV). The lamps spoken of in this passage are what we now call the menorahs. The menorah is one of the oldest symbols of the Jewish faith. It is a seven-branched candelabrum that was used in the temple. The descendants of Aaron lit the menorah in the sanctuary every evening and cleaned it out every morning, replacing the wicks and putting fresh olive oil in the cups.

The menorah has a central shaft that speaks of one. There are three branches on either side. The one speaks of God, and the six branches speak of man. Jesus and His church are to be the light of the world (see Isaiah 42:6–7). Every church is to be a great lampstand with Christ at the center and every member giving light to the world, which is fed by the oil of the Holy Spirit.

The Number Eight

The number eight stands for new beginnings or the new birth. As we learned earlier, there are seven notes in a musical scale, but the eighth note begins the next octave. The eighth day is the first day of the next week. Christians worship on the eighth day.

Jewish children in the Old Testament were circumcised on the eighth day. In Judaism, circumcision is performed as a ritual on every male child when he is eight days old in a ceremony called *brit milah*, which signifies the covenant made between God and Abraham as recorded in Genesis 17:9–14.

Colossians 2:11 speaks of the spiritual significance of circumcision: "In Him you were also circumcised with a circumcision not done with hands, by putting off the body of flesh, in the circumcision of the Messiah." The new birth we receive in Jesus Christ is a symbolic New Testament picture of the Old Testament ritual of circumcision.

Here is another symbolic use of the number eight: it speaks of grace. How many people were saved out of the ark after the flood? Eight people—Noah and his wife, their sons Shem, Ham, Japheth, and their three wives (see Genesis 7:13). First Peter 3:20 speaks of the longsuffering of God when He "waited in the days of Noah while an ark was being prepared; in it, a few—that is, eight people—were saved through water."

When a leper was cleansed of leprosy and was given a fresh start, he was pronounced clean on the eighth day (see Leviticus 14:10–11). When did Jesus Christ rise from the dead? He rose from the dead on the third day, which, if seen on a calendar, was the eighth day of the week, or what we refer to as the Lord's Day today. The resurrection of Jesus on the eighth day is the reason Christians worship on Sunday.

John 20:26 tells us that Jesus appeared to His disciples on the eighth day: "After eight days His disciples were indoors again, and Thomas was with them. Even though the doors were locked, Jesus came and stood among them. He said, 'Peace to you!'"

Here is another interesting symbolic use of the number eight in God's Word. As you know, every number in the Latin alphabet is a letter. For example, a "V" stands for five. Each Greek letter also has numerical significance. Here is the name and numerical significance of the name of Jesus, which is *Iēsous* in Greek:

Iota	10
Eta	8
Sigma	200
Omicron	70
Upsilon	400
Sigma	200
TOTAL	888

The Number Twelve

Twelve is God's governmental number. If you multiply three (the divine number) by four (the earth number), you get twelve. It is God ruling and reigning over the earth. How many apostles were there in the New Testament? Twelve. How many patriarchs were there in the Old Testament? Twelve.

How many thrones do we see other than the one Jesus sits on in glory? Matthew 19:28 tells us, "Jesus said to them, 'I assure you: In the Messianic Age, when the Son of Man sits on His glorious throne, you who have followed Me will also sit on 12 thrones, judging the 12 tribes of Israel.'"

Revelation 4:4 tells us about the worship in heaven, "Around that throne were 24 thrones, and on the thrones sat 24 elders dressed in white clothes, with gold crowns on their heads." All the redeemed of God will be there along with the twenty-four elders who are the twelve patriarchs in the Old Testament and the twelve apostles in the New Testament.

As we have seen, numbers have a scientific significance because God is the God of all nature, and He has built numbers into everything. Numbers also have a symbolic meaning because of God's sovereign wisdom and plan.

The Spiritual Message of Numbers

There are many messages we can interpret from numbers in God's Word, but let me discuss the specific things that God has laid on my heart about this.

The number one tells me there is one God. He is Jehovah. First Corinthians 8:6 declares, "Yet for us there is one God, the Father, from whom are all things, and we for Him; and one Lord, Jesus Christ, through whom are all things, and we through Him." Ephesians 4:6 says, "One God and Father of all, who is above all and through all and in all."

Two tells me that Jesus is the faithful and true witness. God has given us His Word in the divine inspiration of the Old and New Testaments. And He is speaking to you today. John describes Jesus Christ: "Then I saw heaven opened, and there was a white horse! Its rider is called Faithful and True, and in righteousness He judges and makes war. His eyes were like a fiery flame, and on His head were many crowns. He had a name written that no one knows except Himself" (Revelation 19:11–12).

Three tells me that the God of the Bible is a triune God who is Father, Son, and Holy Spirit. Paul gives a blessing in the name of the triune God when he writes, "The grace of the Lord Jesus Christ, and the love of God, and the fellowship of the Holy Spirit be with all of you" (2 Corinthians 13:13). He is the Father omnipotent, omnipresent, and omniscient over all of creation (see 1 Corinthians 15:28). He is Jesus Christ, His Son who gave His life for the forgiveness of sin (see Matthew 3:16–17; John 3:16). He is the blessed Holy Spirit who has come for our edification and encouragement (John 14:16–17; 2 Corinthians 3:17).

Four tells me that the earth is my Father's world. Genesis 1:1 says, "In the beginning God created the heaven and the earth" (KJV). Psalm 24:1–2 says, "The earth is the LORD's, and the fulness thereof; the world, and they that dwell therein. For he hath founded it upon the seas, and established it upon the floods" (KJV). God wants there to be peace on earth. He has a plan where the kingdoms of this world will become the kingdoms of our Lord and His Christ. We are only passing through.

The number five tells me that whatever God begins, He will complete. "I am sure of this, that He who started a good work in you will carry it on to completion until the day of Christ Jesus" (Philippians 1:6). God is in complete control of this world. No matter what happens, we know that the Lamb is the Lion who will reign.

Six tells me that you and I are sinners. Romans 3:23 tells us, "For all have sinned and fall short of the glory of God." God demands absolute perfection, and we cannot provide it on our own. It is only through Christ that we are made perfect in His eyes. First Corinthians 1:30–31 says, "But from Him you are in Christ Jesus, who for us became wisdom from God, as well as righteousness, sanctification, and redemption, in order that, as it is written: 'The one who boasts must boast in the Lord.'"

Seven tells me that God has provided perfection and that perfection is in Jesus. The One who was promised has already come. With His perfect sacrifice upon the cross, He provided for me that perfection that He alone can give. Hebrews 5:8–9 says, "Though a Son, He learned obedience through what He suffered. After He was perfected, He became the source of eternal salvation to all who obey Him."

Eight tells me that every man, woman, and child can have a brand-new life through Jesus Christ. Romans 6:4 says, "Therefore we were buried with Him by baptism into death, in order that, just as Christ was raised from the dead by the glory of the Father, so we too may walk in a new way of life." Eight tells me that I can be born again. He is the God of new beginnings. James 1:17–18 says, "Every generous act and every perfect gift is from above, coming down from the Father of lights; with Him there is no variation or shadow cast by turning. By His own choice, He gave us a new birth by the message of truth so that we would be the first-fruits of His creatures." He is the God who makes all things new.

Twelve tells me that one of these days every child of God will enter heaven through one of the twelve gates, and we will see the Lord rule and reign in glory. First Thessalonians 4:16–17 says, "For the Lord Himself will descend from heaven with a shout, with the archangel's voice, and with the trumpet of God, and the dead in Christ will rise first. Then we who are still alive will be caught up together with them in the clouds to meet the Lord in the air; and so we will always be with the Lord."

Do you think these scientific, symbolic, and spiritual interpretations of numbers are simple happenstance? Or perhaps you think that it is all a grandiose interpretation of overzealous religious types who have nothing better to do. Nothing could be further from the truth!

The Bible is the inspired Word of God. Second Timothy 3:16–17 tells us, "All Scripture is inspired by God and is profitable for teaching, for rebuking, for correcting, for training in righteousness, so that the man of God may be complete, equipped for every good work." And the Book of Revelation is just one incredible portion of the entire revelation of God in His Word.

The Triumph of the Lamb

◄○►

CHAPTER 3

◄○►

Revelation 1:7 heralds the triumphant return of the Lamb—the Lord Jesus Christ—in this way: "'Look! He is coming with the clouds,' and 'every eye will see Him, including those who pierced Him. And all the families of the earth will mourn over Him.' This is certain. Amen." And then the Lord Jesus speaks: "'I am the Alpha and the Omega,' says the Lord God, 'the One who is, who was, and who is coming, the Almighty'" (Revelation 1:8). Are you ready for the triumphant return of Jesus Christ?

A tourist was exploring the sites of Lake Como in northern Italy and came to a beautiful castle called the Villa Asconiti. Feeling brave, he pushed open the gate and went inside. To his delight, everything was beautiful. Flowers were blooming in a rainbow of color. The shrubbery was luxuriously green and magnificently pruned to precision.

Over to the side, the man noticed a gardener on his hands and knees clipping nearly every blade of grass. The man asked, "May I look at the gardens?" The gardener replied, "You're welcome to come right in. I'm glad to have a guest."

The man began to tour the grounds and asked the gardener, "Is the owner here today?"

The gardener replied, "Oh, no. He's away."

"When was the last time you saw him?" he asked.

"Oh, about twelve years ago," said the gardener.

"Twelve years? This place has been empty for twelve years?" exclaimed the tourist.

"Yes," said the gardener.

The tourist asked, "Who tells you what to do?"

The gardener explained that the owner had an agent in Milan.

"Do you ever see him?" asked the tourist.

Still clipping, pruning, and trimming, the gardener answered, "Never. He just sends instructions."

The tourist couldn't believe his ears. "But you have everything so beautiful. It looks like you are expecting him tomorrow."

The gardener replied, "Today, sir. I expect him to come at any time—perhaps today."

Every child of God ought to be living that way—not as if Jesus Christ were returning far off in the future, but as if He were coming today. Someone has said, "We ought to be living as though Jesus died yesterday, rose this morning, and is coming back this afternoon." At any moment, Jesus Christ is coming again. He is coming again in the flesh!

Looking forward to that event makes me wish I had been alive to witness Jesus' humanity when He walked along the rocky shores of Galilee, the banks of the Jordan River, and the dusty hills of Judea. It would have been something to see Him call forth Lazarus out of the tomb. What a privilege it would have been to see the Lord Jesus Christ attend the wedding in Cana and turn sparkling water into wine!

I can only imagine what it must have felt like to be Peter when he saw Jesus walk on the Sea of Galilee in the midst of the storm—the spray of the water on His face, His robes flowing, and His hair blowing as He planted His feet on those waves! I think I would be a better preacher if I had seen Jesus die on the cross. May none of us ever forget Calvary! Can you imagine what it would have been like if we could have seen the Lord Jesus Christ tear the bars of death asunder and come out of the grave? Even though none of us were there when these things happened, every child of God has something magnificent to look forward to—His triumphant return!

Revelation 1:7 tells us that "every eye will see Him." You are going to see Him. Saved or lost, you will see Jesus Christ. Even those who crucified Him will see Him again. "All kindreds of the earth" (KJV) will see the Lord Jesus Christ. Every crusader against Jesus Christ and His followers will see Him. Every pornographer, abortionist, and drug dealer will see Jesus. Everyone—redeemed and unredeemed—will see Him! And we will see Him not as He *was,* but as He *is*—with the veil removed and in all of His glory! And it will be a day of shame and judgment for those who have slandered, abused, and ignored the omnipresent Savior and Lord Jesus Christ.

With all the thousands of Christian books in my library, I have learned that they were all written with just twenty-six letters. Look how Jesus is described in Revelation 1:8: "'I am the Alpha and the Omega,' says the Lord God, 'the One who is, who was, and who is coming, the Almighty.'" Alpha is the first letter and Omega is the last letter in the Greek alphabet. If Jesus were speaking to us today, He would say, "I am the A and the Z." That means He is the first, the last, and all the letters in between. When you've said "Jesus," you've said it all!

Jesus is the omniscient One. He is the accumulated wisdom of Almighty God. He is the beginning; He is the end. He is all the letters in between. He is God's first word, full word, and final word. He is the omniscient One.

Don't say, "I've got Jesus, and I'm moving on." We can learn *more of* Jesus, but Jesus is all we need. You should seek nothing more and settle for nothing less. He is the Alpha and the Omega. He is the omniscient One.

Jesus is also the omnipresent One. Revelation 1:8 tells us that He is "the beginning and the ending" (KJV). He is the bookends of all eternity. He is the One who brought everything into existence (see Genesis 1:1; John 1:1–3). He is the One who will bring everything into consummation (see Romans 11:36; 1 Peter 5:10–11). The One who spoke everything into existence is the One who will speak everything into consummation.

Not only is Jesus the omniscient One and the omnipresent One, but *He is also the omnipotent One.* He is called "the Almighty" in Revelation 1:8. This term is also used of God the Father in Revelation 1:4: "John to the seven churches which are in Asia: Grace be unto you, and peace, from *him which is, and which was, and which is to come;* and from the seven Spirits which are before his throne" (KJV). The same appellative of God is given in both verses. In verse 4 it is God as Father, and in verse 8 it is God as Jesus Christ.

What does "the Almighty" mean in Revelation 1:8? Jesus is Almighty God. We do not just tip the hat to Jesus; we bow the knee. If you miss His omnipotence as God, you miss the gospel message of Christianity. Jesus is not simply a Galilean carpenter, a great teacher, or a wise philosopher. He is the omniscient, omnipresent, omnipotent One.

The triumphant return of the Lamb will be nothing like the humble birth of the baby in Bethlehem. When Jesus came the first time, He came to take the sinner's place to die. When He comes the second time, He will execute judgment upon the unsaved sinner. Jesus came the first time as the Lamb led to slaughter; He is coming again as the Lion enthroned to judge.

He came the first time to save the lost; He is coming the second time to take vengeance on those who have not professed Him as Lord and who have not obeyed His Word. He came the first time as the supreme messenger of love; He is coming the second time as the righteous judge. When Jesus came the first time, He came in the greatest of humility; He will return in awesome power and glory. He came the first time wearing a robe of shame; He is coming back in a robe of glory. Jesus was born in a humble stall and died a horrible death, but He will have an honorable return.

Allow me to refresh your memory on what Jesus went through for the forgiveness of your sin. Before He went to the cross, His persecutors flung lashes upon His back, spit upon His face and pulled His beard, beat Him with clubs, and laid a crown of thorns on His head. His face was so marred that you couldn't tell whether it was the face of a man or of an animal. His flesh was hanging from His back like ribbons, and He was so weak from loss of blood and from shock that He could barely carry the cross. What a dramatic change there will be when He comes in power and glory!

The hour of our Lord's return may happen at any moment! And when it does, you may be caught unaware. Perhaps you are living high, wide, and handsome right now. Maybe you are oblivious to the sufferings of Jesus, the Savior of the world. You may even take the name of the Lord Jesus Christ in vain. This is your hour, but one of these days His hour will come.

Jesus told the women who were weeping alongside the Via Dolorosa that His hour had not come. He said, "Don't weep for me. Weep for yourselves. This is your hour. My hour has not yet come" (see Luke 23:28; John 2:4). First Timothy 6:15 says, "Which *in his times* he shall show, who is the blessed and only Potentate, the King of kings, and Lord of lords" (KJV). What a day that will be!

Revelation 1:9 says, "I, John, your brother and partner in the tribulation, kingdom, and perseverance in Jesus, was on the island called Patmos because of God's word and the testimony about Jesus." The isle of

Patmos is a small, rocky, barren island in the Aegean Sea off the coast of Greece. It is ten miles long and six miles wide.

When John was ninety years old, he was sent to Patmos, the island that was considered the Alcatraz or Devil's Island of its day, where prisoners were sent to spend the rest of their days imprisoned in exile.[3] Most likely, he spent his days working in the rock quarries with a guard at his heels and a whip on his back.

How does John see his exile? He said he was our brother in tribulation. Have you ever thought you would not suffer if you were a good Christian? Many people think their lives will be all cherries and no pits when they become Christians. But the truth is that Jesus did not come to get us *out* of trouble; He came to get *into* trouble with us!

John was not talking about the Great Tribulation when he referred to his tribulation in Revelation 1:9. He was referring to the tribulation to which Jesus refers in John 16:33: "These things I have spoken unto you, that in me ye might have peace. In the world ye shall have tribulation: but be of good cheer; I have overcome the world" (KJV).

There are no "ifs," "ands," or "buts" about it. If you live for the Lord Jesus Christ, you will experience tribulation. And the closer His second coming gets, the more intense the persecution will be. When this tribulation begins, the world will discover who really loves the Lord Jesus. The Sunday benchwarmers who sing, "We will be true to Him 'til death," and do not love Him a dime's worth out of every dollar will scatter.

In the first chapter of Revelation, we learn that John, in spite of tribulation, was worshiping the Lord when he heard a voice that sounded like a trumpet. He turned around to see who was speaking, and it was Jesus! John describes what he saw, and he wrote it down for us.

> I saw seven gold lampstands, and among the lampstands was One like the Son of Man, dressed in a long robe, and with a gold sash wrapped around His chest. His head and hair were white like wool—white as snow, His eyes like a fiery flame, His feet like fine bronze fired in a furnace, and His voice like the sound of cascading waters. In His right hand He had seven stars; from His mouth came a sharp two-edged sword; and His face was shining like the sun at midday. When I saw Him, I fell at His feet like a dead man. He laid His right hand on me, and said, "Don't be afraid! I am the First and the Last, and the

Living One. I was dead, but look—I am alive forever and ever, and I hold the keys of death and Hades" (Revelation 1:12–18).

Let's look at ten things that John saw about the Lord Jesus Christ—not the Lord who was but the Lord who is to come.

The Resurrected Christ with Undiminished Humanity

When John was given the revelation of Jesus Christ, it had been sixty years since he had seen Jesus. In fact, the last time he had seen Him was when He ascended into glory. John was thirty years old; now, he was ninety. But no amount of time could diminish the humanity of Jesus.

Jesus became a man and did not shed His flesh at His ascension. John 1:14 tells us, "The Word became flesh and took up residence among us. We observed His glory, the glory as the One and Only Son from the Father, full of grace and truth." First Timothy 3:16 says, "And most certainly, the mystery of godliness is great: He was manifested in the flesh, justified in the Spirit, seen by angels, preached among the Gentiles, believed on in the world, taken up in glory."

When Jesus decided to step out of glory and be born as a baby in Bethlehem, He did not temporarily become a man. Jesus is a man forever. In order to save us, He knew He had to share in our humanity, and He has decided to share in it for all eternity. In eternity He is the God-man.

When we get to heaven, we will see Jesus. We will see Him as a man with nail scars in His flesh. He will be and is forever like you and me, draped in the flesh of mankind. The first thing John saw was the resurrected Christ with undiminished humanity. Think of it. He forever like us, and we forever like Him!

The Reigning Christ with Unrivaled Majesty

Revelation 1:13 says, "And in the midst of the seven candlesticks one like unto the Son of man, clothed with a garment down to the foot, and girt about the paps with a golden girdle" (KJV). What is the golden girdle? It is the royal regalia of a king and judge. The Lamb has become the Lion. And you will meet Him as king and judge!

No one will be able to hide or escape meeting the Lord Jesus Christ. Jesus is inevitable. Jesus is unavoidable. Jesus is inescapable. "At the name of Jesus every knee should bow—of those who are in heaven and on earth and under the earth—and every tongue should confess that Jesus Christ is Lord, to the glory of God the Father" (Philippians 2:10–11).

And when every knee bows, they will be bowing to a judge. It is not God the Father who judges. It is God the Son who judges. Jesus said, "The Father, in fact, judges no one but has given all judgment to the Son" (John 5:22). The same One who wants to be your Savior will be your Judge. You have a date with deity. And if you do not meet Him as Savior, you will meet Him as Judge. One way or the other, you will meet the Lord Jesus.

Are you a Christian? Do you believe in the One who died to save you from God's wrath and eternal damnation? If not, you will be grouped with those who have cursed Him, ignored Him, begrudged Him, and brought shame to Him. There is no second chance at the day of judgment. Those who are not saved will have passed the divine deadline of repentance, and all that waits is a dreadful day of judgment.

The Righteous Christ with Unblemished Purity

In Revelation 1:14, we read that "His head and hair were white like wool—white as snow." All through Revelation, the color white is a symbol of purity and sinlessness. Even Isaiah referred to the color white as purity: "Come now, and let us reason together, saith the LORD: though your sins be as scarlet, they shall be as white as snow; though they be red like crimson, they shall be as wool" (Isaiah 1:18 KJV).

Jesus is sinless—absolutely pure, holy, and whiter than the virgin snow. Indeed, Jesus is not only the reigning Christ; He is the righteous Christ. He will not overlook the sin of any person. He will never let sin go unpunished. He doesn't wink away our sins by calling Himself a loving Judge. In a court of law, when a guilty man is acquitted, the judge is condemned.

If you think you can get to heaven without being born again, you do not know two things: You do not know how holy God is, and you do not know how sinful you are.

"But I live a good life and follow the teachings of Jesus," you may say. "Surely, God will see my good deeds and let me into heaven." No, He will not. You will go straight to hell, depending on your good deeds. Ephesians 2:8–9 says, "For by grace you are saved through faith, and this is not from yourselves; it is God's gift—not from works, so that no one can boast." Salvation does not come by doing good works or going to church to learn about the life of Christ. Salvation is given to us by believing in the death of Christ for payment of our sin. "Without the shedding of blood there is no forgiveness" of sin (Hebrews 9:22).

"But," you may protest, "I will plead for mercy on the judgment day, and God will hear me." No, He will not. If you want mercy, you may have it—but now, not later. If you want forgiveness, you may have it—but now, not later. Hebrews 9:27–28 says, "And just as it is appointed for people to die once—and after this, judgment—so also the Messiah, having been offered once to bear the sins of many, will appear a second time, not to bear sin, but to bring salvation to those who are waiting for Him." Jesus is the righteous Christ with unblemished purity.

The Revealing Christ with Unhindered Scrutiny

John tells us that Jesus' eyes were like "a fiery flame" (Revelation 1:14). What does that mean? He can see right through you. Jesus sees all; He knows all. Your entire life is laid bare before Him. He knows things that no one else knows about you. He knows every thought.

Jesus knows that answer you stole off your classmate's test paper. He knows that impure thing you did when you were away from your wife and children. He knows the evil sentiment you have toward your neighbor. He knows the Internet site you visit when no one is looking.

Hebrews 4:13 says, "No creature is hidden from Him, but all things are naked and exposed to the eyes of Him to whom we must give an account." All things are open. He knows what you are thinking this very second. And one of these days you will stand before Him.

Here's how an editor responded when criticized for printing bad news. He said, "If you don't want it printed, don't let it happen." I agree! Whether your sin ever becomes public knowledge, God knows all about it. God cannot be disputed. He cannot be discredited. He cannot be deceived. Not only does He see all men, but He also sees *through* all men. He sees the self-centered wickedness that causes the sinner to reject His offer of salvation. You will not be able to fool this Judge when you stand before Him.

The Relentless Christ with Untarnished Integrity

Revelation 1:15 says that the feet of Jesus are "like unto fine brass, as if they burned in a furnace" (KJV). Brass is an emblem of judgment and feet are a symbol of progress. All the vessels in the outer court in the tabernacle were made of brass.

Jesus is pictured as relentless as He goes forth to judge. All hell cannot stop Him. He is not the meek and mild Jesus walking the shore of Lake Galilee. John doesn't lay his head on Jesus' breast as he did when He walked on earth the first time (see John 13:23–25). Now John falls at His feet like a dead man (see Revelation 1:17). This is the Lord Jesus Christ in relentless judgment.

The Bible talks about this in Acts 17:30–31: "And the times of this ignorance God winked at; but now commandeth all men everywhere to repent: because he hath appointed a day, in the which he will judge the world in righteousness *by that man whom he hath ordained;* whereof he hath given assurance unto all men, in that he hath raised him from the dead" (KJV). Who is the ordained man? He is the One with the feet like brass. He is the One who says, "I am the First and the Last, and the Living One. I was dead, but look—I am alive forever and ever, and I hold the keys of death and Hades" (Revelation 1:17–18).

A lot of people do not have a clue about this coming Judge named Jesus. They are unsaved, and yet they get dressed in their finest on Easter and Christmas and come to church. Now, don't get me wrong—I am glad they come when they do.

But do you know what they are coming to celebrate? Their doom if they remain unsaved! That's right. But they don't know it. We just read in Acts 17:30–31 that God will judge the world, and that He has given assurance to every person that He raised Jesus from the dead. You cannot hold court if either the judge or the defendant is dead. The God who raised Jesus from the dead will raise all for the coming judgment. No one can crawl in the grave and pull the dirt over his face and hide from God. Jesus is going forth to judge with justice and integrity.

The Regal Christ with Unchallenged Authority

In Revelation 1:15, we read that Jesus' voice is like "cascading waters." When the unsaved person stands before Him on the judgment day, he will want to talk back, but he will be unable to be heard. He may as well go down to the ocean in the midst of a hurricane and argue with the wind, as to stand before the holy judgment bar of Christ and speak against the One who comes with unchallenged authority.

Psalm 29 is full of analogies about the voice of the Lord:

The voice of the LORD is upon the waters: the God of glory thundereth: the LORD is upon many waters. The voice of the LORD is powerful; the voice of the LORD is full of majesty. The voice of the LORD breaketh the cedars; yea, the LORD breaketh the cedars of Lebanon. . . . The voice of the LORD divideth the flames of fire. The voice of the LORD shaketh the wilderness; the LORD shaketh the wilderness of Kadesh. The voice of the LORD maketh the hinds to calve, and discovereth the forests: and in his temple doth every one speak of his glory (Psalm 29:3–5, 7–9 KJV).

The powerful voice of God will even be heard by the dead: "Do not be amazed at this, because a time is coming when all who are in the graves will hear His voice and come out—those who have done good things, to the resurrection of life, but those who have done wicked things, to the resurrection of judgment" (John 5:28–29). Jesus is the regal Christ with a voice like cascading waters and unchallenged authority.

The Ruling Christ with Unequaled Majesty

In his vision John saw that Jesus had seven stars in His right hand (see Revelation 1:16). Have you ever sung the song, "He's Got the Whole World in His Hands"? According to God's Word, Jesus has more than the world; He has the stars, the planets, and the entire universe in His hands! How can I say that when the Scripture only says "seven stars"? Because if you will remember from the previous chapter, seven is the perfect number. This means that He has it all in His hand.

What does it mean to you that Jesus has the universe in His hands? For me, it brings great comfort. Knowing that God's Son is the ruling Christ with unequaled majesty encourages me to trust Him with even the smallest things that are going on in my life. He rules in majesty.

The Revenging Christ with Unspoiled Victory

"From His mouth came a sharp two-edged sword" (Revelation 1:16). What do you think Jesus will do with a two-edged sword? Revelation 19:15 tells us the answer: "From His mouth came a sharp sword, so that with it He might strike the nations. He will shepherd them with an iron scepter. He will also trample the winepress of the fierce anger of God, the Almighty."

We must be careful here. Remember that the Book of Revelation is filled with symbolism. Hebrews 4:12 tells us that the Word of God is a two-edged sword. With His word, God spoke the world into existence. From His mouth came light and all of creation. He spoke and mountains were heaped, oceans were filled, flowers were planted, birds flew into the air, fish swam in the sea.

A friend and great Bible teacher, John Phillips, says that Jesus will speak two words at the battle of Armageddon, and it will all be over. Jesus will look across the plains and say, "Drop dead!" Jesus is the revenging Christ with unspoiled victory.

The Resplendent Christ with Undimmed Glory

The last part of Revelation 1:16 tells us that Jesus' "countenance was as the sun shineth in his strength" (KJV). His countenance was like the noonday sun. Can you imagine looking into the very face of the sun? The brightness would blind you.

The apostle Paul was blinded when he saw Jesus, but we will not be blinded because at that moment we will share in the nature of the Son. When we see Jesus in His undimmed glory, we will be like Him, so we will be able to look upon Him. First John 3:2 says, "Dear friends, we are God's children now, and what we will be has not yet been revealed. We know that when He appears, we will be like Him, because we will see Him as He is."

The very face of Jesus will be all the light we will need in heaven—no more sun, moon, and stars. Second Corinthians 4:6 promises, "For God, who said, 'Light shall shine out of darkness'—He has shone in our hearts to give the light of the knowledge of God's glory in the face of Jesus Christ." For now, we cannot see Him with our eyes, still we can have Him in our hearts. But think of the brightness of His glory when He comes!

The Reassuring Christ with Undiluted Deity

John said: "When I saw Him, I fell at His feet like a dead man. He laid His right hand on me, and said, "Don't be afraid! I am the First and the Last, and the Living One. I was dead, but look—I am alive forever and ever, and I hold the keys of death and Hades" (Revelation 1:17–18).

If you are saved, this vision of Christ will not cause you to fear. It will only cause you to feel immense reverence and awesome anticipation.

Only love for Christ will well up in your heart. And you will want to fall at His feet because Jesus is your King of kings and Lord of lords.

John MacArthur shares a story of a man who was boasting about his intimacy with Jesus. This man said, "Jesus and I are good friends. Sometimes when I'm shaving, He comes in the bathroom with me."

John said, "Literally?"

"Oh, yes! He comes in His body."

John asked, "What does He do?"

The man replied, "He just puts His arm around my shoulder while I'm shaving."

John said, "Is that right? What do you do then?"

"I just keep on shaving."

John responded, "Then that's not Jesus!"

When we see Jesus, we won't keep on shaving. We will fall at His feet! What a mighty God we serve! What a glorious Savior we have! Hallelujah! Behold, He cometh!

He Holds the Keys

◄o►

CHAPTER 4

◄o►

For most every book that is written, there is a title, target group, subject, author, publisher, and dedication. The Book of Revelation has its *title* right in the first verse: "The revelation of Jesus Christ." The revelation literally means "the unveiling or unfolding of Jesus Christ." What a great title!

The Book of Revelation not only has a title; it also has a *target group*. You'll seldom find a book written "To Whom It May Concern." An author usually has an audience in mind when he writes. Who is the target group? Again, we look to Revelation 1:1: "God gave unto him, to show unto his servants things which must shortly come to pass" (KJV). The target group is God's servants. In the Greek, this word *servants* is *doulō*, which means "bond slaves."

In Bible times, a bondslave was not always subjugated against his will; sometimes he willingly submitted himself to another person. The master was responsible for the protection and care of his slaves. The bondslave did not have to worry about what he was going to wear, what he was going to eat, where he had to be at a certain time, or what would happen to him if he needed medical attention. All these things were his master's responsibility. If he had a caring and thoughtful master, he had a good situation. The same is true today of being a bondslave of Christ.

There is another benefit of being a slave. Not only are you taken care of, but you are also "in the know." Who knew that Jesus turned the water into wine at the wedding in Cana? The master of ceremonies? No! It was the servants who knew (see John 2:9). Why did they know and he did not?

Because servants have a way of knowing what's going on that the others may not know.

Here is what Jesus said to the people who served Him: "I do not call you slaves anymore, because a slave doesn't know what his master is doing. I have called you friends, because I have made known to you everything I have heard from My Father" (John 15:15). Servants have a way of becoming friends and getting into the inner circle. Amos 3:7 says, "Surely the Lord GOD will do nothing, but he revealeth his secret unto his servants the prophets" (KJV). Servants know secrets!

Household servants know things that other people do not know. Isn't that true? That is true in the White House, in the governor's mansion, and the Rogers home! My wife Joyce and I have a dear woman who helps us once a week. She and my wife Joyce fellowship together a lot. One time she walked into the kitchen while I was giving Joyce a big kiss. The average person doesn't get to see that, but a household worker did! When you become a servant of the Lord Jesus you will experience intimacy with the Lord Jesus.

Revelation is a book written to Christ's servants. The only way you will understand this book or any book of the Bible is to submit yourself to Christ. I know this may sound like a contradiction, but there is no greater freedom than being His perfect slave. We are made absolutely free when we become slaves of Jesus Christ.

We have seen that the Book of Revelation has a title and a target group. Now let's look at the *subject* of the book in Revelation 1:1: "Things which must shortly come to pass" (KJV). Do you want to know what the Book of Revelation is about? That's it! It is about things that will happen in the future.

You may be saying, "I don't understand what the Bible means by 'things which must shortly come to pass.' How can that be? That was two thousand years ago!" To answer that, you need to understand the word *shortly*. It is the Greek word *tachei* from which we get a few English words, such as *tachometer*, a gadget that registers speed revolutions per time unit. The word *taxi* is another word derived from *tachei*. What does a taxi do? It gets you to the places where you want to be in a hurry. The word, therefore, means "quickly." It means the events described will come suddenly. The idea is not that these things will happen immediately but that they will burst upon the world rapidly when they come.

We must all understand that in the end times, history picks up speed. Have you noticed the acceleration of technology in the last fifty years? It is like drinking from a fire hose and looking into the end of a loaded cannon, all at the same time. If you pick up your Bible with one hand and a newspaper in the other, you can tell that we are living in the closing shadows of the end of an age. The child of God ought not to be ignorant about these pivotal times in which we are living.

The next thing a book has is an *author*. Revelation 1:4 reveals this: "John: To the seven churches." At about ninety years of age, John was exiled to the island of Patmos. He had a vision and was commissioned to write this book. As a matter of fact, God gave him the outline of the book. Where do most authors get the outline of their books? The publisher? No, not normally. But this is exactly the source from which the author got his outline.

The *publisher* is the Trinity Publishing Company. Read once again from Revelation 1:4–5: "*From* Him which is, and which was, and which is to come; and *from* the seven Spirits which are before his throne; and *from* Jesus Christ, who is the faithful witness, and the first begotten of the dead, and the prince of the kings of the earth. Unto him that loved us, and washed us from our sins in his own blood" (KJV).

John uses the word *from* three times in these verses to emphasize that this revelation is from God the Father, God the Son, and God the Holy Spirit. Normally, when the Trinity is mentioned, we say, "The Father, Son, and Holy Spirit." But here, the order is Father, Holy Spirit, and Son. Why is that? Revelation is particularly about the Lord Jesus Christ, and that is why He is mentioned last for emphasis.

This brings us to the *dedication* of the book. The last part of Revelation 1:5 and verse 6 tell us this dedication: "To Him who loves us and has set us free from our sins by His blood, and made us a kingdom, priests to His God and Father—to Him be the glory and dominion forever and ever. Amen." Most people who write books include a dedication at the beginning. I have dedicated books to my wife, parents, children, grandchildren, congregation, and editors. For the Book of Revelation, John makes the dedication to only one—the hero of the Word of God, the Lord Jesus Christ. Do you have a hero in your life?

Some years ago, a paddlewheel steamboat was going down the Mississippi River. Two men were watching it. One of them said, "Look, there's the captain. Do you see him?"

The other said, "Why are you so excited about the captain?"

"Well," he said, "I fell in the Mississippi River one time, and the captain jumped in and saved my life. Ever since then I just love to point him out."

That is the way I feel about Jesus. I love to say, "Look, there is Jesus!" Let's look at four things about the Lord Jesus Christ: His grace, glory, gentleness, and government.

The Grace of Our Risen Lord

Because of His grace, He has loved us, washed us, and made us kings and priests. Revelation 1:4–5 says, "John to the seven churches which are in Asia: Grace be unto you, and peace, from him which is, and which was, and which is to come; and from the seven Spirits which are before his throne; and from Jesus Christ, who is the faithful witness, and the first begotten of the dead, and the prince of the kings of the earth. Unto him that loved us, and washed us from our sins in his own blood. And hath made us kings and priests unto God and his Father; to him be glory and dominion for ever and ever. Amen" (KJV).

He Loves Us: "Unto Him That Loved Us"

When did Jesus start loving you? He never did—He has always loved you. He loved you before time began. He loved you before He swung this planet into space. You were in the heart and mind of God before the foundation of the world. Ephesians 1:4–6 says, "According as he hath chosen us in him before the foundation of the world, that we should be holy and without blame before him in love: having predestinated us unto the adoption of children by Jesus Christ to himself, according to the good pleasure of his will, to the praise of the glory of his grace, wherein he hath made us *accepted in the beloved*" (KJV).

You are accepted in the Beloved. And it's not because you did anything to deserve His love. This is why we spell love G-R-A-C-E. Jesus doesn't love you because you are valuable; you are valuable because He loves you. Why does He love you? Sheer grace. And nothing can separate you from that grace. Romans 8:38–39 says, "For I am persuaded that neither death nor life, nor angels nor rulers, nor things present, nor things to come, nor powers, nor height, nor depth, nor any other created thing will have the power to separate us from the love of God that is in Christ Jesus our Lord!"

Many people try to make themselves lovable apart from the grace of God. They get the idea that if they could just clean themselves up, maybe

God would love them. Revelation 1:4–5 tells us that He loves us—then He washes us. It doesn't say He washed us so He could love us.

When a dirty little child comes into the house, his mother doesn't wash the child so she can love him. The mother loves the child, so she washes him. God doesn't change us so He can love us; He loves us so He can change us. The love comes before the washing.

Philip P. Bliss said it so beautifully in his hymn, "Jesus Loves Even Me":

> *I am so glad that our Father in Heav'n*
> *Tells of His love in the Book He has giv'n;*
> *Wonderful things in the Bible I see,*
> *This is the dearest, that Jesus loves me.*

He Liberates Us: "Washed Us from Our Sins"

The second thing we learn about the grace of our risen Lord is that He cleanses us from our sin (see Revelation 1:5). The Greek word for "cleanses" is *lusanti*, which means "to loose." It has the idea of using keys to set someone free or the idea of removing pollution. It is a very significant word because it teaches us that Jesus is not only the One who not only loves us but is also the one who has loosed us. His blood has set us free! Only through the blood of Jesus are we set free from the eternal prison of sin and death.

John 8:36 says, "Therefore if the Son sets you free, you really will be free." Romans 6:5–7 also teaches this truth: "For if we have been joined with Him in the likeness of His death, we will certainly also be in the likeness of His resurrection. For we know that our old self was crucified with Him in order that sin's dominion over the body may be abolished, so that we may no longer be enslaved to sin, since a person who has died is freed from sin's claims."

Have you ever thought carefully about the blood of Jesus? There is no other blood like that. His blood is unique. His blood is sinless and uncontaminated. Some people think that Jesus' blood was not unique, because He was born from the womb of Mary. But not a drop of a mother's blood goes into the baby she carries. As a matter of fact, that baby may have one blood type, and the mother may have another blood type.

There was none of Mary's blood in the Lord Jesus. There was none of Joseph's blood in the Lord Jesus because God was His Father. Jesus had the holy blood of God running through His veins. God tells us in Acts 20:28

that He purchased the church with *His own blood*. And this precious blood is the only thing that cleanses us from sin.

Peter said, "For you know that you were redeemed from your empty way of life inherited from the fathers, not with perishable things, like silver or gold, but with the precious blood of Christ, like that of a lamb without defect or blemish" (1 Peter 1:18–19). God purchased the church with His own blood. How grateful I am for the cleansing blood of Jesus Christ.

I am so absentminded that I can lose a pen when I am writing with it. I will take the top off a felt-tip pen, start writing, then something will distract me, and I'll put the pen in my shirt pocket without the top on! Have you ever done that? Sadly, I seem to do this when I am wearing one of my nicest shirts. I hate for my wife Joyce to see it, so I will go into the bathroom to scrub and spray, and scrub some more. I hate to say it, but there is nothing that will take that spot out except a pair of scissors! That stain will not let go.

But how the stain of our sin will let go when it comes into contact with the precious blood of the Lord Jesus Christ! Do you want to be free and clean today? You can be! Revelation 1:5 promises that He can wash you in His blood. It was Robert Lowry who penned these words in the hymn "Nothing but the Blood":

What can wash away my sin?
Nothing but the blood of Jesus;
What can make me whole again?
Nothing but the blood of Jesus.

Oh! precious is the flow
That makes me white as snow;
No other fount I know,
Nothing but the blood of Jesus.

He Lifts Us: "Kings and Priests"

Revelation 1:6 says that Jesus "hath made us kings and priests unto God and his Father; to him be glory and dominion for ever and ever. Amen" (KJV). Have you ever seen a queen or king? Do you want to see one? Go look in the mirror and you will! Jesus has made us kings and priests unto God. Read Romans 8:15–17: "For you did not receive a spirit of slavery to fall back into fear, but you received the Spirit of adoption, by whom we cry out, 'Abba, Father!' The Spirit Himself testifies together with our spirit that we are God's children, and if children, also heirs—heirs of God and co-heirs with Christ—seeing that we suffer with Him so that we may also be glorified with Him."

Perhaps you have trouble relating to that description of yourself. But it is true—you are somebody if you are a child of God! People may not recognize you like they do a movie star when you walk down the street. Some may ignore or even snub you. But if you are redeemed, you are a royal blue blood. You are next of kin to the holy Trinity. Jesus is not ashamed to call you His brother. You are royalty in the family of God

More important than your royalty is your position in Christ. You are a priest. You don't need an intermediary; you can go directly to God. He is no farther away from you than your knees are from the floor. And if you cannot get your knees on the floor, He is no farther away from you than the breath in your lungs and the skin on your body. Praise God for the grace of our risen Lord.

The Glory of Our Risen Lord

"He Is Coming with the Clouds"

Revelation 1:7 says, "Look! He is coming with the clouds, and every eye will see Him, including those who pierced Him. And all the families of the earth will mourn over Him. This is certain. Amen." When John said that Jesus would be coming "with the clouds," he was not referring to cumulus or cirrus clouds. Instead, he was referring to the effulgence of God's glory in which Jesus will be robed—what we call the shekinah glory of God.

Jesus returned to heaven in the clouds of glory. And He is returning to earth in the clouds of glory: "After He had said this, He was taken up as they were watching, and a cloud received Him out of their sight. While He was going, they were gazing into heaven, and suddenly two men in white clothes stood by them. They said, 'Men of Galilee, why do you stand looking up into heaven? This Jesus, who has been taken from you into heaven, will come in the same way that you have seen Him going into heaven'" (Acts 1:9–11).

The shekinah glory led the children of Israel through the wilderness and draped itself over the mercy seat in the ark of the covenant. Exodus 13:21–22 says, "And the LORD went before them by day in a pillar of a cloud, to lead them the way; and by night in a pillar of fire, to give them light; to go by day and night: he took not away the pillar of the cloud by day, nor the pillar of fire by night, from before the people" (KJV).

Once, when Aaron spoke to the Israelites, the glory of the Lord appeared in a cloud: "And it came to pass, as Aaron spake unto the whole congregation of the children of Israel, that they looked toward the wilderness, and, behold, the glory of the LORD appeared in the cloud" (Exodus 16: 10 KJV). Jesus is coming in clouds of glory!

"Every Eye Will See Him, Including Those Who Pierced Him"

What does it mean that every eye will see Jesus? Just that—every eye. Even those who nailed Him to the cross and pierced His side will see Him. The last time the Roman soldiers saw Jesus, He was hanging in shame and stripped naked before their eyes. (He didn't have a beautiful loincloth as later painted by artists—that wasn't the practice of Roman crucifixions.) When they see Him again, He will be resplendent in the royal robes, not just of a king but of the King of kings!

The last time they saw Jesus, His hair was matted with crimson blood. When they see Him again, His hair will be whiter than snow (see Revelation 1:14, which speaks of His holiness and purity). When they saw Him the last time, His eyes were filled with tears of liquid love. When He comes again in glory, His eyes will be like flames of fire that will see right through them (see Revelation 1:14).

The last time they saw Him, they drove a huge spike through His feet. When He comes again, His feet will be like molten brass going forth in judgment (see Revelation 1:15). The last time they saw Him, they put a spear in His side and out came water and blood. When He comes again in glory, He will have a sharp two-edged sword in His mouth with which He will strike the nations (see Revelation 19:15). When they crucified Him, His face was so battered and bruised that people couldn't tell whether they were seeing the face of a man or of an animal. When He comes again in glory, His face will be brighter than the glory of the noonday sun.

Humanity has a date with Jesus. And that humanity will wail when they see Him. "For it is written: As I live, says the Lord, every knee will bow to Me, and every tongue will give praise to God" (Romans 14:11). Jesus Christ is coming again.

The Gentleness of Our Risen Lord

John said, "When I saw Him, I fell at His feet like a dead man" (Revelation 1:17). John was so overwhelmed by the glory, majesty, magnitude, and awesomeness of the glorified, risen, and ascended Lord that he collapsed. If that was all that verse said, we might be afraid to approach Him today. We might even say, "Whoever You are, I'm afraid of You. I don't know whether I want to have fellowship with You, because You are so awesome. All I can do is shrink back from You."

But the verse doesn't end there. Notice Christ's response: "He laid His right hand on me, and said, 'Don't be afraid! I am the First and the Last, and the Living One. I was dead, but look—I am alive forever and ever'" (Revelation 1:17–18). Jesus touched John and said, "Get up, son—don't be afraid." Even though Christ's outward appearance had changed since John first saw Him, His heart had remained the same.

Notice which hand Jesus laid upon John: the right hand. This was the hand that symbolized power and authority. Jesus touched the eyes of the blind, and the blind saw. He touched the ears of the deaf, and the deaf heard. He touched the limbs of the crippled, and the crippled walked.

If Jesus were standing before you right now, how would you feel? Perhaps some people reading this would feel untouchable. Let me assure you that you are not untouchable! Jesus loves you. It matters not *who* you are or *how bad* your condition. That's the reason I love the Bill Gaither song, "He Touched Me":

Shackled by a heavy burden,
'Neath a load of guilt and shame,
Then the hand of Jesus touched me,
And now I am no longer the same.

Since I met this blessed Savior,
Since He cleansed and made me whole,
I will never cease to praise Him;
I'll shout it while eternity rolls.

He touched me, O He touched me,
And O the joy that floods my soul!
Something happened, and now I know,
He touched me and made me whole.

The Government of Our Risen Lord

Isaiah 9:6 says, "For unto us a child is born, unto us a son is given: *and the government shall be upon his shoulder: and his name shall be called*

Wonderful, Counsellor, The mighty God, The everlasting Father, The Prince of Peace" (KJV). Before Jesus was born, Isaiah prophesied that the government would be upon His shoulders. And John explained what that meant.

Revelation 1:18 says that Jesus has "the keys of death and Hades." What does that mean? Keys stand for authority, possession, and privilege. The one who has the keys is the one who is in control. What do keys do? They open things. They lock and unlock things. They liberate and imprison.

What are these keys to? Death and Hades—the two great enemies of man. The New Testament Greek word is *hadēs;* the Old Testament Hebrew word is *sheol.* Both words literally mean "the realm of the unseen, spirit world." When a person dies, death gets the body but hades gets the spirit and the soul.

Jesus is the keeper of the keys to both death and hades. Have you wondered how Jesus got those keys? By His resurrection. When Jesus died, that cruel monarch of terrorists called death clapped his bony hands and laughed his hoarse laugh and said, "We've got Him." But they didn't have Him. Jesus was taken captive by death that He might set the captive free.

Jesus rose from the dead in complete confidence and calmness. As a matter of fact, John 20:7 tells us something about how He neatly disposed of His grave clothes: "The wrapping that had been on His head was not lying with the linen cloths but folded up in a separate place by itself." How did you leave your bedroom this morning? Jesus did not leave His garments on the floor in a resurrection rush! He was in complete control of this situation.

We have so much to be thankful for because our risen, living, victorious Savior owns the keys of death and hell! I can imagine that death shrieked in terror when Jesus rose from the grave. Jesus put His heel on the throat of death, pulled death from his throne, threw him to the dungeon floor, and pulled out the sting of death and in its place ignited a star of hope in the tomb.

In Chicago years ago, there was a nightclub called "The Gates of Hell." Down the street was Calvary Church. As the story goes, a young man wanted to go to that nightclub one day, so he asked a stranger on the street, "Can you tell me how to get to The Gates of Hell?" The stranger replied, "Go right past Calvary and you'll come to the Gates of Hell."

With brokenness in my heart, I want to close this chapter by saying that if you refuse the Lord Jesus Christ and walk past Calvary, you will end up at the very gates of hell. Do you want to be free? Jesus has the key. He loves you and wants to save you from that fiery death. Will you repent and believe upon Him today? "Because we know that Christ, having been raised from the dead, no longer dies. Death no longer rules over Him. For in that He died, He died to sin once for all; but in that He lives, He lives to God. So, you too consider yourselves dead to sin, but alive to God in Christ Jesus" (Romans 6:9–11).

The Golden Key to the Book of Revelation

◄○►

CHAPTER 5

◄○►

Many people find the Book of Revelation hard to understand. They often ask me, "Is there a key to help me understand the Book of Revelation?" Yes! God's purpose is not to conceal but to reveal. This golden key is hanging right on the front door in verse 19 of the first chapter of Revelation. It is John's commission to write the Book of Revelation: "Write the things which thou hast seen, and the things which are, and the things which shall be hereafter" (KJV).

There are three things the Lord Jesus commissioned John to write. First, there were the "things which thou hast seen" (KJV). What did John see? A vision of the Lord Jesus Christ. And so Jesus said, "Write it." This makes up chapter 1 of Revelation. I refer to this as *past things.*

Second, Jesus told him to write about "the things which are" (KJV). This refers to the "present things"—the church age, which is recorded in chapters 2 and 3. In that time, there were seven churches in Asia Minor: Ephesus, Smyrna, Pergamos, Thyatira, Sardis, Philadelphia, and Laodicea (see Revelation 1:11). While these were actual churches, they are representative of all churches throughout all ages. Today, we are living in the time of the "things which are"—the *present things.*

The third thing John wrote about was the "things which shall be hereafter" (KJV). The remaining chapters of Revelation make up this division, which I call the *prophetic things.* These things tell us that Jesus has come. Jesus is here today with us. And He is coming again.

The Book of Revelation is primarily a prophetic book, and only God knows the future. Prophecy is in the realm of God, not the devil. Satan is not omniscient, and his wisdom is perverted. He doesn't understand these things. Can you imagine that he would have the audacity to think he could overthrow God? No! Only God knows the future.

There are a lot of soothsayers, prophets, and prognosticators who try to tell the future. Indeed, there are enough gullible people in America today to keep 10,000 astrologers working full time and another 175,000 working part time!

Did you know you can pay someone to project "healing thoughts" to you? They claim to reveal hidden secrets about your love life, career, finances, health, future, and personal problems. All it will cost you is $3.99 a minute.

If you have any astrological charts or horoscope books, put them in the garbage! "They can't be that bad," you may say. "I just amuse myself with them." Well, you may amuse yourself into hell. Get rid of them. Only God knows the future and those to whom God reveals the future. Isaiah 46:9–10 says, "Remember the former things of old: for I am God, and there is none else; I am God, and there is none like me, declaring the end from the beginning, and from ancient times the things that are not yet done, saying, My counsel shall stand, and I will do all my pleasure" (KJV).

One of the ways we know that the Bible is the inspired, inerrant, infallible Word of God is fulfilled prophecy. What God has already fulfilled is assurance that He will fulfill the rest.

Mathematics professor and author Peter Stoner wrote a book entitled *Science Speaks*. In it he explained the probability of Old Testament prophecies regarding Jesus Christ. There are scores of prophecies in God's Word about Jesus Christ, but Stoner took only eight (Psalm 22:16; Isaiah 53:7; Micah 5:2; Zechariah 9:9; 11:12–13; 13:6; Malachi 3:1). Mathematically, he reasoned that the chance of one man fulfilling all eight prophecies was astronomical. To illustrate the magnitude of this probability, he said:

> If you mark one of ten tickets, and place all the tickets in a
> hat, and thoroughly stir them, and then ask a blindfolded man to
> draw one, his chance of getting the right ticket is one in ten.
> Suppose that we take millions of silver dollars and lay them on
> the face of Texas. They'll cover all of the state two feet deep.
> Now mark one of these silver dollars and stir the whole mass

thoroughly, all over the state. Blindfold a man and tell him that he can travel as far as he wishes, but he must pick up one silver dollar and say that this is the right one. What chance would he have of getting the right one? Just the same chance that the prophets would've had of writing these eight prophecies and having them all come true in any one man, from their day to the present time, providing they wrote them in their own wisdom.[4]

The Book of Revelation gives us a look at history and the future from the eyes of God. Not a guess, but a sure word from Almighty God. Now let's look at a panoramic view of prophecy as told in the Book of Revelation.

The Rapture of the Church and the Departure of the Saints

John says, "After this I looked, and, behold, a door was opened in heaven: and the first voice which I heard was as it were of a trumpet talking with me; which said, Come up hither, and I will show thee *things which must be hereafter*" (Revelation 4:1 KJV).

From this verse to the end of the book, the word *church* is no longer mentioned because the church will be raptured by that point. According to Revelation, the rapture occurs before the tribulation, and the church then stands before the judgment seat of Christ and attends the marriage of the Lamb. Those who remain on earth will enter the Great Tribulation.

The rapture will constitute the end of the church age. This will be explained in detail in chapter 7 of this book. A voice like a trumpet will shout, "Come up hither!" And at that moment I will be gone from this earth. Every child of God will be gone. Are you saved? Then you are a part of the church, which is raptured into glory. First Thessalonians 4:16–18 says, "For the Lord Himself will descend from heaven with a shout, with the archangel's voice, and with the trumpet of God, and the dead in Christ will rise first. Then we who are still alive will be caught up together with them in the clouds to meet the Lord in the air; and so we will always be with the Lord. Therefore encourage one another with these words."

When will the rapture take place? At any moment. We're not looking for some sign. We're not looking for some prophecy to be fulfilled before Jesus can come for His church. It could happen before you finish reading this sentence!

Luke 12:40 says, "You also be ready, because the Son of Man is coming at an hour that you do not expect." Jesus is coming like a thief in the night. First Thessalonians 5:2 says, "For you yourselves know very well that the Day of the Lord will come just like a thief in the night." A burglar never writes a note and says, "I'll be at your house tonight." Do you believe that? If you really believe it, then be ready.

The Rise of the Beast and the Deceptions of the Devil

The church is the salt of the earth. So when the church is raptured, that which preserves, heals, and restrains is removed. This ungodly world system resents salty saints. It wishes we were gone. And one day we will be. That is when corruption will really set in and the beast, with devilish deception, will come on the scene. Revelation 13:1–3 says:

> And I stood upon the sand of the sea [*in Bible prophecy the sea represents peoples and nations*], and saw a beast rise up out of the sea [*out of these nations in turmoil*], having seven heads and ten horns [*seven is the perfect number; ten is the complete number; heads speak of wisdom; ten horns speak of power*], and upon his horns ten crowns [*this speaks of dominion*], and upon his heads the name of blasphemy [*this speaks of his character; he blasphemes God.*]. And the beast which I saw was like unto a leopard, and his feet were as the feet of a bear, and his mouth as the mouth of a lion: and the dragon [*Satan*] gave him his power, and his seat [*his throne*], and great authority. And I saw one of his heads as it were wounded to death; and his deadly wound was healed: and all the world wondered after the beast (KJV, explanatory notes added by the author).

Satan's superman, who is also called the Antichrist (the counterfeit Christ) is coming into this world. And when he does, he will turn the world into a vast concentration camp with all of the inmates numbered. No one will be able to buy or sell unless they have the validating mark given by this man, who is the beast. John Phillips has described the beast in this way:

> He will be a most attractive person—a veritable savior to a world careening like an express train without throttle, wide open, out of control, and without a man at the helm. No doubt his personal charm will be great, his intellectual genius

immense, his wealth and influence proverbial, his authority overpowering, his passions and hatreds extraordinary, his organizing skill unsurpassed, his techniques superb. Men will follow him to death. Women will swoon at his feet and children will say his name as savior of the world and the hope of mankind. Yet for all of that, he will be totally and thoroughly bad. He is the man of sin.

The Great Tribulation and the Devastation of the Earth

Jesus was once the sacrificial lamb, but He will not always be that way. The Lamb becomes the Lion. John said,

> Then I saw Him open the sixth seal. A violent earthquake occurred; the sun turned black like sackcloth made of goat hair; the entire moon became like blood; the stars of heaven fell to the earth as a fig tree drops its unripe figs when shaken by a high wind; the sky separated like a scroll being rolled up; and every mountain and island was moved from its place. Then the kings of the earth, the nobles, the military commanders, the rich, the powerful, and every slave and free person hid in the caves and among the rocks of the mountains. And they said to the mountains and to the rocks, "Fall on us and hide us from the face of the One seated on the throne and from the wrath of the Lamb, because the great day of Their wrath has come! And who is able to stand?" (Revelation 6:12–17).

During the tribulation, not only will the beast deceive the nations, but God will also pour out His fury upon the world. It will be so terrible that people will desire to die and will not be able to do so. Death will flee from them.

In this panorama of prophecy, first there will be the rapture, second will come the rise of the beast, and third will be the Great Tribulation, which will last for seven years. There has never been a time like this. Hell will have a holiday.

Calamities across the world will occur—hail, fire, a burning mountain cast into the sea, a bitter star named Wormwood that poisons the waters, boils, cosmic darkness, locusts (which are really demon spirits), horsemen who ride forth to bring pestilence, and the worship of the Antichrist. The vials of God's wrath will be poured out. The sea and rivers will turn to blood. There will be great heat and great darkness. The Euphrates River will dry up. It will be horrible beyond description.

Armageddon and the Defeat of the Beast and His Armies

The tribulation will end with a battle called Armageddon. At this battle, the beast and his armies will be defeated. John said,

> And I saw three unclean spirits like frogs come out of the mouth of the dragon [*Satan*], and out of the mouth of the beast [*the Antichrist*], and out of the mouth of the false prophet [*the sinister minister of propaganda who counterfeits the Holy Spirit*]. For they are the spirits of devils, working miracles, which go forth unto the kings of the earth and of the whole world, to gather them to the battle of that great day of God Almighty. Behold, I come as a thief. Blessed is he that watcheth, and keepeth his garments, lest he walk naked, and they see his shame. And he gathered them together into a place called in the Hebrew tongue Armageddon (Revelation 16:13–16 KJV, explanatory notes added by the author).

The vast plain you can see from atop Mount Megiddo in Israel is where the battle of Armageddon will take place. John said,

> Then I saw heaven opened, and there was a white horse! Its rider is called Faithful and True, and in righteousness He judges and makes war. His eyes were like a fiery flame, and on His head were many crowns. He had a name written that no one knows except Himself. He wore a robe stained with blood, and His name is called the Word of God. The armies that were in heaven followed Him on white horses, wearing pure white linen. From His mouth came a sharp sword, so that with it He might strike the nations. He will shepherd them with an iron scepter. He will also trample the winepress of the fierce anger of God, the Almighty. And on His robe and on His thigh He has a name written: KING OF KINGS, AND LORD OF LORDS (Revelation 19:11–16).

What a day this will be! The Antichrist will come and rally the demon spirits to draw the world leaders to fight against the Jews and Jerusalem. Then Jesus will come in power and great glory to judge Babylon the Great. At this time, He will be coming not *for* His saints (they will have already been raptured). But instead, Jesus will be coming *with* His saints to defeat the beast and his armies. And according to Revelation 19:15, He will be fighting the battle with one weapon—the sword in His mouth. And what is this sword?

Let me answer that by giving you a New Testament picture of how that sword was used in the Garden of Gethesemane.

When Jesus had finished praying in the Garden of Gethsemane, Judas walked up to Him to identify Him to the Roman guards. Satan had entered Judas, so he is a New Testament picture of the Antichrist. The word *anti* means "against" or "instead of." Judas is even called the son of perdition like the Antichrist.

Nowhere else in the Bible does it say that Satan entered another person. People say, "I've been wrestling with the devil all day." The smallest demons can deal with us, but Judas was truly filled with the devil.

When Jesus saw them, He asked, "Who are you looking for?" And they answered, "We're looking for Jesus of Nazareth. Are you Jesus?" Jesus said, "I AM." At that moment, they fell down like dead men (see John 18:4–6). One word from His mouth, and they dropped.

What a demonstration of His mighty power! How will this battle be fought? By the sword that goes out of the mouth of the Lord Jesus Christ.

The Millennial Reign of Peace and the Dominion of Jesus

Revelation 20:1–6 says:

> Then I saw an angel coming down from heaven with the key to the abyss and a great chain in his hand. He seized the dragon, that ancient serpent who is the Devil and Satan, and bound him for 1,000 years. He threw him into the abyss, closed it, and put a seal on it so that he would no longer deceive the nations until the 1,000 years were completed. After that, he must be released for a short time. Then I saw thrones, and people seated on them who were given authority to judge. I also saw the souls of those who had been beheaded because of their testimony about Jesus and because of God's word, who had not worshiped the beast or his image, and who had not accepted the mark on their foreheads or their hands. They came to life and reigned with the Messiah for 1,000 years. The rest of the dead did not come to life until the 1,000 years were completed. This is the first resurrection. Blessed and holy is the

one who shares in the first resurrection! The second death has no power over these, but they will be priests of God and the Messiah, and they will reign with Him for 1,000 years.

These thousand years will be signified by the reign of Christ, when the lamb and the lion will lie down together and the lamb won't be inside the lion. It will be a millennium of peace. And Satan will get the longest prison sentence in history (and I hope it is with hard labor).

The prophet Habakkuk describes this time: "For the earth shall be filled with the knowledge of the glory of the LORD, as the waters cover the sea" (Habakkuk 2:14 KJV). And Isaiah adds, "And he [Jesus] shall judge among the nations, and shall rebuke many people: and they shall beat their swords into plowshares, and their spears into pruninghooks: nation shall not lift up sword against nation, neither shall they learn war any more" (Isaiah 2:4 KJV).

This is the reason my wife and I pray every Friday for the peace of Jerusalem. There will be ultimate peace in the Middle East only when Jesus comes to rule and to reign. How we need to pray for the second coming of the Lord Jesus Christ! Can you imagine what the millennial reign of Jesus Christ will be like? No war, no disease, and worldwide peace!

The Final Judgment and the Doom of the Lost

Revelation 20:11–15 says:

Then I saw a great white throne and One seated on it. Earth and heaven fled from His presence, and no place was found for them. I also saw the dead, the great and the small, standing before the throne, and books were opened. Another book was opened, which is the book of life, and the dead were judged according to their works by what was written in the books. Then the sea gave up its dead, and Death and Hades gave up their dead; all were judged according to their works. Death and Hades were thrown into the lake of fire. This is the second death, the lake of fire. And anyone not found written in the book of life was thrown into the lake of fire.

How does the millennial reign of Jesus Christ end? With the final judgment of every unsaved man, woman, boy, and girl standing before the great white throne of Jesus Christ. John 5:22–23 says, "The Father, in fact, judges no one but has given all judgment to the Son, so that all people will honor the Son just as they honor the Father. Anyone who does not honor the Son does not honor the Father who sent Him."

Why does God delay the final judgment until this time? Because the waves of sin have not yet hit the shores of eternity. When you drop a pebble in a lake, concentric circles radiate outward to the shoreline. Allow me to illustrate this principle.

Consider the people who are trafficing in pornography. They corrupt one person with their pornography, who then divorces his wife, who rapes someone, who defiles someone else. And on and on and on it goes. But one day these pornographers will die. Even after death, their influence will go on and on, just like the ripple in a lake. But one day that ripple will hit the shoreline.

At that time, God will place the period on the last sentence in the final paragraph upon the final page in the book of history, and mankind will experience cumulative judgment. The unsaved dead will be judged and cast into the lake of fire.

The Final State and the Destiny of Mankind

Revelation 21:6–8 says, "And He said to me, 'It is done! I am the Alpha and the Omega, the Beginning and the End. I will give to the thirsty from the spring of living water as a gift. The victor will inherit these things, and I will be his God, and he will be My son. But the cowards, unbelievers, vile, murderers, sexually immoral, sorcerers, idolaters, and all liars—their share will be in the lake that burns with fire and sulfur, which is the second death.'"

When God created you with a soul, body, and mind, He made you in His image. You could no more cease to exist than God Himself could cease to exist. For all time, your soul will exist somewhere—either in heaven or hell. You have a life to live, a death to die, a judgment to face, and an eternity to endure either in heaven or in hell. And you will not miss hell and go to heaven unless you are twice born.

When the moon and stars fall, the sun is darkened, the mountains crumble, the sky is split, and Jesus comes with His blood-washed armies of heaven, where will your soul be? Revelation 22:17 says, "Both the Spirit and the bride say, 'Come!' Anyone who hears should say, 'Come!' And the one who is thirsty should come. Whoever desires should take the living water as a gift."

How to Keep Your Spiritual Fire Burning

-◄O►-

CHAPTER 6

-◄O►-

In this chapter, I want to address a great problem among Christians. I call this "Ho-hum Christianity," and it consists of yawning in the face of God. There is no fire, zeal, or enthusiasm for the things of God. And the resulting tragedy is a half-hearted church in a hell-bent world.

You will recall in the previous chapter that there are three major divisions of Revelation. The first division is basically a vision of the glorified Christ.

The next grand division deals with the church age and comprises the time between the ascension of Jesus and the rapture of the church. The church age seems to be symbolically described by these seven churches located in John's time in Asia Minor. "Write on a scroll what you see and send it to the seven churches: *Ephesus, Smyrna, Pergamum, Thyatira, Sardis, Philadelphia,* and *Laodicea*" (Revelation 1:11). While these seven churches were actual, they speak of all churches of all time.

Each message to these churches applies to us today. First, they speak to us *prophetically* of the church age, beginning with Ephesus (a church whose love was waning and growing cold), and extending to Laodicea (a church that was lukewarm). Second, they speak to us *practically*. There is not a problem that today's churches will face that is not addressed in these comments to these seven churches.

Third, they speak to us *powerfully*. Revelation 3:22 says, "Anyone who has an ear should listen to what the Spirit says to the churches." Fourth, they speak to us *presently*. This is not just what God *has said;* it is what God *is saying*. And finally, they speak to us *personally*. This is not what God is saying *in general;* it is what God is saying *to us*. The church is made up of people just like you, so open your ears, your mind, and your heart to this message on how to keep your spiritual fire burning.

The Curse of Lukewarm Christianity

To address every one of the messages to these seven churches, I would need to write a separate book! Instead, I will address only one of these churches:

> And unto the angel of the church of the Laodiceans write; These things saith the Amen, the faithful and true witness, the beginning of the creation of God; I know thy works, that thou art neither cold nor hot: I would thou wert cold or hot. So then because thou art lukewarm, and neither cold nor hot, I will spue thee out of my mouth. Because thou sayest, I am rich, and increased with goods, and have need of nothing; and know-est not that thou art wretched, and miserable, and poor, and blind, and naked: I counsel thee to buy of me gold tried in the fire, that thou mayest be rich; and white raiment, that thou mayest be clothed, and that the shame of thy nakedness do not appear; and anoint thine eyes with eyesalve, that thou mayest see. As many as I love, I rebuke and chasten: be zealous there-fore, and repent. Behold, I stand at the door, and knock: if any man hear my voice, and open the door, I will come in to him, and will sup with him, and he with me. To him that over-cometh will I grant to sit with me in my throne, even as I also overcame, and am set down with my Father in his throne. He that hath an ear, let him hear what the Spirit saith unto the churches (Revelation 3:14–22 KJV).

What does the phrase "These things saith the Amen" mean? The word *amen* means "it is so" or "let it be." It means He is the factual Christ. He doesn't just say Amen; He *is* the Amen. Whatever He says, you can bank on it. He will not lie, and He will tell you exactly what you need to hear.

The Lord Jesus Christ is the *factual One*. He is the faithful and the true witness. And not only that, He is the *faithful One*. He is the beginning of the creation of God. He is also the *forceful One*. He created everything and is the sovereign Lord of the church.

As we saw in Revelation chapter 1, the Lord Jesus Christ is standing in the midst of seven golden candlesticks fed by oil. These candlesticks are an illustration of the church, which is the light of the world. "For where two or three are gathered together in My name, I am there among them" (Matthew 18:20). He is in our midst today with a message for you. "He that hath an ear, let him hear" (Revelation 3:22 KJV).

Revelation 3:16 contains a strong warning: "So then because thou art lukewarm, and neither cold nor hot, I will spue thee out of my mouth" (KJV). The Greek word translated "spue" is the word from which we get our English word *emetic*—an agent that induces vomiting. God is saying that there is a sin so vile that it nauseates Him. What is that sin? Lukewarmness. Lukewarmness is just a little too cold to be hot and just a little too hot to be cold. Too cold to boil, too hot to freeze. It's the sin that is probably the most prevalent in the church today.

To whom is our Lord speaking? Not to those who hate Christ; these are already cold and awaiting judgment. Nor is He speaking to those who are on fire for Him—the zealots who have a burning, glowing passion to grow closer to God and give Him glory. Instead, God is speaking to those in between—the self-satisfied, half-hearted Christians. I don't want to hurt your feelings, but I have been pastoring long enough to know that most people who attend church fall into that category. And that breaks my heart.

How do you know if you are lukewarm? Following are six areas in your life that you can examine.

Sanctification

A little girl prayed, "Lord, make me good, not *too* good, just good enough not to get a spanking." That's how many Christians feel about personal holiness. They consider holiness old-fashioned. Jesus knew about this kind of indifference when He said, "Isaiah prophesied correctly about you hypocrites, as it is written: This people honors Me with their lips, but their heart is far from Me" (Mark 7:6).

Do you have a desire to be personally holy before God—to honor Him with your life? You sing gloriously on Sunday mornings in church, but is there a daily burning passion in your heart for holiness? I am not talking about sinless perfection. But is your goal, each and every day, to live a holy life before God?

Our churches are filled with people who live on the edge of personal holiness. For instance, they will not tell out-and-out lies, but they will tell little white lies. They see someone they don't like and say, "It's good to see you." They tell a friend, "I'll pray for you" and never pray for him. They may not steal, but they don't pay their debts. They don't commit adultery, but they laugh at filthy jokes and entertain themselves with lasciviousness on television.

Service

Where are the Bible study teachers who are so burdened for their classes that they weep in prayer over each member? Where are the Christians who are reaching out in love to their unsaved neighbors? Where are the church members who are inviting unsaved people whom they meet in the grocery store or the gym to church? How many preachers do you know who preach with a fiery urgency and tears of conviction?

I remember when I took a seminary course on preaching. My professor said, "Preaching is very much like making any other kind of speech. You don't need to have a preacher tone. You don't need to have preacher mannerisms. It's just like making any other kind of speech."

There was an older man in that class named Famous McElheney, who had been pastoring for a long time. Brother McElheney lifted his hand and said, "Professor, I hear what you're saying, but when I get up to preach, something gets a hold of me."

Somebody described the average preacher as a mild-mannered man standing in front of a mild-mannered people exhorting everybody to be more mild-mannered. Would to God that there were more preachers like Famous McElheney who would preach not only with exactitude and eloquence, but also with a burning fire in their hearts!

Singing

The most important thing about a song is not that it is in perfect pitch and every word is memorized. The most important thing about a song is that it is sung *in the Spirit*. No person should be singing in a choir who is not Spirit-filled. No one should lead music who is not Spirit-filled.

The requirement for singing is this: "And don't get drunk with wine, which leads to reckless actions, but be filled with the Spirit: speaking to one another in psalms, hymns, and spiritual songs, singing and making music to the Lord in your heart" (Ephesians 5:18–19).

We should sing with gladness. We should sing with urgency. We should sing with feeling. We should sing with tears. Our singing should not only bless people; it should exhort and warn people.

Scriptures

Do you truly love the Word of God? Not just when you are sitting in church or in a Bible study, but when you are alone, do you hunger for His Word? So many Christians believe the Bible *in general* but don't believe it *with specificity*. I would venture to say that the average Christian has never read the entire Bible or could name the books of the Bible. Did you know that the entire Bible can be read through in ten months at the pace of only four chapters a day?

Do you believe everything you read in the newspaper? What about the Bible? Now I am going to ask you the hardest question of all: How much time do you spend reading the Bible compared to the time you spend surfing the Internet for news, or reading the newspaper, or watching your favorite television news magazine? If you are like most Christians, you are spending more time with something you do not believe than with something you say you do believe. We are lukewarm about the Scriptures. We do not love the Word of God as we should.

Supplication

So many people in churches around the world are lukewarm about prayer. Would you agree with this statement? *The average Christian doesn't spend ten minutes a day interceding on behalf of others.* When was the last time you missed a meal to pray? When was the last time you missed sleep to pray? When was the last time you fasted and prayed for a day?

The devil looks at the modern lukewarm church today and laughingly says, "You can have your big buildings, your fancy sound systems, your Bible classes, your multilevel organization, and your comforts. You can have it all, as long as you leave out earnest, heartfelt, consistent prayer that goes before Almighty God and will not take no for an answer." Sadly, the good that our churches wish to accomplish often becomes the substitute for the best. We need to learn how to pray. The Bible says, "The intense prayer of the righteous is very powerful" (James 5:16).

Sacrifice

How many Christians do you know who sacrifice their lives daily for the glory of God and the saving of souls? I am not talking about those you know who have given their lives overseas in foreign missions; rather, those who should be concerned about their next-door neighbor.

You don't have to go overseas to sacrifice your life for the Lord Jesus Christ. Sacrifice is laying down your life daily for God's use. First John 3:16 says, "This is how we have come to know love: He laid down His life for us. We should also lay down our lives for our brothers."

Some people will not allow themselves to be embarrassed by bringing a Bible to work and putting it on their desks. Some are ashamed of the Lord Jesus Christ and will not even bow their heads to give thanks for their meal in a public place.

What about you? Do you give a little, but not so much that your life is inconvenienced? Most of our giving has not changed our lifestyle. In 1874 Frances Havergal wrote this pledge:

> *Take my voice, and let me sing always, only, for my King.*
> *Take my lips, and let them be filled with messages from Thee.*
> *Take my silver and my gold; not a mite would I withhold.*
> *Take my intellect, and use every power as Thou shalt choose.*

What do we do instead? We use our voices in compromising testimonies, we pass on opportunities to tell others about Christ, we hold on to our silver and gold with all our might, and we use our intellect and power for our own glory. We pray without fasting, we give without sacrifice, we witness without tears. Is it any wonder that we sow without reaping?

Soul Winning

Do you have a passion for your next-door neighbor, who is doomed to hell without Jesus? Maybe you don't believe in hell. Maybe you don't believe the Great Commission was addressed to you. Maybe you don't believe that it is your solemn responsibility and glorious privilege to share the gospel of our Lord and Savior Jesus Christ. But Paul said, "Therefore, whether you eat or drink, or whatever you do, do everything for God's glory. Give no offense to the Jews or the Greeks or the church of God, just as I also try to please all people in all things, not seeking my own profit, but the profit of many, that they may be saved. Be imitators of me, as I also am of Christ" (1 Corinthians 10:31–11:1).

Why does our Lord say, "I wish that you were cold or hot" (Revelation 3:15)? He had rather have you against Him than pretending to love Him with a lukewarm heart. Lukewarm Christians have done more to harm the cause of Jesus Christ than all the prostitutes, bartenders, pornographers, and drug pushers combined.

Lukewarm Christians are the alibi of sinners; they double-cross Christ. Jesus had rather have you on the wrong side of the fence than sitting *on* the fence. I am convinced that if only one-tenth of those who name the name of Christ were on fire for the Lord Jesus Christ, we would see a mighty revival sweep across our land. But we cannot reach the goal for stumbling over our own players.

G. Campbell Morgan, one of the greatest Bible expositors who ever lived, said, "Lukewarmness is the worst form of blasphemy." Now that is a mouthful. Lukewarm Christians say, "Jesus, I believe in you, but you just don't excite me. I believe in you, but I don't intend to serve you with fire and fervor." What an insult to yawn in the face of Almighty God!

Why is lukewarmness so harmful? Because it sets us up for other sins. The lukewarm Christian is a sitting duck for the devil. Let me illustrate. A husband and wife are happily married, but the wife begins to feel less and less passionate. She starts to read love stories and begins to daydream about another life outside her home and marriage. One day at the health club, she meets a man who seems to personify all the men she has read about in her novels. And before she knows it, her lukewarm heart has led her down the pathway of unfaithfulness.

How do you remain faithful to your husband and not run off with another man? How do you remain faithful to your wife and not run off with another woman? Stay in love. A person who is deeply in love will not go off with someone else.

The Cause of Lukewarmness

The indifference of the Laodiceans was caused by their ignorance. They did not even know what their need was, which was to see their need. Revelation 3:17 sums up the cause of their lukewarmness in two phrases—"thou sayest" and "knowest not": "Because *thou sayest*, I am rich, and increased with goods, and have need of nothing; and *knowest not* that thou art wretched, and miserable, and poor, and blind, and naked" (KJV).

The lukewarm Christian is generally the last one to know that he is lukewarm. There are none so blind as those who refuse to see. There are none so deaf as those who have ears but will not hear. That's the reason John says, "Anyone who has an ear, should listen to what the Spirit says to the churches" (Revelation 3:22).

The Laodiceans were self-satisfied. Notice what John says in Revelation 3:18: "I advise you to buy from Me gold refined in the fire so that you may be rich, and white clothes so that you may be dressed and your shameful nakedness not be exposed, and ointment to spread on your eyes so that you may see."

Laodicea was famous for three things: its famous wool, its wealth in gold, and for its medical center for the treatment of blindness. So, God is making a play here on words. He says, "In spite of your wool and your wealth and your medicine, you need a holy fire."

How did their self-satisfaction and complacency begin? People cool down by degrees. To show this, let's look at the degrees of separation from Ephesus, which was the first church exhorted in Revelation, and move to Laodicea, the last church.

When God addressed the church at Ephesus, He spoke about their programs, their power, and their purity (see Revelation 2:1–3). As you read, you may say to yourself, "My, what a wonderful church!" And yet God said one thing to the church at Ephesus: "Nevertheless I have somewhat against thee, because thou hast left thy first love" (Revelation 2:4 KJV).

The Ephesians were not exhorted because they did not love the Lord. They had simply left their *first* love. If you are married, perhaps you remember your honeymoon. Somebody has jokingly said that the honeymoon is that period of time between "I do" and "You'd better." The honeymoon ought never to end.

If you don't love your spouse more today than you did when you married, you love him or her less. How sad it is when people leave their first love. First love is enthusiastic. First love is reckless. First love doesn't count the cost. First love says, "I love you with all my heart, all my soul." We must keep that love hot and glowing and growing. That is what God means when He says "first love."

Somebody has said that an average church is so lukewarm that you have to backslide to be in fellowship. Was there ever a time when you loved Jesus Christ more than you do right now? If so, then to that degree you are backslidden; you are beginning to cool down, and before long you will be room temperature. And when you do, you'll look around and say, "I must not be so bad. I'm like everybody else." If you really get on fire for the Lord Jesus Christ, people will think that you're odd.

How do you become lukewarm? You begin by assuming that you are all right, but instead you are cooling down by degrees.

The Cure for Lukewarmness

Let's look again at Revelation 3:18: "I advise you to buy from Me gold refined in the fire so that you may be rich, and white clothes so that you may be dressed and your shameful nakedness not be exposed, and ointment to spread on your eyes so that you may see."

The Laodiceans needed the gold of God's glory that had been through the fire. They needed the garments of God's righteousness. They thought they were clothed; they came to the worship service and looked so fine. And yet, God said, "You are naked." First Corinthians 2:14 says, "But the natural man does not welcome what comes from God's Spirit, because it is foolishness to him; he is not able to know it since it is evaluated spiritually."

Do you remember Hans Christian Andersen's story, "The Emperor's New Clothes"? A couple of conniving men pretended to be tailors. Knowing the king's vanity about his clothes, they began a scheme to weave invisible garments. And the king bought into it! He took off all his clothes and put on the invisible suit. He walked in a royal procession down the streets to show everyone his magnificent clothes. At first everyone exclaimed praises over what he was "wearing." Then one little boy had the audacity to say, "Look at the king. He is altogether as naked as the day he was born!"

Are you rich today? Add up everything you have that money cannot buy and death cannot take away. That is how you will know how rich you are.

What happens to someone who is lukewarm? God says, "As many as I love, I rebuke and chasten: be zealous therefore, and repent" (Revelation 3:19 KJV). Ask yourself: "Do I love the Lord my God with all my heart? If not, am I willing to repent?" If you do not, He will rebuke and chasten you. You cannot simply waltz to heaven in a lukewarm condition without God meeting you along the way to chasten you. His Word says, "Repent!"

Lukewarmness is not weakness; it is wickedness. It is not a small sin; it is a great sin. If the greatest commandment is to love God with all your heart, then the greatest sin is not to do so. In the last days, our Lord says that lukewarmness will be the condition of the average church.

And God graciously says, "Listen! I stand at the door and knock. If anyone hears My voice and opens the door, I will come in to him and have dinner with him, and he with Me. I will give him the right to sit with Me on My throne, just as I also won the victory and sat down with My Father on His throne. Anyone who has an ear should listen to what the Spirit says to the churches" (Revelation 3:20–22).

God is speaking to those who are in the church but are lukewarm. He says, "I am knocking at your heart's door." What a loving Lord He is. How much He loves you, even if you are lukewarm. Do not let this moment pass you by. Make Him Lord of your life.

The Midnight Cry and the Rapture of the Church

◄◇►

CHAPTER 7

◄◇►

We enter into the third grand division in the Book of Revelation—the rapture of the church. If you remember, John was told to write about the things that he had seen, the things which are, and things which would occur in the future.

The church age ends at the rapture of the church. At the midnight cry Jesus will come for His own. Those who are saved and are still living will be miraculously transformed with glorified bodies and caught up in the air to meet the Lord. Those whose bodies sleep in the earth will be raised from their sleeping place to meet their heavenly spirits with the Lord in the air.

The Bible calls this the blessed hope. And you need to be ready, but you don't have to be fearful. Remember that sorrow looks back, worry looks all around, but hope looks up. We are on a collision course with destiny, and we cannot afford to be ignorant. Let's begin with Revelation 4:1: "After this I looked, and there in heaven was an open door. The first voice that I had heard speaking to me like a trumpet said, 'Come up here, and I will show you what must take place after this.'"

From this point on, we will be studying everything that will transpire after the rapture of the church. To help you remember these things, I will be asking four questions: What? Who? When? and Why?

What Is the Sacred Mystery of the Rapture?

A Bible mystery is not a story you might read in a novel; instead, it is a truth that has been hidden, a truth that no one can understand apart from God. And it can only be revealed by divine revelation in the Word of God. The only way that people today know about the mystery of the rapture is by studying not what the Old Testament prophets had to say, but what the New Testament prophets had to say. This was revealed to the apostle Paul who said, "Listen! I am telling you a mystery: We will not all fall asleep, but we will all be changed, in a moment, in the twinkling of an eye, at the last trumpet. For the trumpet will sound, and the dead will be raised incorruptible, and we will be changed. Because this corruptible must be clothed with incorruptibility, and this mortal must be clothed with immortality" (1 Corinthians 15:51–53).

Paul explained the church age, *the things which are.* This is that interval between the time when Jesus came the first time and when He will come again the second time. What a majestic and mysterious thing the rapture will be that ends the church age.

In Revelation 4:1, we learn that John was caught up through a door in the heavens and heard a voice that said, "Come up here, and I will show you what must take place after this." A corresponding New Testament verse about the rapture of the church is 1 Thessalonians 4:13: "We do not want you to be uninformed, brothers, concerning those who are asleep, so that you will not grieve like the rest, who have no hope."

At the time this was written, the Thessalonian church was ignorant of what had happened to those who had died before Jesus' return. Some of their brothers and sisters had died, and they were wondering if they would miss the coming of the Lord. Sooner or later, most of us will go to a graveside to say good-bye to a loved one who knows Jesus Christ, but we do not have to be without hope. First Thessalonians 4:14–15 gives us this promise: "Since we believe that Jesus died and rose again, in the same way God will bring with Him those who have fallen asleep through Jesus. For we say this to you by a revelation from the Lord: We who are still alive at the Lord's coming will certainly have no advantage over those who have fallen asleep."

God's Word teaches us that when the rapture occurs, the body of the believer will awaken from the grave and be reunited with his spirit that is with the Lord. The body will ascend from the earth, and the spirit will descend from the heavens.

Paul thought it was feasible that Jesus could return in his lifetime, because he used the personal pronoun "we" in the plural sense in verse 15 and again in verse 17. Here is the promise of His return: "For the Lord himself shall descend from heaven with a shout, with the voice of the archangel, and with the trump of God: and the dead in Christ shall rise first: Then we which are alive and remain shall be caught up together with them in the clouds, to meet the Lord in the air: and so shall we ever be with the Lord" (1 Thessalonians 4:16–17 KJV).

The phrase "caught up" in the Greek is *harpazē* and in the Latin it is *rapto,* which means "to seize," "to catch away," or "to pluck." This is what will happen. One of these days, God the Father will turn to His Son and say, "It's time. Go get your bride." The trumpet will sound. And Jesus will rise from His throne in the lofty heavens with a voice that will echo through the subterranean tombs of this earth. Miraculously, those who know the Lord Jesus Christ will have their ears tuned to Him, and we will be glorified and rise to meet the Lord. They will come from the swelling bosom of the sea, the winding sheets of desert sands, the battlefields of this world, and country graveyards all around.

If you were to sprinkle silver, gold, zinc, copper, and iron on the ground, then sweep a giant electromagnet over those particles, some of the metal would rise to meet the magnet, but others would stay in the ground. The silver, gold, zinc, and copper would stay on the ground. But the iron would rise. Why? Because it has the same nature as the magnet. When Jesus comes again, those who are heaven-born will be heaven-bound.

Some may ask, "Do you really believe in the rapture?" Yes! "Well," they may say, "doesn't that smack a little bit of supernaturalism?" Yes, indeed, it does. But the apostle Paul began his explanation of the mystery of the rapture by saying: "Since we believe that Jesus died and rose again" (1 Thessalonians 4:14). So if you believe that Jesus died and rose again, it should not be difficult for you to believe in the rapture.

I believe in the rapture because I believe the gospel—the death, burial, and resurrection of Jesus Christ. The rapture is linked to His redemption. If you have Calvary without the rapture, it is like having up without down or night without day. You cannot have the incarnation without the coronation. I believe Jesus has already gone through the grave and has come out on the other side, because Paul said, "For we say this to you by a revelation from the Lord" (1 Thessalonians 4:15).

Who Is the Select Multitude of the Rapture?

The select multitude of the rapture is represented by twenty-four elders as Revelation 4:4 explains: "Around that throne were 24 thrones, and on the thrones sat 24 elders dressed in white clothes, with gold crowns on their heads."

Some people have surmised that these twenty-four elders are angels. But they are not, since Revelation 5:11 makes a distinction between angels, beasts, and elders. Others think that they are inanimate symbols. Wrong again. The elders cannot be symbols because symbols do not talk to one another (see Revelation 5:5).

Elders are representatives of God's people. For instance, every minister is an elder of his church. Why twenty-four elders? Twelve, you may recall, is God's governmental number—the number that denotes the rule of God on earth. (Four is the earth number. Three is the divine number. Three times four is twelve.) Here, we have twelve times two, which is twenty-four. These twenty-four elders are the dead in Christ and living saints who have been transformed from earth into heaven.

Further on in the Book of Revelation, we learn that there are twelve gates in the new Jerusalem, which is the place that we call heaven or glory. The names of each of the twelve patriarchs of the tribes of Israel are inscribed on those twelve gates. In addition, the twelves apostles are named for the foundations of the city. Twelve patriarchs from the Old Testament and twelve apostles from the New Testament. Put them together and they make twenty-four. These twenty-four elders represent the saints of God. And one day you will meet all of these men!

Notice how John describes these elders. They are saints clothed in white and wearing crowns on their heads. Their white clothing represents the righteousness of Christ manifested in their lives. White is mentioned elsewhere in Revelation 19:8: "She [the Bride of Christ—the church] was permitted to wear fine linen, bright and pure. For the fine linen represents the righteous acts of the saints" (explanatory note added by author).

The crowns of gold on their heads were placed there when they came before the judgment seat of Christ. Every believer will stand before Christ's judgment seat. "And when the chief Shepherd appears, you will receive the unfading crown of glory" (1 Peter 5:4). None of us will receive our crowns until that time.

At the beginning of this section, I said there would be a select group in the rapture. Let me explain. Not everybody will be raptured, because

Jesus said, "I tell you, on that night two will be in one bed: one will be taken and the other will be left. Two women will be grinding grain together: one will be taken and the other left. [Two will be in a field: one will be taken, and the other will be left.] 'Where, Lord?' they asked Him. He said to them, 'Where the corpse is, there also the vultures will be gathered'" (Luke 17:34–37).

Sometimes when I am preaching, I look out upon my congregation and wonder if the rapture will occur before I finish my sermon. Everyone looks alike more or less, but if I had the eyes of Christ I could look into every heart and see a completely different picture, "for the LORD seeth not as man seeth; for man looketh on the outward appearance, but the LORD looketh on the heart" (1 Samuel 16:7 KJV). And that is what separates the saved from the lost—those who are ready for Jesus Christ to come and those who are not.

At the rapture, the person sitting next to you at the dinner table will go and you will remain. Or you may go and that person will remain. Two will be sitting in church. One will be taken and the other left. There is a select multitude—only the saved will be going.

When Will the Rapture Take Place?

There is no question—the rapture will happen! And it will happen suddenly and immediately. John had been looking at the churches and describing the church age, when suddenly the trumpet sounded and he was immediately caught up into heaven. Here is how he described what happened: "After this I looked, and there in heaven was an open door. The first voice that I had heard speaking to me like a trumpet said, 'Come up here, and I will show you what must take place after this.' Immediately I was in the Spirit, and there in heaven a throne was set. One was seated on the throne" (Revelation 4:1–2).

Today we are living in the church age (discussed in the beginning of the Book of Revelation), which is also called the age of grace. After Revelation chapter 3, you will notice that the word *church* is no longer mentioned, because the church is raptured! And this begins the next phase of God's work on earth.

When is Jesus coming for His church? I don't know. You don't know. Nobody knows, though we have a lot of soothsayers, prognosticators, astrologers, and so-called prophets trying to predict when this will happen. But they're not prophetic; they're pathetic!

No one has a shred of an iota of a scintilla of information about when this will happen. No one sitting in the Pentagon, on Capitol Hill, or in executive offices and financial institutions has a clue. If some high muckety-muck comes along and tells you, "I've set a date for the coming of Jesus," you need to ask him, "Will you give me the deed to your house effective the day after your set date and do it now?"

No one but God alone knows when His Son will return. Why? It is a sacred mystery known to God alone. Jesus said:

> Now concerning that day and hour no one knows—neither the angels in heaven, nor the Son—except the Father only. As the days of Noah were, so the coming of the Son of Man will be. For in those days before the flood they were eating and drinking, marrying and giving in marriage, until the day Noah boarded the ark. They didn't know until the flood came and swept them all away. So this is the way the coming of the Son of Man will be: Then two men will be in the field: one will be taken and one left. Two women will be grinding at the mill: one will be taken and one left. Therefore be alert, since you don't know what day your Lord is coming. But know this: If the homeowner had known what time the thief was coming, he would have stayed alert and not let his house be broken into. This is why you also should get ready, because the Son of Man is coming at an hour you do not expect (Matthew 24:36–44).

We see all kinds of events that seem to indicate that the coming of Jesus is soon; but no sign proves that, and no lack of signs disproves it. Let me see if I can give you an illustration. Shortly after Halloween, many retail stores start displaying Christmas decorations. When you see those decorations, does that mean Christmas is right around the corner? No, it means Thanksgiving is coming!

Now indeed Christmas is coming, but Thanksgiving will come first. The signs we see may be of the great events that will take place after the rapture of the church, but the rapture must come first. There will be plenty of signs after the rapture that foretell the final climax of history and signs before the rapture that speak of events that take place after the rapture. Yet there is no sign or event that must take place before the rapture can happen.

Certainly there are signs that would seem to point toward Christ's return. But are they signs of the times? Yes and no. Writers of the New Testament thought *they* were living in the end times because of the signs they witnessed. If certain signs have to occur before Jesus can come, then why does Paul tell us, "For you yourselves know very well that the Day of the Lord will come just like a thief in the night" (1 Thessalonians 5:2)? And Peter tells us, "But the Day of the Lord will come like a thief; on that day the heavens will pass away with a loud noise, the elements will burn and be dissolved, and the earth and the works on it will be disclosed" (2 Peter 3:10).

If you say, "I don't think He's coming today," this is a good sign that He might! Do you expect a thief every night? No. But you probably live prepared and protected in case it happens. The apostle Paul expected Jesus to return in his own lifetime. Was Paul wrong? No, he was absolutely right. Every Christian is right to be expecting Christ in his lifetime. And every Christian from Christ's ascension until now should be living with that "thief in the night" mentality.

A while back I heard that the average individual blinks his eyes twenty thousand times a day. I am always suspicious of statistics like that, because when you think about it, who will sit for an entire day and count the number of times someone blinks his eyes? But the statistic does remind me that perhaps twenty thousand times every day I may hear the trumpet sound because God's Word says, "In a moment, in the twinkling of an eye, at the last trumpet. For the trumpet will sound, and the dead will be raised incorruptible, and we will be changed" (1 Corinthians 15:52).

Why Will the Rapture Take Place?

There is a threefold reason for the rapture: reception, rescue, and reunion. John said, "And immediately I was in the spirit: and, behold, a throne was set in heaven, and one sat on the throne" (Revelation 4:2).

Think of the reception! Jesus said, "In My Father's house are many dwelling places; if not, I would have told you. I am going away to prepare a place for you. If I go away and prepare a place for you, I will come back and receive you to Myself, so that where I am you may be also" (John 14:2–3).

My first thrill in heaven will be to see my Lord Jesus Christ. What a day that will be! The closest day that brings this kind of joy is a wedding day. I always enjoy seeing the bride come down the aisle. There is such joy on the faces of the bride and groom!

We will see not only His majesty, but we will also glorify His ministry as our High Priest. The high priest in the Old Testament wore a breastplate with twelve precious stones that represented the people of God. The first and the last stones (the alpha and omega) are the same stones in Revelation 4:3: "And he that sat was to look upon like a jasper and a sardius stone" (KJV).

Have you ever seen jasper? Most likely it is like a diamond because it is pure and sparkling white. How do we know that? The Bible speaks of the heavenly city as being "arrayed with God's glory. Her radiance was like a very precious stone, like a jasper stone, bright as crystal" (Revelation 21:11). This sounds like a diamond to me. Jesus is sparkling, pure, transparent, and translucent. At the same time, Jesus appears as a sardias, which is blood red. These are two very important representations of our Lord, which I believe speak of His purity and His blood sacrificed for the church.

The second reason for the rapture is the rescue of God's people. Notice in Revelation 4:3 that there is a rainbow around the throne. This word *rainbow* in the Greek is *iris,* which means "halo." All around this throne is a rainbow, but there is something different about this rainbow. It is the color of emerald green—the color of life.

Do you remember what the rainbow stood for in the Old Testament? The covenant of God with His people. Genesis 9:13–15 says, "I do set my bow in the cloud, and it shall be for a token of a covenant between me and the earth. And it shall come to pass, when I bring a cloud over the earth, that the bow shall be seen in the cloud: and I will remember my covenant, which is between me and you and every living creature of all flesh; and the waters shall no more become a flood to destroy all flesh" (KJV).

Can you imagine the carnage, wreckage, slime, and everything else that Noah saw when he stepped out of the ark? But when he looked up at the vault of heaven, there was a glorious rainbow—like a multicolored scarf thrown over the shoulders of the storm.

Notice that this rainbow around the throne is a perfect circle. In our limited vision, all we can see is the shape of a bow. But if we saw the rainbow from God's perspective, we would see a perfect circle. What does the circle represent? Eternity. It has no beginning and no end. It is green, the color of life. This emerald circle speaks of eternal life.

In the storms of our lives, we never see the full picture. But one day we will see it all; one day the circle will be complete. In his hymn, "Some Time We'll Understand," Maxwell Cornelius wrote:

Not now, but in the coming years,
It may be in the better land,
We'll read the meaning of our tears,
And there, sometime, we'll understand.

Then trust in God through all the days;
Fear not, for He doth hold thy hand;
Though dark thy way, still sing and praise,
Some time, sometime we'll understand.

The third reason for the rapture is the reunion. Revelation 4:4 speaks of twenty-four elders, which represent all who will be caught up to meet the Lord in the air. What does that mean to us?

First, we must *learn* about the return of Jesus. Second, we should *live* for His return. Third, we should *look* for His return. Fourth, we should *long* for His return. The last prayer in the Bible is for Jesus to come again (see Revelation 22:20).

Steven Covey wrote a book about how people need to prioritize things. He illustrated his point by saying that a professor walked into a class with a wide-mouth jar. In that jar he put some big rocks and asked the students, "Is the jar full?" They nodded their heads in agreement. He said, "No, the jar's not full."

The professor took some gravel and sprinkled it on top of the rocks, shook it down, and smoothed it off. Then he asked his students, "Is the jar full now?" They said, "Yes, it's full now." "No," he said, "it's not full." Then he poured some sand on top of the gravel, shook it down good, and smoothed it off.

When he asked the students if the jar was full, some of the students were hesitant to answer because he had proven them wrong before. He said, "I'll answer for you. It's not full yet." Then he poured some water over the sand, and it filled every little crevice. Then he asked, "Now is the jar full?" They timidly nodded their heads yes. He said, "You're right! What is the lesson?"

One student lifted his hand and said, "Things are not always as they appear to be." Another said, "There's always room for more." The professor said, "These are good things, but that is not the real lesson. Here is the lesson: If I had not put the big rocks in first, it would be too late to put them in."

What are the big rocks? Get right with God by giving your heart to Jesus Christ. Those are the things that count. A lot of things you think are important will turn out to be gravel, sand, and water. Are you saved? Get that settled, and you'll be ready for the rest.

*W*orthy Is the Lamb

◄o►

CHAPTER 8

◄o►

I want to start this chapter by asking you a few questions. Do you have a cause worth living for? Is what you are living for worthy of Jesus' dying for? When you get to where you are headed, where will you be? Many of us are shoveling smoke and plowing water. When this world is over, much of what we have done will make no difference whatsoever.

Years ago, *Reader's Digest* reported that in order for a person to have a meaningful life, he needs three things. First, he needs someone to love. Second, he needs something to do. Third, he needs something to hope for. I think *Reader's Digest* is right, and the answer to all three of these things is Jesus. He is the One we love, the One we serve, and the One in whom we hope. Jesus Christ is the only One worthy of my love, my life, my all—and yours.

The fifth chapter of Revelation talks about this One—Jesus Christ. And it brings home the fact that each of us will never have satisfaction and fulfillment or understand why God created us until we come to worship the One who is worthy. Let's look at three things that this chapter says about our glorious Savior and Lord, Jesus Christ.

Jesus Is Exclusively *Worthy*

John wrote the following about his vision of heaven:

> Then I saw in the right hand of the One seated on the
> throne a scroll with writing on the inside and on the back,
> sealed with seven seals. I also saw a mighty angel proclaiming
> in a loud voice, "Who is worthy to open the scroll and break its

seals?" But no one in heaven or on earth or under the earth was able to open the scroll or even to look in it. And I cried and cried because no one was found worthy to open the scroll or even to look in it. Then one of the elders said to me, "Stop crying. Look! The Lion from the tribe of Judah, the Root of David, has been victorious so that He may open the scroll and its seven seals" (Revelation 5:1–5).

We will see that this scroll is the title deed to the earth. The one who can break the seals and open the book is the one to whom it rightfully belongs.

John wants the seals of this book broken, but an angel challenges him: "Who is worthy to open the scroll and break its seals?" (Revelation 5:2). The angel did not ask, "Who is willing?" Instead, the angel asked, "Who is worthy?" Indeed, there were plenty willing, but "no one in heaven or on earth or under the earth was able to open the scroll or even to look in it" (Revelation 5:3). None who has died or is living can open the book.

John begins to weep—and these aren't just the tears of one solitary man. These are great salty tears representing every person from the time that Adam and Eve looked on the dead body of their son Abel, murdered by another of their sons, Cain. He cries, "Is there no hope for planet earth, which has become such a mess? Is the devil just going to inherit it all?"

Perhaps you have cried these tears at one time or another when you looked out upon our world saturated with buckets of blood and oceans of tears and have asked, "Is there no hope for creation?" Yes. "Then one of the elders said to me, 'Stop crying. Look! The Lion from the tribe of Judah, the Root of David, has been victorious so that He may open the scroll and its seven seals'" (Revelation 5:5). Who is the Root of David? Jesus. He is worthy and has bought back what was legally lost in creation. Let me explain.

When God created the world, He turned it over to Adam and Eve and gave them dominion. But then Satan crawled his slimy, con-artist frame onto the pages of history and beguiled Eve in the Garden of Eden. In turn Adam fell as well. At that moment, Adam and Eve turned over to Satan the dominion that God had given to them. To put it in simple terms, Adam and Eve sold the farm. Satan went away with the title deed to all creation. Second Peter 2:19 says, "They promise them freedom, but they themselves are slaves of corruption, since people are enslaved to whatever defeats them."

When Satan overcame Adam and Eve, they became slaves of Satan, and all those who came after Adam became slaves to Satan. Satan owns the slave, and he owns all that the slave owns. Every man, woman, and child is born into slavery, and we are bankrupt. There is no way we can redeem ourselves. There is no way we can buy back what Adam lost, because we do not have what it takes.

Did God recognize Satan's usurped authority? Yes, He did. As a matter of fact, Luke 4:6–7 tells us that one of the temptations that Satan offered Jesus in the wilderness was that he would give the kingdoms of this world to Jesus: "The Devil said to Him, 'I will give You their splendor and all this authority, because it has been given over to me, and I can give it to anyone I want. If You, then, will worship me, all will be Yours.'"

Basically, Satan was saying, "Adam gave me the power and glory of this world. Now I can give it to You if You will simply bow down and worship me." Did Jesus say to Satan, "It is not yours to give"? No. Jesus knew that Adam had legally lost his dominion to "the god of this age" (2 Corinthians 4:4).

Let me illustrate this biblical truth: I had a teenage friend whose father gave him a brand-new car. Do you know what he did with that car? He gave it to somebody else. Now how would you feel if you were his dad? It legally became the car of his son's friend. In the same way, God gave Adam dominion. Then Adam gave it to Satan. It was legally lost; and now it has to be legally regained. How could this be done?

In the Old Testament, God gave property rights to the people. It was His to give, so He gave it. Sometimes, though, a man would foolishly lose his possession, or he would become poor and have to sell it. In times like this, God provided a way that the man's possession could be restored. There had to be a kinsman-redeemer—someone related and who was wealthy enough to pay the price. Leviticus 25:25 says, "If thy brother be waxen poor, and hath sold away some of his possession, and if any of his kin come to redeem it, then shall he redeem that which his brother sold" (KJV).

That's the reason Jesus came to earth. He came as the second Adam to put back what was right. He was not the son of Adam; He was the Son of God. If He had been the son of Adam, He would have been a slave, and all that belonged to Adam would belong to Him. But Jesus was born of a virgin so He would be sinless—the only one worthy to redeem man and open the scroll. The Holy Spirit of God generated the holy life of Jesus Christ in the womb of Mary. He was Son of Man and Son of God.

First Peter 1:18–19 says, "For you know that you were redeemed from your empty way of life inherited from the fathers, not with perishable things, like silver or gold, but with the precious blood of Christ, like that of a lamb without defect or blemish." Jesus had to be the perfect, sinless sacrifice. Only the sinless blood of Jesus Christ could pay the debt. Jesus is our only hope.

There is absolutely no way that anyone will go to heaven apart from Jesus Christ. God's Word is clear: "Jesus told him, 'I am the way, the truth, and the life. No one comes to the Father except through Me'" (John 14:6). And in Acts 4:12 we read: "There is salvation in no one else, for there is no other name under heaven given to people by which we must be saved."

Our kinsman-redeemer Jesus is the only one worthy to break the seal and buy back what Adam lost. Our inheritance was lost by a man; it had to be redeemed by a man—but not just any man. Only Jesus could pay the price. Only Jesus Christ is exclusively worthy.

If you were to take all the billions of people on earth and put them in single file, then have each one pass by and put into a receptacle all of his inherent goodness, then put that goodness into one man, that one man would not be worthy to open this book. There is only one who could do it. Our redeemer, the Lord Jesus Christ, paid the price.

Jesus Is Exceedingly Worthy

Jesus is exceedingly worthy for three reasons: He is worthy because of creation, because of Calvary, and because of conquest.

He Is Worthy Because of Creation

Revelation 4:10–11 says, "The 24 elders fall down before the One seated on the throne, worship the One who lives forever and ever, cast their crowns before the throne, and say: 'Our Lord and God, You are worthy to receive glory and honor and power, because You have created all things, and because of Your will they exist and were created.'"

Everything was created by Him and for Him (see Colossians 1:16). People talk about creating life in the laboratory, but no one can create life in this way. Men can only take what God has created and synthesize that lifelike substance in the laboratory.

Suppose my father is a master builder and he can build magnificent houses. One day, while my father is away I decide to get his tools, plans, and materials, and I build a dog house. Then I point to that dog house and say, "That proves my father doesn't exist." That is what men say when they think they are creating life and they don't need God.

Here's another imagined story to prove my point. A scientist got into an argument with God. "You're not the only creator," he declared. "I can make a man."

So God said, "Let's see you do it."

The man walked over to some dirt. But God stopped him and said, "Get your own dirt."

There is only One who can create. His name is Jesus. He is worthy. He is worthy because of creation.

He Is Worthy Because of Calvary

Revelation 5:6–7 says, "And I beheld, and, lo, in the midst of the throne and of the four beasts, and in the midst of the elders, stood a Lamb as it had been slain, having seven horns and seven eyes, which are the seven Spirits of God sent forth into all the earth. And he came and took the book out of the right hand of him that sat upon the throne" (KJV).

John was weeping at the beginning of Revelation 5 because no one was able to open the book. Now a Lamb "as it had been slain" appears. The Greek word for "lamb" used elsewhere in the New Testament is *amnos*. But here in the Book of Revelation, the word for lamb is *arnion*. This latter word means a little pet lamb. It is used in the plural form in the Bible where Jesus said to Peter, "Feed My lambs" (John 21:15).

What a surprise! John was expecting to see a lion, because the elders had said, "Look! The Lion from the tribe of Judah, the Root of David, has been victorious so that He may open the scroll" (Revelation 5:5). And instead he saw a lamb, and not just any lamb. He saw the most helpless creature—an *arnion*—a little pet lamb. No animal could have symbolized anything weaker than a little lamb.

Where else have you read about a sacrificial lamb? Perhaps you recall the Passover, where God instructed the Jews to sacrifice a lamb—but not just any lamb off the streets. They were to select a perfect lamb, a firstling from their flock without spot or blemish. After they had selected the lamb, they were to keep it in their home for four days. Can you imagine how your children would feel if you had a little lamb in your home for four days? They would cuddle and snuggle with it until they had identified with it.

This Lamb is different from most helpless lambs written about in God's Word. First, although it had the marks of death upon His body, this Lamb was now standing. How does a lamb that has died now stand up? Because this Lamb was not any lamb; this was the resurrected Lamb of God. He is the reigning Lamb. He is the Lamb as described by John the Baptist: "Here is the Lamb of God, who takes away the sin of the world" (John 1:29).

This Lamb is also significant because the perfect number seven is mentioned three times. First, He has seven horns, which speaks of the omnipotence of the Lamb. He is all-powerful. Second, the Lamb has seven eyes, which speaks of the omniscience of the Lamb. He sees everything (see 2 Chronicles 16:9; Proverbs 5:21). Then notice that there are "seven spirits of God sent into all the earth" (Revelation 5:6). He is omnipresent. There is nowhere that He is not.

The Lamb of God is the Lord Jesus—the redeeming Lamb, the resurrected Lamb, and the reigning Lamb who comes against them all.

He Is Worthy Because of Conquest

Let's return to Revelation 5:5: "And one of the elders saith unto me, Weep not: behold, the Lion of the tribe of Judah, the Root of David, hath prevailed to open the book, and to loose the seven seals thereof" (KJV). This word *prevailed* is from the Greek word *nikē*, which speaks of victory. He is the One who has won the victory.

Perhaps you have heard about the first U.S. Army Air Defense Artillery guided-missile system called the Nike Ajax. It is a system far superior to conventional anti-aircraft weapons. No doubt, you have also heard of the sporting goods manufacturer called Nike. It's the symbol of victory.

If you were to ask the Lord Jesus how He was able to open the book, He would answer, "I am worthy, first of all because of creation. I made everything. Second, I am worthy because of Calvary. I have redeemed mankind. Third, I am worthy because of conquest. I have prevailed."

Jesus Is Eternally Worthy

There has never been a time when Jesus was not worthy. There will never be a time when He is not worthy. Jesus is eternally worthy forever and ever. This is the eternal song of the ages.

When He took the scroll, the four living creatures and the
24 elders fell down before the Lamb. Each one had a harp and
gold bowls filled with incense, which are the prayers of the
saints. And they sang a new song: "You are worthy to take the
scroll and to open its seals; because You were slaughtered, and
You redeemed people for God by Your blood from every tribe
and language and people and nation. You made them a kingdom and priests to our God, and they will reign on the earth."
. . . I heard every creature in heaven, on earth, under the earth,
on the sea, and everything in them say: "Blessing and honor
and glory and dominion to the One seated on the throne,
and to the Lamb, forever and ever!" The four living creatures
said, "Amen," and the elders fell down and worshiped
(Revelation 5:8–10, 13–14).

In this passage, praise is symbolized by harps, and prayer is symbolized by bowls of incense. In the Old Testament, we read that many of the
psalms were sung to harp music. Psalm 98:5 says, "Sing unto the LORD
with the harp; with the harp, and the voice of a psalm" (KJV). As for the
bowls of incense, when the high priest went into the temple, he would take
a bowl of incense so the aroma would perfume the air.

Someone has asked, "Will we pray in heaven?" I believe that the
prayers mentioned here have already been prayed. They may have been
prayed by your grandmother, great grandfather, or by the apostle Paul.
God has not forgotten a single prayer but has gathered them in heaven,
and now they are offered as sweet smelling savor in the nostrils of God.

Your praise is a sacrifice of prayer. Hebrews 13:1 says, "Therefore,
through Him [Jesus] let us continually offer up to God a sacrifice of praise,
that is, the fruit of our lips that confess His name."

Maybe you think that since you don't *see* your prayers answered, perhaps they have been forgotten. Or since you don't *see* God working,
perhaps God is *not* working. Let me ask you a question: Have you ever
prayed the prayer found in Matthew 6:10: "Thy kingdom come. Thy will
be done in earth, as it is in heaven" (KJV)? Now I want to ask you another
question: Has God's kingdom come? Not yet. Is His will being done on
earth as it is in heaven? Not yet.

Did you offer a prayer, therefore, that was not answered? No. Every
prayer is heard. And one of these days, you will see the answer to that

prayer, because His kingdom will come, and the kingdoms of this world will become the kingdoms of our Lord and His Christ.

And we will shout about it! Revelation 5:12 says, "They said with a loud voice: 'The Lamb who was slaughtered is worthy to receive power and riches and wisdom and strength and honor and glory and blessing!'" Think of the reach of that song. It will echo and thunder from the highest heaven to the lowest hell.

Revelation 5:9 says they sang a new song. It's not new in the sense that nobody's ever heard it before. It's new because the singers are now redeemed and up in glory. In the words of Katherine Hankey:

I love to tell the story, for those who know it best
Seem hungering and thirsting to hear it like the rest.
And when, in scenes of glory, I sing the new, new song,
'Twill be the old, old story that I have loved so long.

Do you know what we will be singing in heaven? We will sing about the Lamb. Revelation 5:13–14 says, "I heard every creature in heaven, on earth, under the earth, on the sea, and everything in them say: 'Blessing and honor and glory and dominion to the One seated on the throne, and to the Lamb, forever and ever!' The four living creatures said, 'Amen,' and the elders fell down and worshiped."

From every possible sphere, they will give the Lord Jesus Christ glory. Everybody will confess it. "I have sworn by myself, the word is gone out of my mouth in righteousness, and shall not return, that unto me every knee shall bow, every tongue shall swear" (Isaiah 45:23 KJV).

Jesus Christ is exclusively worthy. There is none other. He is exceedingly worthy because of Calvary, because of creation, because of conquest. He is eternally worthy forever and ever and ever.

Let me end this chapter with the same questions with which I began. Do you have a cause worth living for? Is what you are living for worthy of Jesus' dying for? When you get to where you are headed, where will you be? If I had a thousand lives, I'd give every one to Jesus Christ.

The Wrath of the Lamb and the Coming Tribulation

◄o►
CHAPTER 9
◄o►

Revelation 6 involves the third phase of the prophecy of God in the Book of Revelation. In Revelation 1–3, John had a vision of the Lord Jesus Christ and delivered messages to seven churches: Ephesus, Smyrna, Pergamos, Thyatira, Sardis, Philadelphia, and Laodecia. As we learned, this was the period that church historians call the church age.

In Revelation 4 and 5, God prophesies about the return of His Son, the rapture of His church, and tells us about the great scroll with seven seals that the Lamb of God has been deemed worthy to open. At the close of Revelation 5, the elders have dropped down to worship the Lamb as He takes the scroll to open it and reveal its contents.

As we come to the opening of these seven seals, there is a feeling of great humility and a spirit of anticipation and awe. The first verse of Revelation 6 says, "And I saw when the Lamb opened one of the seals, and I heard, as it were, the noise of thunder, one of the four beasts saying, Come and see" (KJV).

Come and see. Some people think they already know what the future holds. But no one knows. I do not know what tomorrow holds. Neither do you. Nor does Satan. Only God knows the future. All we know is what God has revealed in His Word. In this chapter, we want to look at the things that God has revealed about the world being on a collision course with judgment. I know that is not a popular subject, but it is certainly true.

What does it mean that God will judge the world? Many people think that judgment only involves the active stance a judge takes when he delivers a sentence to the guilty party. But the judge can just as easily take a passive stance, letting the chips fall where they may and allowing the consequences of one's behavior to serve as the judgment. The latter is how God will judge the world. He will simply let the world have its own way. And ironically, when the world gets what it wants, it will not want what it gets.

Revelation 6:15–17 speaks of this time when people will want to escape, but it will be too late: "Then the kings of the earth, the nobles, the military commanders, the rich, the powerful, and every slave and free person hid in the caves and among the rocks of the mountains. And they said to the mountains and to the rocks, 'Fall on us and hide us from the face of the One seated on the throne and from the wrath of the Lamb, because the great day of Their wrath has come! And who is able to stand?'"

Most people reading this probably do not think of a lamb as having wrath. But this isn't just any lamb; this is the Lamb of God. When Jesus was on earth, He warned about a time known as the Great Tribulation: "For at that time there will be great tribulation, the kind that hasn't taken place since the beginning of the world until now, and never will again! Unless those days were cut short, no one would survive. But because of the elect those days will be cut short" (Matthew 24:21–22).

What will happen to the world when the church is removed? First, we need to describe the church. We read in Matthew 5:13–16 that Jesus said the church was like salt and light to the world. Salt preserves, and light gives warmth and illumination. What happens when you take away the salt? Putrefaction sets in. What happens when you remove the light? Darkness ensues. This is the time of the Great Tribulation. Are you ready to open the scroll? Let's begin with what is behind the first seal.

The Four Beasts

The spiritual barometer is dropping, the storm clouds are rolling, and there's distant thunder. A storm is brewing as John's vision continues: "And I saw when the Lamb opened one of the seals, and I heard, as it were the noise of thunder, one of the four beasts saying, Come and see" (Revelation 6:1 KJV).

Who are these four beasts? Actually, they are not beasts in a horrendous sense. The Greek word for "beasts" in this passage is *zōon*. It is the word from which we get our English word *zoo*, and it means "four living ones." We see these in Revelation 4:7, the four beasts around the throne:

"And the first beast was like a lion, and the second beast like a calf, and the third beast had a face as a man, and the fourth beast was like a flying eagle" (KJV). Notice that God's Word prefaces each description of the beasts with the word *like*. This is comparative symbolism to describe four living creatures around the throne of God. I believe these living creatures are the highest class of angels that praise the grace, glory, and government of God.

What does this comparative symbolism mean? The first one had a face like a lion. What do you think of when you envision a lion? I think of authority and power. I call this the *majesty* of the Lord Jesus Christ. The second had a face like a calf, which reminds me of servitude and sacrifice. This speaks of the *ministry* of the Lord Jesus Christ. The next one had a face like a man, which speaks of the *humanity* of the Lord Jesus Christ. And the last one had a face like an eagle. What comes to mind when you think of an eagle at the throne of God? I think of the *deity* of the Lord Jesus Christ. These living creatures reflect the majesty, ministry, humanity, and deity of the Lord Jesus Christ.

Furthermore, the four living creatures are symbolized in the four Gospels. Matthew deals with the majesty of the lion—depicting Jesus Christ as the King of the Jews. Mark deals with the ministry of the Suffering Servant who was crucified for our sins. The Gospel of Luke shares much about the humanity of Jesus Christ—for one reason. Luke goes into the greatest detail about the virgin birth of our Lord. John shares much about the deity of the Lord Jesus Christ.

Militant Conquest

We have heard of the four horsemen of the Apocalypse. Here they are, riding forth after the rapture. We can almost hear their distant hoofbeats.

As these seals are broken, the first vision that appears is of someone who comes in power to rule. Revelation 6:2 says, "I looked, and there was a white horse. The horseman on it had a bow; a crown was given to him, and he went out as a victor to conquer." Look at the symbolism here. The white horse symbolizes a conqueror, the bow symbolizes power, and the crown symbolizes dominion. Could this be the Lord Jesus Christ? No. Jesus Christ is shown in Revelation 19 as coming on a white horse to rule and to reign. Then who is this? This is the Antichrist—the one who imitates the Lord Jesus Christ.

The prefix *anti* means "against" and "instead of." The Antichrist will be the devil's false messiah. He was prophesied in the Old *and* New Testaments. In the Old Testament, the Book of Daniel spoke of the man of sin, the Antichrist: "And through his policy also he shall cause craft to prosper in his hand; and he shall magnify himself in his heart, and by peace shall destroy many: he shall also stand up against the Prince of princes; but he shall be broken without hand" (Daniel. 8:25 KJV). The Antichrist is described here as a man with crafty policies who is a consummate egotist.

In the New Testament, Jesus prophesied about this false messiah when He said, "I have come in My Father's name, yet you don't accept Me. If someone else comes in his own name, you will accept him" (John 5:43). When the Antichrist begins to go forth, everyone will proclaim that a savior has come to bring world peace. Indeed, at that moment in time, the world will be ripe for the devil's messiah. And he will take full advantage of his hero status.

The world will worship at his feet. Little children will speak his name with reverence. Men will lay down their lives for this man, which we are told will be Satan's superman. He will personify all of the Caesars, Napoleons, Hitlers, and Stalins rolled into one, and he will have sinister plans for military conquest.

Murderous Conflicts

The second seal is opened, and it reveals that there will be murderous conflicts. The prophecy of Revelation 6:3–4 says, "And when he had opened the second seal, I heard the second beast say, Come and see. And there went out another horse that was red: and power was given to him that sat thereon to take peace from the earth, and that they should kill one another: and there was given unto him a great sword" (KJV).

When Satan's superman appears on the world stage with ideas of world conquest infesting his evil brain, war will follow as night follows day. That is the reason John has seen a horse that is red. It is a symbol of the bloodthirsty plans of this evil man. Indeed, there will be worldwide havoc and destruction as was prophesied by Jesus: "You are going to hear of wars and rumors of wars. See that you are not alarmed, because these things must take place, but the end is not yet" (Matthew 24:6). The Bible never prophesies that the world will get better, but to the contrary—the world will become worse and worse.

One evidence of this is the frightening escalation of weaponry technology. There are enough nuclear weapons in the world today to annihilate every human being on earth hundreds of times over, but we continue to build and stockpile more and more. Recently our city's newspaper carried the headline: "Doomsday Scenario Laid Out." Here is a statement from the article: "A million people could die if terrorists launch a biological attack that widely disperses smallpox, Anthrax, Ebola virus, or other agents, according to the analysis of the damage that could be caused by weapons of mass destruction." The technology is there for massive destruction.

Why do I bring this up? Because when the Antichrist comes, a spirit of hatred will inflame the depraved hearts of men (see Matthew 24; Mark 13; Luke 21). According to God's Word, Jesus prophesied that there would be wars between nations, and also wars between classes of people, races, and religions. Brother will kill brother, and parents will gladly slay their children.

In addition, God spoke this prophecy to the prophet Ezekiel: "And I will call for a sword against him throughout all my mountains, saith the Lord GOD: every man's sword shall be against his brother" (Ezekiel 38:21 KJV). Without the Prince of Peace and the salt and light of the church, the restraints of hatred in the world will be removed. Swords will drip with blood. The stench of decaying human flesh will rise up from every corner of the globe. Now let's move to the third seal.

Meager Crops

What is behind the third seal is revealed in Revelation 6:5–6: "And when he had opened the third seal, I heard the third beast say, Come and see. And I beheld, and lo a black horse; and he that sat on him had a pair of balances in his hand. And I heard a voice in the midst of the four beasts say, A measure of wheat for a penny, and three measures of barley for a penny; and see thou hurt not the oil and the wine" (KJV).

This rider is on a black horse and is carrying old-fashioned scales and balances in his hands. What does he say? "A measure of wheat for a penny, and three measures of barley for a penny" (KJV). He is talking about food that is being carefully rationed. Let's look at this further. What does he mean by a penny and a measure?

The penny in this passage does not carry the same worth as the copper penny with which we are familiar. It's the Greek word *dēnariou*, which meant the pay for a day's labor for people in John's generation. In addition, it took about a quart (a measure) of milled wheat to bake a loaf of bread. If you had lived during this time, you would have been forced to work a full day to get one meal.

What does this prophecy tell us? It tells us there will be a time of limited productivity and economic deprivation. This time, the horse does not symbolize war but famine. When people go to war, they no longer till the fields. And the transportation that brings food to the needy is immobilized. Can you imagine what it will be like to live where there is a worldwide famine?

A man will be fortunate to have a job for which he will be paid just enough for one meal. What if he has a family? Does he give a little bit to each member so they starve together? Does he feed one and neglect another? Will he succumb to the temptation to steal another person's bread? What a tragic picture this prophecy paints! Even Jesus prophesied about this when He said, "Woe to pregnant women and nursing mothers in those days!" (Matthew 24:19). Little children with bloated bellies will die of malnutrition. Little babies will gnaw at dry breasts. People will starve because of the meager crops.

Manifold Carnage

The prophecy hidden within the fourth seal is revealed in Revelation 6:7–8: "And when he had opened the fourth seal, I heard the voice of the fourth beast say, Come and see. And I looked, and behold a pale horse: and his name that sat on him was Death, and Hell followed with him. And power was given unto them over the fourth part of the earth, to kill with sword, and with hunger, and with death, and with the beasts of the earth" (KJV).

The Greek word for the pale color of the horse is *chlōros*. A famous bleach manufacturer has a product whose name closely resembles this. When you pour bleach on colored fabric, the fabric will turn a pale, greenish yellow. What happens to the color? It dies.

There is a chain reaction happening. The first seal ushers in the Antichrist upon a white horse. The second seal brings war with a rider upon a red horse. Famine is the result when the third rider on the black horse strides upon the scene. Now the rider sits upon a pale horse bringing death. Sin causes hatred. Hatred causes war and bloodshed. War brings famine. Famine produces death. And after death come hell and the judgment.

There is often more death after a war than when the war was underway. This happens because of the disease epidemics and famine that grow out of war. You can see this in Revelation 6:8, which says that death was given power to "kill with sword, and with hunger, and with death, and with the beasts of the earth" (KJV).

We have seen how men will die by the sword in war and by starvation in famine, but now God's Word tells us that they will die "with death." Does that phrase sound a little redundant to you? The word for "death" in the Greek is *thanatō*, which means "plagues." I think of the thousands of men, women, and children who have lost their lives because of the AIDS epidemic. CNN has reported that if forty million people with AIDS do not get life-prolonging drugs, the number of deaths from AIDS will surpass those from the Black Death of the fourteenth century.

The next way that death will kill is "with the beasts of the earth" (KJV). In explaining the meaning of Revelation 6:1–2 earlier, we discussed the word *beasts*. Here in Revelation 6:8, the word *beasts* is a different word in the Greek—it is *thērion*. What kind of animal do you think of when you think of a beast? A bear? A tiger? A rhinoceros? Beasts come in many sizes. If you look up the word in a dictionary, the definition may define a beast only as a four-footed mammal.

Do you know what beasts carried the Black Death? Rats. These tiny four-footed mammals carried a bubonic bacterium that killed more than twenty-five million people in a five-year period. At the time, that was one-third of the population of Europe! David Jeremiah said, "I have another theory about these beasts since they accompany famine and plagues. The most destructive creature on the earth is the rat. He is a menace to human health and food supplies, and the nasty creature comes in more than one hundred species. Rats are extremely prolific, producing five or more litters of eight to ten each year. It has been estimated that rats are responsible for the loss of more than one billion dollars' worth of food each year in the United States alone. Typhus killed an estimated 200 million people in four centuries. The disease was transmitted by rat fleas."

Martyred Christians

Revelation 6:9–11 tells us that there will be many martyrs who die during the tribulation: "When He opened the fifth seal, I saw under the altar the souls of those slaughtered because of God's word and the testimony they had. They cried out with a loud voice: 'O Lord, holy and true, how long until You judge and avenge our blood from those who live on the earth?' So a white robe was given to each of them, and they were told to rest a little while longer until the number of their fellow slaves and their brothers, who were going to be killed just as they had been, would be completed."

If Jesus Christ came today and raptured His church, multiplied millions would remain. And many of these will come to Christ in the world's great revival *after* the rapture. But in doing so, these people will pay a great price. They will refuse the mark of the beast and will not bow down and worship his image. Because of this, they will become the object of Satan's wrath. It will be a time of great persecution for these saints. As Jesus said, "Then they will hand you over to persecution, and they will kill you. You will be hated by all nations because of My name" (Matthew 24:9).

Have you read about women in the Middle East who are being killed for allegedly committing adultery? They are brought out before their accusers, then forced to kneel (sometimes these events are held in soccer stadiums). On one occasion I read about a man cutting off a woman's head with a great sword. What was the reason for that? I believe it was to strike terror in those who saw it.

Do you know the chief weapon that Satan will use to kill the martyrs during the Great Tribulation? The guillotine, or if not the guillotine, he will use another instrument of decapitation. Revelation 20:4 says, "Then I saw thrones, and people seated on them who were given authority to judge. I also saw the souls of those who had been beheaded because of their testimony about Jesus and because of God's word, who had not worshiped the beast or his image, and who had not accepted the mark on their foreheads or their hands. They came to life and reigned with the Messiah for 1,000 years."

Satan can take off their heads, but he can't destroy their souls! Jesus promised, "Don't fear those who kill the body but are not able to kill the soul; but rather, fear Him who is able to destroy both soul and body in hell" (Matthew 10:28).

"But," you may say, "why do I have to get saved now if people will be saved in the Great Tribulation? Can't I just wait until then?" No, you can't. Today, you have a knowledge of what it means to be saved. During the tribulation, you will believe a lie. God says this about anybody who has heard the truth and turned from the truth: "And with all deceivableness of unrighteousness in them that perish; because they received not the love of the truth, that they might be saved. And for this cause *God shall send them strong delusion, that they should believe a lie:* that they all might be damned who believed not the truth, but had pleasure in unrighteousness" (2 Thessalonians 2:10–12 KJV).

If you openly, knowingly, willingly refuse to accept Jesus Christ as your Lord and Savior in this day and age, there is no doubt that according to this Word from God, you will believe the devil's lie when he comes as the Antichrist.

Massive Cataclysms

What do you think would happen if the all-powerful Creator decided to relax His grip on nature just a bit? Revelation 6:12–14 tells us that massive cataclysmic acts will happen on earth and in space: "Then I saw Him open the sixth seal. A violent earthquake occurred; the sun turned black like sackcloth made of goat hair; the entire moon became like blood; the stars of heaven fell to the earth as a fig tree drops its unripe figs when shaken by a high wind; the sky separated like a scroll being rolled up; and every mountain and island was moved from its place."

This will happen to millions who refused the Lord Jesus Christ and wanted nothing to do with the One of which the Bible says, "Because by Him everything was created, in heaven and on earth, the visible and the invisible, whether thrones or dominions or rulers or authorities—all things have been created through Him and for Him. He is before all things, and by Him all things hold together" (Colossians 1:16–17).

A great earthquake of such magnitude will be felt around the world. The light of the sun will die out, the moon will hang in the sky like a clot of blood, and the stars will fall to the earth. This will not be a localized event like a tornado popping up in America's heartland or a tremor felt in the Sierra Nevada. This will be an environmental catastrophe that has never been predicted or recorded on any radar screen or seismometer.

Have you ever thought about how large a star is? One star is of much greater magnitude than the earth. A 984-foot wide asteroid was discovered and labeled as potentially hazardous by NASA. It came within 516,000 miles of the earth as it whizzed past. Scientist Don Yeomans, manager of the NEAT (Near Earth Asteroid Tracking) program office, said, "Think of it as Mother Nature's wake-up call to us."

Yeomans goes on to say, "The probability of an asteroid impacting Earth is low, but it is also a high-consequence event that is hard for most people to grasp." Further information in the article stated that the last major asteroid to cause damage on Earth occurred in a sparsely populated region of Siberia in 1908. Seven hundred square miles of forest land and some wildlife were killed, but no human deaths were reported.

In 1994, an asteroid came within 64,200 miles of the earth. And the scientists that I read afterward said, "If this had landed, for example, if it had hit in the San Francisco Bay area, there would be nothing but utter devastation in a 100-mile radius." But then he said, "If it landed not there, but in the ocean, it would be even more devastating because it would ruin the entire Pacific Ocean basin, and great tidal waves and floods would come."

A NASA astronomer is writing a book about this. He said that every million years the earth is struck by asteroids. Other astronomers claim that about two thousand asteroids larger than a kilometer in diameter and capable of generating waves sixteen feet high and threatening a nuclear winter could strike at any time. Here's what one of them said: "A day will surely come when the sheltering sky is torn apart with a power that staggers the imagination. It has happened before. Ask any dinosaur, if you can find one. The earth is a dangerous place to live."

Another news magazine said, "Only 10 percent or so of the potential earth-hitting asteroids have been detected, as astronomers believe, and without a systematic early warning system, earth could be taken by surprise."

On May 1, 1989, *Time* magazine asked this question: "Where were you on the night of March 23rd? Out dancing perhaps, or attending a PTA meeting, or just sitting at home watching *L.A. Law*? If so, you did not realize how close you came to disaster. While you were blissfully unaware of the danger, a huge asteroid whizzed past the earth coming closer than any other such heavenly bodies seen in 52 years. If the giant clump of rock, a half mile across by one estimate, had hit the planet, it would have packed the wallop of thousands of H-bombs and possibly killed millions of people."

The same article goes on to ask, "Is there any way to avoid collisions with asteroids and comets?" "Perhaps a nuclear warhead aimed right at the small asteroid could vaporize it," said Allen Harris, an astronomer at the Jet Propulsion Laboratory in Pasadena, California, "but the warhead might also simply break the rock in pieces that would hit the earth anyway. The most sensible thing to do about earth-grazing asteroids is to try and not think about it."

Revelation 6:14 speaks of the heavens parting like a scroll. This Scripture is not as far-fetched as some people think. Do you know what a nuclear blast does in the atmosphere? It causes a vacuum—then the air rushes back in and the heavens roll up upon themselves.

There is another possibility here, however. God may be speaking in symbolic terms of a great cataclysmic shaking of the entire fabric of society. The writer of the Book of Hebrews talked about God's shaking everything that can be shaken so that which cannot be shaken may remain (Hebrews 12:27). Also, Jesus said that before His coming in glory the powers of the heavens will be shaken: "Immediately after the tribulation of those days shall the sun be darkened, and the moon shall not give her light, and the stars shall fall from heaven, and the powers of the heavens shall be shaken: And then shall appear the sign of the Son of man in heaven: and then shall all the tribes of the earth mourn, and they shall see the Son of man coming in the clouds of heaven with power and great glory" (Matthew 24:29–30 KJV).

Whatever this shaking is—literal or figurative—there will be cataclysm beyond compare during the tribulation.

There is coming a day when every one of these six seals will be opened, one by one. And when all of that happens, there will be a colossal prayer meeting: "Then the kings of the earth, the nobles, the military commanders, the rich, the powerful, and every slave and free person hid in the caves and among the rocks of the mountains. And they said to the mountains and to the rocks, 'Fall on us and hide us from the face of the One seated on the throne and from the wrath of the Lamb, because the great day of Their wrath has come! And who is able to stand?'" (Revelation 6:15–17).

Isn't this amazing? They reject the Rock of Ages and pray to the rocks. You would think they would be praying to God. But instead they are praying to the forces of nature. The more sensible thing is not to be here when all this happens. If you want to go through the Great Tribulation, help yourself, but I do not plan to be here. I am counting on meeting the Lord in the air on that glorious reunion day! Thank God, there is a way out—and it is the way up. It is Jesus!

What a Mighty God We Serve!

◄o►
CHAPTER 10
◄o►

Revelation 7 reminds us one more time that we may be the rapture generation—that last generation of the church age caught up into glory to meet the Lord in the air. What a day that will be!

I want you to be ready. But not so ready that your head is in the clouds of prophecy and not on the pavement of serving and soul winning. The blessed hope for which we await is not an incentive to rest but to work. Jesus said, "Occupy till I come" (Luke 19:13 KJV). He didn't mean for us to take up space; He meant for us to get to work because we know the future. Our occupation is our job, and we need to stay at it. And because your future is secure, your present is something into which you can put all of your heart, soul, and energy.

As I read Revelation 7 over and over, one phrase keeps echoing in my mind. It is a chorus entitled "What a Mighty God We Serve!" that our church often sings:

What a mighty God we serve!
What a mighty God we serve!
Angels bow before Him,
Heaven and earth adore Him,
What a mighty God we serve![5]

How do we know we serve a mighty God? Because God made everything. He created the universe. He made the galaxies, the sun, the moon, and the stars. He flung the world into space. Nothing is too difficult for Him.

The angel said to Abraham, "Is any thing too hard for the LORD? At the time appointed I will return unto thee, according to the time of life, and Sarah shall have a son" (Genesis 18:14 KJV). And then, again Jeremiah said, "Ah Lord GOD! Behold, thou hast made the heaven and the earth by thy great power and stretched out arm, and there is nothing too hard for thee" (Jeremiah 32:17 KJV).

In Revelation 7 we learn more about what this great God can do. Here we will learn about the greatest harvest of souls the world has ever known. During the Great Tribulation, God will save great multitudes—so many that we cannot count them all. What a mighty God we serve!

There Is No Promise Too Hard for God to Keep

There are thirty thousand promises in the Word of God, and "every one of God's promises is 'Yes' in Him. Therefore the 'Amen' is also through Him for God's glory through us" (2 Corinthians 1:20). And Jesus said, "I assure you: Until heaven and earth pass away, not the smallest letter or one stroke of a letter will pass from the law until all things are accomplished" (Matthew 5:18). There is no promise too hard for God to keep.

Let's look at how this is illustrated in Revelation 7:1–8:

> After this I saw four angels standing at the four corners of the earth, restraining the four winds of the earth so that no wind could blow on the earth or on the sea or on any tree. Then I saw another angel rise up from the east, who had the seal of the living God. He cried out in a loud voice to the four angels who were empowered to harm the earth and the sea: "Don't harm the earth or the sea or the trees until we seal the slaves of our God on their foreheads." And I heard the number of those who were sealed: 144,000 sealed from every tribe of the sons of Israel: 12,000 sealed from the tribe of Judah, 12,000 from the tribe of Reuben, 12,000 from the tribe of Gad, 12,000 from the tribe of Asher, 12,000 from the tribe of Naphtali, 12,000 from the tribe of Manasseh, 12,000 from the tribe of Simeon, 12,000 from the tribe of Levi, 12,000 from the tribe of Issachar, 12,000 from the tribe of Zebulun, 12,000 from the tribe of Joseph, 12,000 sealed from the tribe of Benjamin.

Many years ago, God made a promise to Abraham—the first Hebrew and the brightest star in the Hebrew heaven: "Now the LORD had said unto Abram, Get thee out of thy country, and from thy kindred, and from thy father's house, unto a land that I will show thee: And I will make of thee a great nation, and I will bless thee, and make thy name great; and thou shalt be a blessing: And I will bless them that bless thee, and curse him that curseth thee: and in thee shall all families of the earth be blessed" (Genesis 12:1–3 KJV).

God made this promise to Abraham two thousand years before John wrote the Book of Revelation (and two thousand years have passed since then!). Has God kept that promise? Yes! Numbers 23:19 says, "God is not a man, that he should lie; neither the son of man, that he should repent: hath he said, and shall he not do it? or hath he spoken, and shall he not make it good?"(KJV). What does that mean? It means that if God says it, you can bank on it. Every family has been and will be blessed through Abraham. They may have refused the blessing, but it has come.

In Revelation 7 we learn that God's promise to Abraham will be consummated with a unique group of 144,000. Various groups have claimed to be the 144,000—the Jehovah's Witnesses, Seventh-Day Adventists, Sabbath Keepers, and one even called the Flying Roll. Some others say that this group is the New Testament church, which is spiritual Israel.

There is a spiritual Israel, and the church is part of that; but we must remember that God has not cast away His chosen people—the Israelites. The Bible teaches that this race of people will not pass away. The Jew will be here until Jesus comes. The nation of Israel cannot be obliterated. God's promise will stand. You can bank on it.

So who are these 144,000? They are a select group of actual Jews— God's chosen people. Some people who call themselves amillennialists believe that God is finished with Israel as a nation. They do not believe that there is a future for national Israel, nor do they believe that there will be a literal thousand-year millennium or reign of peace on this earth. They take the truth concerning the church as spiritual Israel and endeavor to make that all of the truth. But to make part of the truth all of the truth is to make even that part of the truth an untruth. In the face of direct promises concerning the literal nation Israel, they still take the Old Testament prophecies and promises that God gave to Israel and apply them to the church. In a strange way, they take to themselves the blessings and leave the curses to Israel.

When an amillennialist says that the church is a part of the 144,000, I simply want to ask, "Which tribe?" The Bible is very clear that these are the tribes of Israel. It is black print on white paper: "And I heard the number of those who were sealed: 144,000 sealed from every tribe of the sons of Israel" (Revelation 7:4). Let's look at the 144,000.

They Are Selected

Why does God select 144,000 out of the Jewish people? To answer that question, let's review what we learned in chapter 2 about the symbolic use of numbers in the Book of Revelation.

Three numbers make up the figure 144,000. They are three, four and ten. Four is the earth number, as we have seen; three is the divine number, and ten speaks of completeness.

Three times four is twelve.

Twelve times twelve gives us 144.

Ten times ten times ten gives us 1,000.

Together we have 144,000.

God has taken His governmental number and intensified it. He has said in essence, "These are My chosen ones to do My will and to fulfill My purpose."

Many have asked if 144,000 is a literal number. I see no reason why it should not be a literal number. But let's focus on the main interpretation of this passage in God's Word. God has a plan with Israel, and He is going to complete that plan.

They Are Sealed

John said, "Then I saw another angel rise up from the east, who had the seal of the living God. He cried out in a loud voice to the four angels who were empowered to harm the earth and the sea" (Revelation 7:2).

The angel is carrying a seal of the living God for these 144,000 souls. This seal signifies a mark of ownership. In the days when the Bible was written, a seal basically stood for three things: possession, protection, and preservation. In the same way, God has put a seal of possession, protection, and preservation upon these 144,000 souls. Why? Because God has a special job for them, and they must be kept safe. Otherwise, the Antichrist would obliterate these people.

Before we move to the next point, did you know that you also are sealed? Ephesians 4:30 says, "And don't grieve God's Holy Spirit, who sealed you for the day of redemption." Some people think the devil can take born-again believers out of the hand of God. If you think that, it's time you changed your view.

Thank God for His provision, protection, and preservation of His people. The Holy Spirit seals every person who has placed his or her trust in the almighty power of God for salvation. The reason we are kept saved is that we are sealed from the very beginning. This is a wonderful truth.

Revelation 7:3 tells us that the angel said, "Hurt not the earth, neither the sea, nor the trees, till we have sealed the servants of our God in their foreheads" (KJV). Will this seal be a literal mark upon the foreheads of the saved? Maybe and maybe not. It could be an impression of truth in their minds that God is their Father. Revelation 14:1 teaches: "Then I looked, and there on Mount Zion stood the Lamb, and with Him were 144,000. who had His name and *His Father's name written on their foreheads.*" I don't know whether this means that the name of the Father is in their mind, or whether it is a literal mark, but I do know the 144,000 are sealed.

They Are Servants

Revelation 7:3 says that those who are sealed are the "servants of our God" (KJV). And they will serve the Lord by preaching the gospel of our Lord and Savior, Jesus Christ. Can you imagine what will happen during the Great Tribulation when God turns loose 144,000 evangelists? It seems to me that Paul must have had these 144,000 in mind when he spoke of himself as a pattern to those who would later believe. "Howbeit for this cause I obtained mercy, that in me first Jesus Christ might show forth all longsuffering, *for a pattern to them which should hereafter believe on him to life everlasting*" (1 Timothy 1:16 KJV).

Of whom was Paul a pattern? Certainly not a pattern to believers in the church age. The normal conversion experience today does not follow after the pattern of Paul's dramatic experience on the Damascus Road.

See how Paul's conversion seems to picture and prophesy these Jewish evangelists of the end time. At one time Paul was a blasphemer who was putting Christians to death. Then the Lord miraculously appeared and spoke to him. He was blinded by a light and fell to the ground. When Ananias told him what the Lord had said, the scales fell from his eyes and he prayed, "Lord, what would You have me to do?" (see Acts 9). Then Paul became an evangelist to the Gentile nations. He was a pattern for the 144,000 Jews who will also have a dramatic, divine encounter with the Almighty. One day they will become flaming evangelists to reach the world for the Lord Jesus Christ.

"This is all fine and good," you may be saying, "but why did you start this section saying that there is no promise too hard for God to keep?" Because other nations have been absorbed and obliterated, but not the Jews. The Jews exist forever, and there is no one or no thing that can destroy the nation of Israel. God is keeping His promise today. To the Bible-believing Christian, Israel's significance is beyond measure. Israel is the lightning rod of the nations today. Israel is on the front page of almost every newspaper in America almost every day.

Let me give you a key verse about this: "And in that day will I make Jerusalem a burdensome stone for all people: all that burden themselves with it shall be cut in pieces, though all the people of the earth be gathered together against it" (Zechariah 12:3 KJV). God prophesied that Israel would be disobedient, dispersed, and discredited, but not destroyed.

In order to destroy Israel, first you will have to destroy the power that regulates the universe. You will have to remove God from His throne, then snatch the sun, moon, and stars from His hand. Jeremiah 31:35–37 says:

> Thus saith the LORD, which giveth the sun for a light by
> day, and the ordinances of the moon and of the stars for a light
> by night, which divideth the sea when the waves thereof roar;
> The LORD of hosts is his name: If those ordinances depart from
> before me, saith the LORD, then the seed of Israel also shall
> cease from being a nation before me for ever. Thus saith the
> LORD; If heaven above can be measured, and the foundations of
> the earth searched out beneath, I will also cast off all the seed
> of Israel for all that they have done, saith the LORD (KJV).

Every Jew you see and every headline you read are sermons about the faithfulness of God. God made a promise to Abraham that "in thee shall all families of the earth be blessed" (Genesis 12:3 KJV). And you will never see that promise more greatly fulfilled than during the Great Tribulation, when the 144,000 preach the everlasting gospel to all the peoples on the face of this earth and there is a great harvest of souls.

Not one promise of God will fail. And not only the promises of what God has said to Israel, but what God has said to you. "For every one of God's promises is 'Yes' in Him. Therefore the 'Amen' is also through Him for God's glory through us" (2 Corinthians 1:20).

There Is No Person Too Hard for God to Save

Revelation 7:9–14 says:

After this I looked, and there was a vast multitude from every nation, tribe, people, and language, which no one could number, standing before the throne and before the Lamb. They were robed in white with palm branches in their hands. And they cried out in a loud voice: "Salvation belongs to our God, who is seated on the throne, and to the Lamb!" All the angels stood around the throne, the elders, and the four living creatures, and they fell on their faces before the throne and worshiped God, saying: "Amen! Blessing and glory and wisdom and thanksgiving and honor and power and strength, be to our God forever and ever. Amen." Then one of the elders asked me, "Who are these people robed in white, and where did they come from?" I said to him, "Sir, you know." Then he told me: "These are the ones coming out of the great tribulation. They washed their robes and made them white in the blood of the Lamb."

As a result of the great witness of the 144,000, there is a great harvest of souls. Thousands and thousands have been saved and dressed in white robes signifying the righteousness of Christ. And in their hands are palm branches, which are used to celebrate the Feast of Tabernacles.

Why are so many people going to be saved during the Great Tribulation and not before? Because of the climate of the tribulation. When the church is raptured, the Antichrist will tell a perverted lie. Perhaps he will say it is God's judgment on those who are gone—that God got us out of the way and sent us to hell. I don't know. No one knows. But it is *the* lie. It is the big one that will set the stage for his reign on earth. Can you imagine the confusion and conviction that will come to this world when the church is raptured?

The second reason many will be saved is that their false security will be taken away. Do you remember what we learned in Revelation 6 about war, famine, calamities, and disasters? Imagine living in a world that chaotic. People will be asking, "What is happening? Where are the answers? What must we do?" Compound their uncertainties by 144,000 flaming evangelists who have been sealed. The Antichrist cannot kill them, and they will be preaching the glorious gospel of our Lord and

Savior Jesus Christ. Many will not believe the lie of the Antichrist. They will be listening.

I often notice when a flight attendant is explaining the life-saving procedures and devices of a plane that most people are not paying attention. But I guarantee you that if the pilot announced that the plane was going down in five minutes, I would grab that little manual from the back of the seat and begin to read everything it says. This gives you an idea of what will happen during the Great Tribulation. People will not be casual about God as some are today. And God will save a great, great multitude.

Acts 2:20–21 speaks of this time: "The sun will be turned to darkness, and the moon to blood, before the great and remarkable day of the Lord comes; then whoever calls on the name of the Lord will be saved." A lot of people will be inclined to call on the name of the Lord in that day, and they will be saved.

God can save anyone. There is no one too hard for God to save. It doesn't matter how bad a sinner you are; God will save you. Conversely, it doesn't matter how good you *think* you are; you need to be saved. God will not save someone who refuses to believe, but it is not because He *could not*. It is just that He *will not* because of their unbelief. Here is a letter from someone that the world would have given up on, but not God:

> *Dear Pastor Rogers,*
>
> *I had to write to let you know what effect your ministry has had on my life. Many times I sat and watched your program and thought what you said was stupid. How you expressed Christ was a joke. I laughed at your God by ignoring Him. He wasn't really there.*
>
> *I was a satanist as well as part of the Nazi movement. As bad as it sounds, Christians were nothing more than lower life forms to myself and my friends. I didn't need your God. I sold my soul to the devil. I signed a pact with my own blood. And after doing so, I read the small print. If I tried to get out of the group, I could be killed.*
>
> *I remembered the prayer line at your church. I called the number and someone prayed with me and I received Christ. I got a Bible and read and reread it. God saved me. Why would He do that? Because I was so evil and hurt Him so badly. I had been living with my boyfriend. He saw the change in me, too. He got saved and we finally got married. We both love the*

*Lord so much because we see the love of the Lord through
your church. Jesus can save anyone. He saved me. Thanks for
your prayer line, your church, and your TV ministry.*

There is no one so bad that he cannot be saved and no one so good that
he need not be saved. All who are saved will be saved by the precious blood
of the Lord Jesus Christ. What a mighty God we serve! There is no promise too hard for God to keep. There is no person too hard for God to save.

These saved ones, according to Scripture that we have read, will be
praising God. The Bible says they are waving palm branches. Palm
branches were used in the Feast of Tabernacles as a symbol of joy. All
heaven breaks loose with praise. Look in verses 11–12 of Revelation 7:
"All the angels stood around the throne, the elders, and the four living
creatures, and they fell on their faces before the throne and worshiped
God, saying: 'Amen! Blessing and glory and wisdom and thanksgiving and
honor and power and strength, be to our God forever and ever.'" Those are
the angels praising Him. Why are they praising Him? The angels are
praising Him when they see what God has done by His grace for us and
for these tribulation saints.

I thought of that old song that we used to sing about praising our
great God in glory.

> *Holy, holy is what the angels sing,*
> *And I expect to help them to make the courts of heaven ring.*
> *But when we sing salvation's story,*
> *They must fold their wings,*
> *For angels never knew the joy that our salvation brings.*

Indeed the angels may be praising the Lord. Yet saints have even more
reason to praise than angels do.

These tribulation saints will be martyred. Millions and millions will
go to heaven through the gates of torture. When they get saved they
will refuse the mark of the beast. They will disavow their allegiance to the
Antichrist. Most of them will be put to death by the guillotine. What a
terrible, horrible thing it will be. But then they will awaken in glory.

Do you know what some people are thinking today? "If all of these
people are going to get saved in the Great Tribulation, I will just wait until
then to be saved." Pardon me, but that's ignorance. Let me give you four
reasons why that is foolish.

First, you may die before the Great Tribulation. And if you do, you will go straight to hell without Jesus Christ. If I were unsaved, I wouldn't wait five minutes to give my heart to Jesus Christ, knowing what I do today.

Second, you will not believe on the Lord Jesus Christ during the Great Tribulation. Millions will, but not you because 2 Thessalonians 2:11–12 says, "For this reason God sends them a strong delusion so that they will believe what is false, so that all will be condemned—those who did not believe the truth but enjoyed unrighteousness." There is not one iota of hope for anybody who has knowingly refused Jesus Christ.

Third, even if you could be saved during the Great Tribulation, that would be a foolish decision. Do you really want to endure the sorrow, horror, and pain, and perhaps be decapitated for the cause of Christ? If it were me, I would rather go another way.

Fourth, you will miss knowing Jesus today. People say, "Get right with Jesus. You may die!" But, I say: "Get right with Jesus. You may live!" There is no greater joy than knowing Jesus Christ!

There Is No Problem Too Hard for God to Solve

No one is immune to problems. Job 14:1 says, "Man that is born of a woman is of few days, and full of trouble" (KJV). But we must remember that there is no problem that God cannot solve. Just read the glorious finale in Revelation 7:15–17: "For this reason they are before the throne of God, and they serve Him day and night in His sanctuary. The One seated on the throne will shelter them: no longer will they hunger; no longer will they thirst; no longer will the sun strike them, or any heat. Because the Lamb who is at the center of the throne will shepherd them; He will guide them to springs of living waters, and God will wipe away every tear from their eyes."

Jesus didn't say you will get out of this world unscathed with no problems. He said just the opposite. There is no fine print in the contract. Jesus said, "I have told you these things so that in Me you may have peace. In the world you have suffering. Be courageous! *I have conquered the world*" (John 16:33).

Perhaps God is not working in a timely fashion or in the way that you prefer. You must remember what the prophet Isaiah said: "For my thoughts are not your thoughts, neither are your ways my ways, saith the LORD. For as the heavens are higher than the earth, so are my ways higher than your ways, and my thoughts than your thoughts" (Isaiah 55:8–9 KJV). None of us will ever understand why God does what He does every time He does something.

What do you say to a couple at the graveside of their little child? What do you say to a man who loses his lifelong companion just days away from celebrating their sixtieth wedding anniversary? What do you say to a man who has lost his job, has no savings, and feels embarrassed that he cannot take care of his family? What do you say to a person who is being tortured for his faith?

I'll tell you what to say: This is not God's final plan! Romans 8:18 promises, "For I consider that the sufferings of this present time are not worth comparing with the glory that will be revealed to us." There will come a day when our Lord will wipe away all tears. He will turn every tear into a pearl. He will take every hurt and transform it into a hallelujah. He will arch the rainbow of His glory over the storms of your life.

Many people will say, "If there is no promise that God can't keep, there is no person that God cannot save, there is no problem that God cannot solve, why are there so many unsaved people?" Because of their unbelief. It is not God's problem; it is theirs. In the city of Nazareth, Jesus "did not do many miracles there because of their unbelief" (Matthew 13:58).

There was a little girl who put her hand down in a very expensive vase and could not get it out. The family did everything they knew to do, but they couldn't get her hand out. Finally, they had to break the vase. When they broke the vase, they saw that her little fist was clenched. They opened it up and found a penny in her hand. Her father asked her, "Honey, why didn't you open your hand?" She said, "I'd lose my penny."

This is a timeless illustration of how many of us are clinging to the most foolish things in life rather than setting our old lives down and giving our hearts to Jesus. May we never forget that there is no promise too hard for God to keep, no person too hard for God to save, and no problem too hard for God to solve. What a mighty God we serve!

When Demons Dominate

◄◦►
CHAPTER 11
◄◦►

In studying the Book of Revelation, we now come to a time of silence between the seals. Revelation 8:1 says, "When He opened the seventh seal, there was silence in heaven for about half an hour." I cannot tell you for certain, but this may be the longest silence ever experienced in heaven.

What is this silence? It is an *ominous* silence—the lull before the storm. Have you ever been in a tornado alert? Everything gets very still, and the atmosphere is sometimes clammy. Perhaps you have been in a courtroom when the jury comes back in after a long deliberation. The defendant, the prosecutor, and the judge are sitting there, and there is an eerie silence while everyone waits for the verdict. That is the kind of silence John described in this verse.

The seal was opened, and John saw "the seven angels who stand in the presence of God; seven trumpets were given to them" (Revelation 8:2). A trumpet was used in Bible times for positive events like gathering a convocation or announcing a coronation. But it was also used to gather troops for war—very much like a siren to warn of an air raid or tornado.

The Silence: A Lesson on Prayer

But before these trumpets are sounded, God puts a parenthesis here, and we learn a wonderful lesson on prayer:

> Another angel, with a gold incense burner, came and stood at
> the altar. He was given a large amount of incense to offer with
> the prayers of all the saints on the gold altar in front of the
> throne. The smoke of the incense, with the prayers of the saints,

went up in the presence of God from the angel's hand. The
angel took the incense burner, filled it with fire from the altar,
and hurled it to the earth; there were thunders, rumblings,
lightnings, and an earthquake. And the seven angels who had
the seven trumpets prepared to blow them (Revelation 8:3–6).

Incense in the Bible has often been used as an illustration of what happens when we pray. In the Old Testament, the priest sprinkled the blood
of the sacrifice upon the altar. The coals from this offering would then be
placed in a golden censer, or container, and the smoke would rise to heaven
as incense. In much the same way, our prayers are like a sweet fragrance
in the nostrils of God.

In Revelation 8:3–4, we read that the priest mingled the prayers of the
saints with the incense. In this passage, the incense is the worth of the Lord
Jesus Christ. We are to come before God with both hands filled with the
Lord Jesus. Ephesians 5:2 tells us to "walk in love, as the Messiah also loved
us and gave Himself for us, a sacrificial and fragrant offering to God."

Have you ever prayed when you didn't feel like praying? Sometimes
you have to take yourself by the nape of the neck and say, "It's time to
pray." You don't want to pray. But you must remember that your feelings
have little to do with prayer. You are to pray when you feel like it. You are
to pray when you *don't* feel like it. It is *His presence* that makes your
prayers powerful, *not* how you feel about it. When you pray in the name
of Jesus, you are mingling your prayer with the incense of Jesus' worth,
and that's a sweet smell in the nostrils of Almighty God.

The Altars: The Sacrifice of Christ

What do these altars represent? The golden altar represents the fire of
worship. The altar of judgment represents the death of Jesus Christ for our
sins (every Old Testament altar spoke of Jesus' death on the cross). Why
would the death of Jesus bring judgment? If you do not repent of your sin
and receive Jesus Christ's sacrifice for your forgiveness, His sacrifice that
is meant to be a blessing will become a curse. The gospel is a double-edged
sword. It is a savor of life unto life or death unto death. If the death of
Jesus Christ does not save you, the death of Jesus Christ will condemn
you. His blood will testify either for or against you.

After the angel mingled the prayers of the saints with incense, "the
angel took the incense burner, filled it with fire from the altar, and
hurled it to the earth; there were thunders, rumblings, lightnings, and an

earthquake. And the seven angels who had the seven trumpets prepared to blow them" (Revelation 8:5–6). The horrors of the Great Tribulation are about to intensify for those who have refused Jesus Christ, and yet He died for their sins.

The Trumpets: The Announcement of Judgment

The First Trumpet

The first trumpet announced the judgment on the land and the things that grow on earth. Revelation 8:7 says, "The first angel blew his trumpet, and hail and fire, mixed with blood, were hurled to the earth. So a third of the earth was burned up, a third of the trees were burned up, and all the green grass was burned up."

What man-made device or natural phenomenon could cause this? Could it be an atomic explosion? Perhaps. But could there be a symbolic meaning of these things? I think the grass and the trees may symbolize leaders and people. Isaiah 40:6–7 says, "The voice said, Cry. And he said, What shall I cry? All flesh is grass, and all the goodliness thereof is as the flower of the field: the grass withereth, the flower fadeth: because the spirit of the LORD bloweth upon it: surely the people is grass" (KJV).

The Second Trumpet

The second trumpet sends forth judgment upon the oceans and the things that live in the sea. Revelation 8:8–9 says, "The second angel blew his trumpet, and something like a great mountain ablaze with fire was hurled into the sea. So a third of the sea became blood, a third of the living creatures in the sea died, and a third of the ships were destroyed."

This could literally be an erupting volcano that sends forth fire and burning lava into the sea. Which sea? It could be the Mediterranean, which John knew about when he wrote this book. But I wonder if there is not a deeper, more symbolic meaning. In the Bible, a mountain speaks of kingdoms.

For example, Babylon [now the nation known as Iraq] is spoken of as a destroying mountain in Jeremiah 51:25, when God says, "Behold, I am against thee, O destroying mountain, saith the LORD, which destroyest all the earth: and I will stretch out Mine hand upon thee, and roll thee down from the rocks, and will make thee a burnt mountain" (KJV). This sounds very similar to what we find here in the Book of Revelation.

This mountain is cast into the waters, which stand for a wicked and restless people. The prophet Isaiah said, "But the wicked are like the troubled sea, when it cannot rest, whose waters cast up mire and dirt. There is no peace, saith my God, to the wicked" (Isaiah 57:20–21 KJV). I believe the symbolism of this second trumpet is that this wicked, violent, Babylonish kingdom of Antichrist will bring great trouble to the wicked people who are like the troubled sea when it cannot rest.

The Third Trumpet

The third trumpet heralds judgment upon the rivers and the men who walk on earth. Revelation 8:10–11 says, "The third angel blew his trumpet, and a great star, blazing like a torch, fell from heaven. It fell on a third of the rivers and springs of water. The name of the star is Wormwood, and a third of the waters became wormwood. So, many of the people died from the waters, because they had been made bitter."

There are two ways to look at the interpretation of these verses. First, if an asteroid hit the earth, do you think it could be seen as a burning star like a lamp? We spoke of asteroids in chapter 9, and I believe there may be literal asteroids to hit earth that could poison the atmosphere and waters and kill many. Second, Satan is symbolized as a fallen star (see Isaiah 14:12), and the waters speak of people (see Revelation 17:15). A fallen star (Satan) could poison the water of life, thereby killing off human society in a devastating way.

The Fourth Trumpet

The fourth trumpet sounds, and God sends judgment upon the skies and the very light that shines from heaven. Revelation 8:12–13 says, "The fourth angel blew his trumpet, and a third of the sun was struck, a third of the moon, and a third of the stars, so that a third of them were darkened. A third of the day was without light, and the night as well. I looked, and I heard an eagle, flying in mid-heaven, saying in a loud voice, 'Woe! Woe! Woe to those who live on the earth, because of the remaining trumpet blasts that the three angels are about to sound!'"

The drama of the end of the ages has now intensified threefold. Notice the eagle said, "Woe! woe! woe." The sun, moon, and stars are darkened. What would cause that? If volcanoes and atomic blasts are sending smoke and ashes into the atmosphere, then the light of the sun, moon, and stars would be dimmed.

From the beginning, men have hated the light. Jesus said, "For everyone who practices wicked things hates the light and avoids it, so that his deeds may not be exposed" (John 3:20). Now these men will have their share of the darkness.

Symbolically, the sun, moon, and stars speak of ruling authority. The pastors of the church, for example, are symbolized as stars in the early verses of Revelation. One explanation of this passage is that when the fourth trumpet sounds, the structure of society comes apart. The things that God ordained to give guidance and light are now obliterated. The demon of darkness (Satan) becomes the prince of this world in the form of his Antichrist, who brainwashes the multitudes.

The Fifth Trumpet

The fifth trumpet sounds, and there is an invasion from the bottomless pit. Revelation 9:1–2 says, "And the fifth angel sounded, and I saw a star fall from heaven unto the earth: and to him was given the key of the bottomless pit. And he opened the bottomless pit; and there arose a smoke out of the pit, as the smoke of a great furnace; and the sun and the air were darkened by reason of the smoke of the pit" (KJV).

Demons will be released upon the earth from a bottomless pit. The Greek word for "bottomless pit" is *abussou*, from which we get our English word *abyss*. Who are these demons? They will be especially vile, malicious, and powerful. In fact, they are so diabolical that God in His mercy prepared a special pit in which to lock them away until the appointed time.

These demons are not like the demons who have roamed the earth since they fell from heaven. They dread to go to the pit! When Jesus cast the demons [called Legion] out of a man, "they besought him that he would not command them to go out into the deep" (Luke 8:31 KJV). The "deep" is the same word for the bottomless pit. This is also the place Peter referred to when he said: "For if God spared not the angels that sinned, but cast them down to hell, and delivered them into chains of darkness, to be reserved unto judgment" (2 Peter 2:4 KJV).

I defined the fallen star as Satan in the last section. Here, Almighty God has given him permission to open the door of the bottomless pit to set the demons free.

The Demons: The Dominion of the Antichrist

There are eleven things we need to learn about the demons from the abyss:

1. They are *degenerate spirits*. They are the vilest of the vile. I have already talked at length about this.

2. They are *darkening spirits*. In Revelation 9:2 we learn that a demonic darkness will come upon the earth that will choke out the light. Martin Luther calls Satan the "prince of darkness" in his hymn "A Mighty Fortress Is Our God."

3. They are *devouring spirits*. Revelation 9:3–4 says, "Then out of the smoke locusts came to the earth, and power was given to them like the power that scorpions have on the earth. They were told not to harm the grass of the earth, or any green plant, or any tree, but only people who do not have God's seal on their foreheads." In the Middle East, swarms of locusts have swarmed like great clouds and blotted out the light of the sun and the moon. They devour every bit of plant life in their path like an army—every blade of grass, every flower in the field, every seed and stalk of grain, sometimes even stripping the bark from the trees. But these particular locusts will not feed upon *green* things. They will feed upon the hearts and souls of men. And as they do, they will inflict torment like a scorpion.

4. They are *debilitating spirits*. Revelation 9:5–6 says, "They were not permitted to kill them, but were to torment them for five months; their torment is like the torment caused by a scorpion when it strikes a man. In those days people will seek death and will not find it; they will long to die, but death will flee from them." When I a boy, I was helping my dad clean the yard, and he asked me to get a piece of canvas from the pump house so we could sweep the leaves on it. I unrolled it, and a scorpion began stinging me on the tip of one of my fingers. When I saw that hideous thing I reached over and grabbed him with the other hand, and he stung me on both fingers. Suddenly, I became nauseous. The glands under my arms began to swell, my knees weakened, and the pain began to throb. But here's the good thing—the pain went away. What if the pain had lasted five months, as stated in Revelation 9:10? People will want to die but will not be able to do so.

5. They are *dauntless spirits*. Revelation 9:7 says, "The appearance of the locusts was like horses equipped for battle." Picture a team of mighty horses pawing the ground, snorting in fury, and covered with armor.

Think of their ability to gallop quickly into battle. They are eagerly daunt-less for their mission of doom. Now picture yourself standing in front of them and trying to stop them. No amount of money will be able to do it. The military cannot help. And even medicine will not work. They are dauntless.

6. They are *domineering spirits*. Look again at the next phrase in verse 7: "On their heads were something like gold crowns." Satan has always wanted to wear a crown. Now hell has a holiday, and the world has said to Jesus Christ, "We will not have you rule over us." Instead, they crown Satan and his demons to rule. Demons will have dominion in the Great Tribulation. No human ingenuity will be able to stop them. It will be a reign of terror.

7. They are *deceptive spirits*. Notice the last part of verse 7: "Their faces were like men's faces." What does that mean? "Like men's faces" is a symbol of intelligence. The Antichrist will be crafty and subtle. Jesus said, "False messiahs and false prophets will arise and perform great signs and wonders to lead astray, if possible, even the elect" (Matthew 24:24). Satan has a cunning plan. When He sends the Antichrist into this world, he will be able to make people think that white is black, black is white, up is down, and down is up. This may sound hard to believe, but I think the Antichrist will be so conniving that he will make you murder your mother and think you are doing God a service.

8. They are *defiling spirits*. Revelation 9:8 says, "They had hair like women's hair; their teeth were like lions' teeth." A woman's hair is a symbol of seduction and defilement. God has given women their hair for their glory, and it is a beautiful thing, but these demons will use that as a trap. In many ways, these deceptive demons will seem alluring. The Bible speaks of seducing spirits (see 1 Timothy 4:1). But they will have teeth like lions. This is the picture of Satan that we see in 1 Peter 5:8: "Be sober! Be on the alert! Your adversary the Devil is prowling around like a roaring lion, looking for anyone he can devour." These evil spirits will be hideously beautiful and brilliantly deceptive.

9. They are *defiant spirits*. Revelation 9:9 says, "They had chests like iron breastplates; the sound of their wings was like the sound of chariots with many horses rushing into battle." These demons will be wearing impenetrable armor, so the groans, cries, and shrieks of their victims will be meaningless to them. They will not be moved from their course of action. And wave after wave, they will come. You can hear the chariots

rumble. They cannot be stopped. They cannot be outrun. There is no place to hide.

10. They are *durable spirits*. Revelation 9:10 says, "And they had tails with stingers, like scorpions, so that with their tails they had the power to harm people for five months." Five months is the normal lifespan of a locust. Five is also the number of completeness. What does this mean? Until their deed is done they cannot be stopped. Nothing but the hand of Almighty God can stop these durable spirits. They cannot be destroyed. There is no weapon against them.

11. They are *diabolical spirits*. Revelation 9:11–12 says, "They had as their king the angel of the abyss; his name in Hebrew is Abaddon, and in Greek he has the name Apollyon. The first woe has passed. There are still two more woes to come after this." Apollyon is Satan himself.

Can you imagine what would happen if all the prison doors in America were flung open? If every rapist, murderer, pervert, arsonist, abuser, and thief were free to roam the earth, and no police force could protect us? That is the idea here. Now imagine just one more thing: What if, by some means, all of these criminals were organized under one ruler. There is a ruler—his name is Apollyon.

But the story doesn't end there. The Bible has wonderful news! First Thessalonians gives us two bright notes to end this chapter. Chapter 1, verse 10 says, "And to wait for His Son from heaven, whom He raised from the dead—Jesus, *who rescues us from the coming wrath*." Isn't that wonderful? Here's the second great news: "For God did not appoint us to wrath, but to obtain salvation through our Lord Jesus Christ, who died for us, so that whether we are awake or asleep, we will live together with Him. Therefore encourage one another and build each other up as you are already doing" (1 Thessalonians 5:9–11).

God will not pour out His wrath upon the church. God will chastise us, but He will never pour His wrath upon His bride. What husband would pour out his wrath upon his bride just before the marriage supper? The church is the bride of Christ. One of these days another trumpet will sound, and this is the trumpet that will call us to meet the Lord Jesus Christ in the air. And just as the Lord took Lot out of Sodom before fire and brimstone, and the Lord put Noah in the ark before the flood, He will call His beloved home before the Great Tribulation.

I was on an airplane a while back, and the flight attendant said, "This plane is headed for Cincinnati, Ohio. If Cincinnati is not in your plans today, I suggest you disembark now." This world is headed for hell and judgment, and if you don't intend to go there, may I suggest you avoid this path by giving your heart to Jesus Christ.

Gone Wild

CHAPTER 12

Do you ever look at the world around you and think that everything not nailed down is coming loose, and that the world has gone wild? Where is God? Doesn't He know? If He knows, doesn't He care? If He knows and cares, can't He do anything about it? We will find out in this chapter that God does know, God does care, and God does have a plan.

In the last few chapters, we have studied the future period of time known as the Great Tribulation, which is described by the seven-sealed book. As the seals were broken and the book was opened, we saw the horrors prophesied about the Great Tribulation. Let's pick up where we left off in the last chapter with Revelation 9:13–21:

> The sixth angel blew his trumpet. From the four horns of the gold altar that is before God, I heard a voice say to the sixth angel who had the trumpet, "Release the four angels bound at the great river Euphrates." So the four angels who were prepared for the hour, day, month, and year were released to kill a third of the human race. The number of mounted troops was 200 million; I heard their number. This is how I saw the horses in my vision: The horsemen had breastplates that were fiery red, hyacinth blue, and sulfur yellow. The heads of the horses were like lions' heads, and from their mouths came fire, smoke, and sulfur. A third of the human race was killed by these three plagues—by the fire, the smoke, and the sulfur that came from their mouths. For the power of the horses is in their mouths and in their tails, because their tails, like snakes, have heads, and they inflict injury with them. The rest of the people,

who were not killed by these plagues, did not repent of the works of their hands to stop worshiping demons and idols of gold, silver, bronze, stone, and wood, which are not able to see, hear, or walk. And they did not repent of their murders, their sorceries, their sexual immorality, or their thefts.

As we look around at a world that has seemingly gone wild, how much more will it look chaotic during the Great Tribulation! Thankfully, the church will be raptured and we will not have to experience that torment. For what we are seeing today, there are five factors that we can apply from this text to help us understand that God knows, God cares, and God has a plan.

The Prayer Factor

Revelation 9:13 says, "And the sixth angel sounded, and I heard a voice from the four horns of the golden altar which is before God" (KJV). What is the golden altar? In the tabernacle in heaven there is a golden altar called the altar of prayer. In the days when the Israelite priests worshiped in the earthly tabernacle, there was also a golden altar.

If you had been able to go into the earthly tabernacle, the first thing you would have seen was the outer court where a fire burned continually in a brazen altar. This fire represented the holiness of God and His judgment against sin. The priests would sacrifice a spotless animal on that altar, which represented the Lord Jesus Christ dying for our sins.

The inner court (the Holy of Holies) contained the golden altar (the mercy seat). It had four protuberances or four horns on each corner (the horns speak of power). On the Day of Atonement each year, the high priest walked into the Holy of Holies and sprinkled blood from an animal sacrifice upon the golden altar. This offering represented the sacrifice of Jesus Christ—the propitiation for our sins. When the offering was burned, the high priest then burned incense on the golden altar from morning until evening. This incense represented our prayers to heaven in the power of the blood.

Let me give you some Scriptures that support this: Revelation 5:8 says, "And when he had taken the book, the four beasts and four and twenty elders fell down before the Lamb, having every one of them harps, and golden vials full of odours, which are the prayers of saints" (KJV). Psalm 141:2 says, "Let my prayer be set forth before thee as incense; and the lifting up of my hands as the evening sacrifice" (KJV).

Knowing our prayers are like incense before His throne gives us a little more insight into our prayer life. But do you ever feel like you pray and pray, and yet nothing happens? Perhaps you think God hasn't heard your prayer or God heard and said no. Others share in how you feel:

And when he had opened the fifth seal, I saw under the altar the souls of them that were slain for the word of God, and for the testimony which they held: *And they cried with a loud voice, saying, How long, O Lord, holy and true, dost thou not judge and avenge our blood on them that dwell on the earth?* And white robes were given unto every one of them; and it was said unto them, that they should rest yet for a little season, until their fellowservants also and their brethren, that should be killed as they were, should be fulfilled (Revelation 6:9–11 KJV).

God says, "Wait. There are more who must stand with you, for the battle is not yet over." Revelation 8:3 says that the angel offered the incense with the prayers of "all saints" (KJV). Are you a saint? You are if you are saved. Your prayer has been heard. Ron Dunn, who was an outstanding preacher before he went home to heaven, said that prayer is the Christian's secret weapon and that it is like an intercontinental ballistic missile. He went on to give five factors about prayer.

1. *Prayers can be fired from any spot.* Sometimes I will take a young person to a certain spot in my office and I will say, "Do you see that spot on the carpet? You can go to anywhere in the world from that spot." In the same way, you can launch a prayer from any spot on earth.

2. *Prayers can travel undetected at the speed of light.* I don't know where heaven is or how far away it is, but your prayer can reach heaven faster than the speed of light.

3. *Prayers hit the target every time.* The Father is always listening to His children, and He hears each and every prayer.

4. *Satan has no defense against prayer.* Satan does not have an anti-prayer missile that can prevent your prayer from reaching heaven.

5. *Prayers often have a delayed detonation.* Prayer delayed is not prayer denied. God has His own schedule, and if you prayed to God about something, that prayer did not fall to the ground; that prayer is still in heaven.

The Power Factor

It is so easy to divert our eyes from God and get deceived by Satan's power. Indeed, I would venture to say that all of us at one time or another have thought that God was up in heaven wringing His hands and walking around saying, "What am I going to do?" But we must recognize the power factor.

Revelation 9:14 says, "Say to the sixth angel who had the trumpet, 'Release the four angels bound at the great river Euphrates.'" The Euphrates River is both the cradle and the grave of human civilization. It is the river that divides the east from west. We say, "East is east and west is west, and never the twain shall meet." One of these days, in the Great Tribulation, they will meet in a great conflict.

The Book of Genesis tells us: "And a river went out of Eden to water the garden; and from thence it was parted, and became into four heads" (Genesis 2:10 KJV). One of the "heads" of that river was the Euphrates (see Genesis 2:14). Nimrod (who was an Old Testament picture of the Antichrist, see Genesis 10:8–10) built the Tower of Babel, the first world empire, alongside the Euphrates River (see Genesis 11:1–9). And it is alongside the Euphrates where Saddam Hussein previously reigned in Iraq. Despots like these are only tools and boys in the hands of the prince of Babylon.

In His sovereign wisdom and power, God is restraining four of the most wicked and powerful of all the demonic fallen angels (I call them the filthy four) who have been given dominion over the four world empires. When He is ready in the fullness of time, God will give His permission to release them. And when that happens (and I do not mean this flippantly), all hell will break loose.

To understand a little about these four demonic powers, let's look at a prayer Daniel offered that God did not answer immediately. "An angel came and said to Daniel: 'Do not fear, Daniel, for from the first day that you set your heart to understand, and to humble yourself before your God, your words were heard; and I am come because of your words. But the prince of the kingdom of Persia withstood me twenty-one days; and behold, Michael, one of the chief princes, came to help me, for I had been left alone there with the princes of Persia" (Daniel 10:12–13 NKJV).

Who is the prince of the kingdom of Persia? It certainly wasn't an earthly man who could do battle with an angel. I believe the prince of the kingdom of Persia was one of these four angels that is bound here. The story continues: "Then said he [*the angel to Daniel*], "Do you know why I have come to you? And now I must return to fight with the prince of Persia; and when I have gone forth, indeed the prince of Greece will come. But I will tell you what is noted in the Scripture of Truth. No one upholds me against these, except Michael your prince *(of the people of God and Israel especially]*" (Daniel 10:20–21 NKJV, explanatory notes added by the author).

There are wicked demons who rule over world empires. How do we know this? Paul said, "For our battle is not against flesh and blood, but against the rulers, against the authorities, against the world powers of this darkness, against the spiritual forces of evil in the heavens" (Ephesians 6:12). Have you ever wondered why government officials are unable to negotiate with some of these countries? It is because they are trying to negotiate with men and not the evil power behind those men's actions.

But let us never forget that despite the power of these rulers of darkness, there is only so much they can do. Satan cannot do whatever he wants when he wants. The Bible says, "You are from God, little children, and you have conquered them [the spirits of darkness], because the One who is in you is greater than the one who is in the world" (1 John 4:4).

God allows Satan to do certain things. Satan wanted to sift Peter as wheat, but he had to get God's permission (see Luke 22:31–32). Satan wanted to harm Job, but he had to get God's permission (see Job 1:6–12). In some measure, Satan is restrained on a leash. There is not some sort of conflict that has God on one side and Satan on the other, while we wait to see who will win. Satan is a created being. He may be sinister, but God is sovereign.

Robert Louis Stevenson told a story about a ship on a rocky coastline during a storm. The sailors beneath the waterline were being tossed and turned. They knew the danger and were wondering how they were going to make it. One of the sailors could take it no longer, so he left his duty, went up to the pilothouse, pushed open the door, and saw the captain steering the ship. The captain knew the sailor was worried and without saying a word, he turned and smiled. The sailor returned below deck and said, "Don't worry. It's all right. I have seen the captain, and he smiled at me." Corrie ten Boom said, "Look at the world, you'll be distressed. Look within, you'll be depressed. Look at Christ, you'll be at rest." We must keep our eyes on Him in a world gone wild.

The Purpose Factor

Revelation 9:15 says, "So the four angels who were prepared for the hour, day, month, and year were released to kill a third of the human race." If you read that without much thought, you might have interpreted the time to be thirteen months. But the Greek says, "This very hour and day and month and year."

God has a purpose and a plan for a specific hour when these angels will be loosed. And not a speck of dust moves in this universe unless God gives permission. Not a blade of grass moves in the wind without God's permission. God is strategically moving in His world in His own timing. I remember reading about a mission of the space shuttle Columbia getting called off because the computer was off by one twenty-fifth of a second. Can you imagine the waste for one twenty-fifth of a second? Timing is important.

God said to Abraham, "I am going to give you Canaan" (see Genesis 17:8). But God had one condition: "Abraham, there will be four hundred years before your people will be able to possess it" (see Genesis 15:13–14). Why? "The iniquity of the Amorites is not yet full" (Genesis 15:16 KJV). God waited as the iniquity of the Amorites went into the reservoir of His wrath drop by drop for four hundred years.

Imagine how long people prayed for the Messiah, who had been prophesied over and over again. Second Peter 3:4 says people were asking, "Where is the promise of His coming? For ever since the fathers fell asleep, all things continue as they have been since the beginning of creation." And Peter reassured them, "Dear friends, don't let this one thing escape you: with the Lord one day is like 1,000 years, and 1,000 years like one day" (2 Peter 3:8). God is never ahead of time, and God is never late. He does not punch a clock when He goes to work. The day of the Lord will come. The Epistle to the Galatians tells us: "Even so we, when we were children, were in bondage under the elements of the world: *But when the fulness of the time was come,* God sent forth his Son, made of a woman, made under the law, to redeem them that were under the law, that we might receive the adoption of sons" (Galatians 4:3–5 KJV).

Just because it has been two thousand years since our Lord stepped into glory, don't think for one scintilla of a second that God has forgotten His promise. One day the trumpet will sound, the sky will roll back, and Jesus will rise from His throne and step down to receive His own. He is coming. One of my favorite Scriptures is 1 Timothy 6:14–15, where Paul exhorts Timothy to "keep the commandment without spot or blame until the appearing of our Lord Jesus Christ, which God will bring about in His own time. He is the blessed and only Sovereign, the King of kings, and the Lord of lords."

If you want to know where God is, He is on time. With God, timing is more important than time.

The Perversity Factor

Revelation 9:16 tells us that John saw and heard an army of two hundred million. How can that be? When John saw this revelation, there weren't two hundred million people living on the earth. In World War II, the greatest number of soldiers the United States had at one time was twelve million. And yet, here is an army of two hundred million! You might be tempted to ask: "John, are you sure you put your decimal point in the right place?"

When God gives His permission to release the filthy four from the Euphrates River, an incredible battle will begin and there will be armies of great number. It will not be the battle of Armageddon, but it will set the stage for Armageddon. Satan is a devil of war, and his demons are demons of war. Revelation 16:14 says, "They are spirits of demons performing signs, who travel to the kings of the whole world to assemble them for the battle of the great day of God, the Almighty." Demon spirits move the hearts of terrorists and warmongers toward destruction and battle.

> And thus I saw the horses in the vision, and them that sat on them, having breastplates of fire, and of jacinth, and brimstone: and the heads of the horses were as the heads of lions; and out of their mouths issued fire and smoke and brimstone. By these three was the third part of men killed, by the fire, and by the smoke, and by the brimstone, which issued out of their mouths. For their power is in their mouth, and in their tails: for their tails were like unto serpents, and had heads, and with them they do hurt (Revelation 9:17–19 KJV).

The war described here may be a symbolic description of modern war. There are breastplates of fire and of jacinth (the color of the hot, blue flame that could come from a gun). These instruments of war shoot fire, smoke, and brimstone. They have tails like the tails of serpents. It sounds very much like the kinds of tanks, helicopters, and rockets that we would see today. What if God had given John the vision of when man landed on the moon? John may have described what he saw as a great spider sending forth fire and brimstone. Of course, nobody knew anything about helicopters, airplanes, or tanks back then. But they knew something about horses prepared for battle.

I want to give you a possible scenario of what may happen from the prophecies we have read in God's Word. A political union will arise in Europe—a kind of "United States of Europe." The Antichrist will arise out of western Europe (the old Roman Empire) and gather together the military and economic power that has been latent in Europe. His first task will be to make a treaty with Israel. It will be a logical move of diplomacy because an independent third party seems to be the only solution in the Middle East. He will say, "Come under our wings, and we will protect you and make your borders safe."

And so this alliance, with the support of the United States, will make a treaty with Israel that unconditionally guarantees her voice. When that happens, it will incite the passions of the Muslim world stretched along the Euphrates River to the former Soviet Empire. There will come a war along the Euphrates, and two hundred million soldiers will march in the ultimate jihad. When this happens, the United States of Europe and Israel will come against this horde (see Ezekiel 37–39).

Next, the Bible says there will come a great shaking in the land of Israel. Will it be an earthquake? An atomic war? We will see. But the West will prevail, and in that geo-political vacuum, the Antichrist will be enthroned as the world leader. The world will wonder after the beast, and will say, "Who is like this man? Who is able to make war against him?"

Another possible scenario is this. This army of 200 million may be wave after wave of demos released from the pit. These have already been spoken of in this chapter. Whether this army is one of human beings or of demon forces, it will bring colossal chaos to this earth.

When will this happen? It seems it is going to happen after God removes His church. Then He will remove His hand of mercy and announce that the four angels can be let loose. For man, who has wanted to live his own life his own way, will now be vulnerable to the full reign of terror from Satan.

The Pride Factor

After reading about all of these things, you may think that men will fall on their faces and cry out for mercy to God. Yet, look at Revelation

9:19–21: "For the power of the horses is in their mouths and in their tails, because their tails, like snakes, have heads, and they inflict injury with them. The rest of the people, who were not killed by these plagues, did not repent of the works of their hands to stop worshiping demons and idols of gold, silver, bronze, stone, and wood, which are not able to see, hear, or walk. And they did not repent of their murders, their sorceries, their sexual immorality, or their thefts."

Instead of being horrified, men have become hardened. Men are not changed because of punishment. You can put a person in a prison, but it won't change his heart. Proverbs 17:10 says, "A reproof entereth more into a wise man than an hundred stripes into a fool" (KJV). Men are not beaten into submission.

Do you know what people are doing in hell? Jesus said that they are gnashing their teeth (see Matthew 13:42). Do you know what it means to gnash your teeth? It means to snarl. They are snarling against God. They are not asking God for mercy. They are still participating in their wicked course of demons, astrology, and Satan worship.

Revelation 9:21 tells us that in this time men will be neither sorrowful nor repentant of their sins of murder, sorcery, fornication, and thievery.

Murder. May God have mercy on the murderers of unborn babies in our world today. May God send His Spirit to bring repentance to every man and woman who has participated in this most heinous act against defenseless little ones. Beyond abortion the streets run red with carnage in every corner of the world.

Sorcery. The word *sorcery* comes from the Greek word *pharmakōn.* It is the word from which we get the English word *pharmacist.* Do you know what a pharmacist does? He dispenses drugs. In the Great Tribulation, men will be reduced to rubble through their abuse of drugs.

Fornication. This word comes from the Greek word *porneias,* from which we get our word *pornography.* It speaks of sexual perversion and immorality. God left Sodom and Gomorrah with their smoking ruins as a testimony to those who choose to live ungodly lives (see 2 Peter 2:6). But mankind will not learn. And Jesus tells us that the world will experience an even worse judgment than Sodom and Gomorrah (see Matthew 10:15).

Thefts. In the Great Tribulation, people will steal openly from one another. There will be no restraints or negative consequences from civil authorities for their behavior. God knows that even in this time, punishment and suffering will not bring these people to Himself.

God says, "My spirit shall not always strive with man" (Genesis 6:3 KJV). There will come a time in the Great Tribulation when man will have crossed God's deadline and His hand of mercy will be removed. What is the application for our lives today? "Today, if you hear His voice, do not harden your hearts" (Hebrews 3:15).

Someone has written these words:

> As the tree falls, so must it lie.
> As a man lives, so will he die.
> As a man dies, so will he be
> Through all the years of eternity.

God loves you. Lay aside your pride. May the mercy of God through His Son bring the saving judgment of eternal life to you today, so you will not be lost in the fires of His judgment for all eternity.

Jesus Christ, the One and Only

—◄o►—
CHAPTER 13
—◄o►—

The Islamic faith calls Jesus Christ a prophet, but He is more than a prophet. The liberal calls Him a philosopher, a teacher, or an example for us to follow. But He is much more, so much more as we are about to discover in Revelation 10.

Right in the middle of talking about the Great Tribulation, John gives us a parenthetical passage about the Lord Jesus Christ. The sixth trumpet has blown, and now God takes a break from revealing the end times to remind us of His grace and power in a glorious picture of the Lord Jesus Christ. John says, "Then I saw another mighty angel coming down from heaven, surrounded by a cloud, with a rainbow over his head. His face was like the sun, his legs were like fiery pillars" (Revelation 10:1).

I believe this mighty angel is the Lord Jesus Christ. John knew the Old Testament. Jesus is depicted as an angel in Genesis 22:15: "And the angel of the LORD called unto Abraham out of heaven the second time" (KJV). Also, Isaiah 63:9 says, "In all their affliction he was afflicted, and the angel of his presence saved them: in his love and in his pity he redeemed them; and he bare them, and carried them all the days of old" (KJV). These Old Testament appearances of Christ as the angel of the Lord are called theophanies. There are four things I want you to learn about our Savior, Jesus the One and Only, in this tenth chapter of Revelation.

The Majesty of His Person

In Revelation 10:1 we see that Jesus is "clothed with a cloud: and a rainbow was upon his head, and his face was as it were the sun, and his feet as pillars of fire" (KJV). This is the same Jesus that John talked about in Revelation 1:7: "Behold, He cometh with the clouds; and every eye shall see Him" (KJV).

The Glory of Jesus

"Clothed with a cloud." Jesus is clothed in the shekinah glory of God. The cloud is the garment of divine presence. We have a picture of this happening elsewhere in the New Testament. Matthew records what happened when Jesus took Peter, James, and John to a mountain (now referred to as the Mount of Transfiguration). Matthew 17:2 says, "And [Jesus] was transfigured before them: and his face did shine as the sun, and his raiment was white as the light" (KJV). Matthew 17:5 says, "While [Jesus] yet spake, behold, a bright cloud overshadowed them: and behold a voice out of the cloud, which said, This is my beloved Son, in whom I am well pleased; hear ye him" (KJV).

Peter, having seen all of this, wanted to build a tabernacle and worship Jesus on the mountaintop. That was not God's plan. The lesson we learn about our Lord in this story is the lesson of His glory. Worship is not centered in a place; it is centered in a glorious person, and His name is Jesus. Thank God we can worship this One anywhere.

The Grace of Jesus

"A rainbow was upon his head." What did we learn earlier in the Book of Revelation about rainbows? They are a sign of God's covenants with man. God hung a rainbow in the sky after the flood to remind people of the covenant of His grace (see Genesis 9:13–17). Can you imagine how Noah must have felt when he got out of that ark and saw that creation had been utterly destroyed? Then he looked up and saw how God had placed a rainbow like a scarf on the shoulders of the storm.

In that glorious rainbow was every color ever conceived in the mind of God—red, orange, yellow, green, blue, indigo, violet, and more. And God said, "I will remember my covenant, which is between me and you and every living creature of all flesh; and the waters shall no more become a flood to destroy all flesh" (Genesis 9:15 KJV). Thank God that He will never break His Word.

The Greatness of Jesus

"*His face was as it were the sun.*" In the Book of Revelation, we learn that the sun is a symbol of God's strength. For instance, Revelation 1:16 says, "He had in his right hand seven stars: and out of his mouth went a sharp twoedged sword: and his countenance was as the sun shineth in his strength" (KJV). Think of the incredible power of the sun that hangs in our solar system. That is but a pint-sized picture of the radiant strength of God.

Years ago, astronomers thought the earth was the center of our solar system. And yet, when they compiled their observations and made their mathematical computations, nothing ever seemed to come together. Then along came a man named Copernicus. After considerable study, he discovered that the earth was not the center of our solar system, but that the earth and other planets revolved around the sun. When Copernicus shared this wonderful truth with the rest of the world, everything fell into place.

It is going to be the same way in your life. When you make the Son of Righteousness, the Lord Jesus Christ, the center of your life, things that have never fallen into place will finally make sense. Jesus is the One who holds everything together by His strength.

The Governance of Jesus

"*His feet as pillars of fire.*" Revelation 1:15 tells us that the Lord Jesus Christ had "feet like fine bronze fired in a furnace." Fire consumes. Fire cleanses. Fire spreads. This is a picture of how the Lord Jesus Christ will go forth in holiness to judge.

As I studied the Book of Revelation, I grew to love, appreciate, adore, and fear the Lord Jesus Christ. I am convinced that our churches need to learn how to totally worship the Lord Jesus Christ.

What is worship? Worship is how you respond to all that He is. Do you worship Him? I hope as you study the Book of Revelation that you will not just get facts and figures, but that you will see the Lord Jesus Christ. Revelation is an unveiling of Jesus Christ—His glory, grace, greatness, and governance.

The Mastery of His Power

Revelation 10:2 says, "And he had a little scroll opened in his hand. He put his right foot on the sea, his left on the land." When the book was first given to Him, it was sealed. Now Jesus has opened the seals to show He is coming to judge the earth and to take His purchased possession back with Him. It is His by creation. It is His by Calvary. It is His by conquest.

In Bible times, when a conqueror overthrew a nation and occupied a piece of land that had a shoreline, he would put one foot in the water and another foot on the land and raise his hand in victory. This gesture meant that he had conquered the area. Just as God told Joshua, "Every place that the sole of your foot shall tread upon, that have I given unto you, as I said unto Moses" (Joshua 1:3 KJV).

This gesture by the mighty angel Jesus Christ symbolized that every drop of water and every grain of sand belongs to Him. It is all His. People ask, "What is the world coming to?" It is coming to Jesus. It was all made by Him and for Him, and it is coming to Him. Colossians 1:16 says, "Because by Him everything was created, in heaven and on earth, the visible and the invisible, whether thrones or dominions or rulers or authorities—all things have been created through Him and for Him."

If His majesty causes my total worship, His mastery should cause my total surrender. He is Lord. "That at the name of Jesus every knee should bow—of those who are in heaven and on earth and under the earth—and every tongue should confess that Jesus Christ is Lord, to the glory of God the Father" (Philippians 2:10–11). Jesus is the One and Only.

The Mystery of His Plans

Revelation 10:3–7 says:

And [the mighty angel] cried with a loud voice, as when a lion roareth: and when he had cried, seven thunders uttered their voices. And when the seven thunders had uttered their voices, I was about to write: and I heard a voice from heaven saying unto me, Seal up those things which the seven thunders uttered, and write them not. And the angel which I saw stand upon the sea and upon the earth lifted up his hand to heaven, and sware by him that liveth for ever and ever, who created heaven, and the things that therein are, and the earth, and the things that therein are, and the sea, and the things which are therein, that there should be time no longer: but in the days of the voice of the seventh angel, when he shall begin to sound, the mystery of God should be finished, as he hath declared to his servants the prophets (KJV).

Out of the seven seals came seven trumpets. And as the last trumpet was about to sound, John heard the seven thunders, but he was told to "write them not." This message was a mystery to him for many reasons.

It Was a Startling Message

The Lion has prevailed, and now the Lion roars. Revelation 10:3 tells us that the mighty angel "cried with a loud voice." The Greek word for "angel" is *aggelos,* and it means "messenger." This angel is One who speaks for God like the roar of a lion. Elsewhere in God's Word, Jesus is depicted as a sacrificial Lamb; but in the Book of Revelation Jesus is pictured as the sovereign King. Jesus is not only the Lamb of God, but He is also the Lion of the tribe of Judah. Revelation 5:5 says, "Then one of the elders said to me, 'Stop crying. Look! The Lion from the tribe of Judah, the Root of David, has been victorious so that He may open the scroll and its seven seals.'"

Why does a lion roar? It is to terrify his foes. Joel 3:16 says, "The LORD also shall roar out of Zion, and utter his voice from Jerusalem; and the heavens and the earth shall shake: but the LORD will be the hope of his people, and the strength of the children of Israel" (KJV).

Jesus the Lamb of God "was oppressed, and he was afflicted, yet he opened not his mouth: he is brought as a lamb to the slaughter, and as a sheep before her shearers is dumb, so he openeth not his mouth" (Isaiah 53:7 KJV). When Jesus was crucified, He said, "This is your day; My day is not yet come." But one of these days the Lion of Judah will roar.

It Was a Sealed Message

After Jesus cried with a loud voice, John said, "Seven thunders spoke with their voices. And when the seven thunders spoke, I was about to write. Then I heard a voice from heaven, saying, 'Seal up what the seven thunders said, and do not write it down'" (Revelation 10:3–4).

John was amazed at what he heard and was about to write everything down when God told him to put his pen down. Why? The mysteries of God are too wonderful for explanations, and some things are too terrible for description. It is amazing how many people will try to explain what God has instructed us not to explain. Will Rogers, the philosopher from Oklahoma, said, "People don't show their ignorance by not knowing so much, as they do by knowing so much that ain't so." There are some things we will not understand until they come to pass.

Can you live with that? I wouldn't have any confidence in a God *you* could understand, much less one *I* could understand. No. God's ways, thoughts, and plans are above and beyond us. We don't live by explanations; we live by promises.

The classic passage for this is Daniel 12:8–9: "And I heard, but I understood not: then said I, O my Lord, what shall be the end of these things? And he said, Go thy way, Daniel: for the words are closed up and sealed till the time of the end" (KJV). Daniel heard what God said, but he didn't understand it. Have you ever picked up the Bible and said, "Lord, I can read Your Word, but I don't know what it means"? Does this mean that you are unspiritual or that you are out of the will of God? No, you might be a Daniel.

There are certain things in God's Word that we will never be able to explain. People ask, "What will our resurrection body be like?" Or, "We've got a little baby in heaven. What will my baby be like when I meet him? Will he be a man? Will he still be a baby?" First John 3:2 says, "Dear friends, we are God's children now, and what we will be has not yet been revealed. We know that when He appears, we will be like Him, because we will see Him as He is."

It Was a Sure Message

Revelation 10:5–6 says, "Then the angel that I had seen standing on the sea and on the land raised his right hand to heaven. He swore an oath by the One who lives forever and ever, who created heaven and what is in it, the earth and what is in it, and the sea and what is in it: 'There will no longer be an interval of time.'"

God the Son swore by Himself that time should be no more. God had done this before when He swore by Himself to seal the promise to Abraham that his seed would increase as the stars of heaven. Hebrews 6:13 says, "For when God made a promise to Abraham, since He had no one greater to swear by, He swore by Himself." In essence, God said, "If I don't keep My word, I will cease to be God. By My very existence these things will come to pass." Do you know why God's Word is a sure word of prophecy? Because God stands on His Word.

It Was a Solemn Message

What did the Lord mean when He said that there would "no longer be an interval of time" (Revelation 10:6)? Did He mean that history will cease? No, because after this period in the end times, God's Word tells us that a millennium of peace will follow when Jesus will reign on earth. The word *time* in the Greek is *chronos,* which may be translated "delay." Jesus knew one more trumpet judgment was to come; then the mystery of God would be revealed.

Sin has been on a rampage, and one of these days the clock of sin will stop. No longer will righteousness suffer. Everything will come to a conclusion. God will have given the inhabitants of the earth time to repent; then time will run out. The clock will strike its last note. As I've said before in this book, we must not have the idea that we have time before the rapture to get right with God. The rapture may come at any moment.

I read a story about a man who rushed into a railroad station one morning. He was almost out of breath, and he asked the agent, "What time does the 8:01 train leave?"

The agent said, "At 8:01."

The man said, "Well, it's 7:59 by my watch. It's 7:57 by the town clock. And it's 8:04 by the station clock. Which one should I go by?"

The agent replied, "You can go by any clock you want, but it's too late. The 8:01 has already left the station."

If you are not on God's train, you will be left.

The majesty of Jesus Christ is worthy of our total worship. The mastery of His power is worthy of our total confidence. The fourth thing I want you to see is the ministry of His people.

The Ministry of His People

Revelation 10:8–10 says, "And the voice which I heard from heaven spake unto me again, and said, Go and take the little book which is open in the hand of the angel which standeth upon the sea and upon the earth. And I went unto the angel, and said unto him, Give me the little book. And he said unto me, Take it, and eat it up; and it shall make thy belly bitter, but it shall be in thy mouth sweet as honey. And I took the little book out of the angel's hand, and ate it up; and it was in my mouth sweet as honey: and as soon as I had eaten it, my belly was bitter" (KJV).

The "little book" represents the Word of God. It is the title deed to all creation, and it belongs to the Lord Jesus Christ. It is His by creation; He made it. It is His by Calvary; He died for it. It is His by conquest; He will come in power and great glory.

The Lord instructed John to take this book and eat it. In a sense we should all do the same thing, but not just take and eat of it. Jesus said,

"Thou must prophesy again before many peoples, and nations, and tongues, and kings" (Revelation 10:11 KJV). We are to go forth and tell others about it.

Imagine the Lord Jesus standing before you right now and extending His nail-pierced hand to you to ask you to take His Word. Are you willing to take it? Before we can tell others, we must first appropriate the Word of God for ourselves. Then we are to assimilate that Word. It is not enough to read the recipe book; we are to cook, eat, and digest what we cook. Jesus said, "Man must not live on bread alone, but on every word that comes from the mouth of God" (Matthew 4:4).

We are to feed upon God's Word. Job said, "I have esteemed the words of his mouth more than my necessary food" (Job 23:12 KJV). Have you appropriated the Word of God? Have you assimilated the Word of God? If you have, then you will know that it will be both bitter and sweet. We hear so much about the love of God today that we have a world suffering from spiritual diabetes. There are some sad and horrifying things in the Book of Revelation. This world is headed for judgment.

God is a God of righteousness and justice and judgment. You cannot read the Book of Revelation without seeing that. There are a heaven and a hell, death and life, salvation, condemnation, bitterness and sweetness. It is all in the Bible. Second Corinthians 2:16–17 says, "To some we are a scent of death leading to death, but to others, a scent of life leading to life.

After we appropriate and assimilate the Word of God, we are to disseminate it. And not just part of it—all of it! If you preach the love of God without the wrath of God, you are dishonest. If you preach the wrath of God without the love of God, you are dishonest. Remember, if you take part of the truth and make part of the truth all of the truth, that part of the truth becomes an untruth. We are to preach all the Word of God—the bitter part and the sweet part. May God keep us from loveless truth or truthless love.

When Prophets Will Be Persecuted

◄o►

CHAPTER 14

◄o►

Persecution for religious beliefs is not an archaic practice of days gone by. Christians are being martyred for their faith all over the world *right now*. Indeed, God's Word tells us, "Yea, and *all that will live godly in Christ Jesus* shall suffer persecution" (2 Timothy 3:2 KJV). If everyone who is godly will suffer persecution, then why are some not? Because everyone is not living a godly life in Christ Jesus. When the times of this earth draw to a close, many prophets will be persecuted.

Some amazing end-time prophecies are being fulfilled today. For example, God said that He would bring the people of Israel back to their land: "For I will take you from among the heathen, and gather you out of all countries, and will bring you into your own land" (Ezekiel 36:24 KJV). That has happened, hasn't it? Plus, that prophecy solves the question about whose land the Israelites occupy.

But there is another prophecy in Revelation 11 about Jerusalem: The temple is to be rebuilt. If you visit Jerusalem today, you will see the Mosque of Omar on the temple mount (which is the most contested piece of real estate in the world). Some people call this site the Dome of the Rock. The only part of the temple that is left is the western part of the platform known as the Western Wall or the Wailing Wall. What happened to the temple?

In A.D. 70, a Roman general named Titus laid siege against Jerusalem. To hold true to his tradition as a Roman, he did not destroy the temple

(Romans preserved temples). Instead, Titus declared that Herod's temple in Jerusalem was to be preserved, but somehow it caught on fire—then was looted for its treasures. Parts of the temple were overlaid with gold, and everyone suspected there were great treasures down in the vaults. In the fire, the gold melted into the crevices of the stones. People pried apart each stone to get the gold, so there is no temple left today.

Jesus predicted in Matthew 24:1–2 that the temple would be destroyed: "As Jesus left and was going out of the temple complex, His disciples came up and called His attention to the temple buildings. Then He replied to them, 'Do you not see all these things? I assure you: Not one stone will be left here on another that will not be thrown down.'"

In Revelation 11, we learn that God told John to measure the temple—a difficult task, since nothing was there! "Then I was given a measuring reed like a rod, with these words: 'Go and measure God's sanctuary and the altar, and count those who worship there. But exclude the courtyard outside the sanctuary. Don't measure it, because it is given to the nations, and they will trample the holy city for 42 months" (Revelation 11:1–2).

This Scripture says that the temple will be rebuilt. And the Jews believe this will happen. Today, rabbinic schools are training young Jewish priests (the descendants of Levi) to offer sacrifices in the temple. I have been to the Temple Institute, where seamstresses are weaving clothing for the priests to wear, artisans are making vessels of silver and gold for temple worship, and carpenters are fashioning musical instruments to replicate the worship in the Bible. They are getting ready to rebuild the temple! Some have even tried to lay the foundation stone of the new temple, and it caused all kinds of mayhem.

The Hasmonean Tunnel that was discovered and excavated several years ago is located at the foot of the perimeter of the temple mount. It is also called the Rabbi Tunnel; it served as an aqueduct in the Hasmonean period or Maccabbean era. There is a sign on the wall of that tunnel that suggests this spot is closest to the Holy of Holies. If you ask a Hasidic Jew what he is praying for at the Western Wall, he will tell you that he is praying for Messiah to come and for the temple to be rebuilt.

The interesting thing to know about the rebuilding of the temple is that the temple is the precursor of the Antichrist. Jesus said that the Antichrist will enter the temple to abominate it and make it desolate (see Matthew 24:15). Daniel the prophet also said that an abomination of desolations would stand in the holy place (see Daniel 11:31; 12:11). The apostle Paul prophesied:

> Now concerning the coming of our Lord Jesus Christ and our being gathered to Him: we ask you, brothers, not to be easily upset in mind or troubled, either by a spirit or by a message or by a letter as if from us, alleging that the Day of the Lord has come. Don't let anyone deceive you in any way. For that day will not come unless the apostasy comes first and the man of lawlessness is revealed, the son of destruction. He opposes and exalts himself above every so-called god or object of worship, so that he sits in God's sanctuary, publicizing that he himself is God. Don't you remember that when I was still with you I told you about this? (2 Thessalonians 2:1–5).

At the end of Revelation 11:2 we read that there is a distinct period when Jerusalem will be made desolate. It is a period of "forty and two months" (KJV). This is translated to be 1,260 days, or as the Bible calls it "time, and times, and half a time" (Revelation 12:14 KJV). Basically three and one-half years. Why this time period? Because three and one-half is seven divided and speaks of the division and danger that will occur when the Antichrist moves into the temple to declare to the world that he is God.

From Revelation 11:3 to the end of the chapter, we read that God will bring two mighty prophets during this horrendous period to prophesy and teach. There has never been a time when God did not have His prophets. Amos 3:7 says, "Surely the Lord GOD will do nothing, but he revealeth his secret unto his servants the prophets" (KJV). God does not move without letting a prophet know what is about to happen. Before the flood, God spoke to Enoch and Noah. Before the exile of the Israelites, God spoke to Elijah and Jeremiah. Let's look at five truths about these two prophets.

They Will Be Spiritually Prepared

Revelation 11:3–4 says, "I will empower my two witnesses, and they will prophesy for 1,260 days, dressed in sackcloth. These are the two olive trees and the two lampstands that stand before the Lord of the earth." These men are described as olive trees and lampstands. The olive trees speak of fruitfulness, and the lampstands speak of light. These prophets were to be fruitful as they proclaimed a witness of God's light.

The olive oil burned in the lampstands is symbolic of the Holy Spirit of God. What does God's Word say about our light? "You are the light of the world. A city situated on a hill cannot be hidden. No one lights a lamp and puts it under a basket, but rather on a lampstand, and it gives light for all who are in the house. In the same way, let your light shine before men, so that they may see your good works and give glory to your Father in heaven" (Matthew 5:14–16).

These witnesses were spiritually prepared. It would be foolish and wicked to try to do God's work without God's power. For instance, to let your light shine, you must learn to burn the oil and not the wick. If you burn the wick, you will burn out and do nothing but make a lot of smoke.

What else do we notice about these men and their spiritual preparation? They were clothed in sackcloth, the drab garments that people wore in Bible times when they were in mourning and sorrow. If you preach judgment, you ought to do it in the sackcloth of a broken heart. Multitudes upon multitudes are marching into hell. Is your heart broken over that? Is it broken enough that you are willing to get spiritually prepared to tell others about what is going to happen?

I believe in heaven. And I believe in hell. I also believe that if preachers taught more about hell in the pulpits, we would have less ungodly living in our communities. The first thing about these prophets that I want you to see is that they are spiritually prepared.

They Will Be Sovereignly Protected

Revelation 11:5 says, "If anyone wants to harm them, fire comes from their mouths and consumes their enemies; if anyone wants to harm them, he must be killed in this way." The fire coming from their mouths may be symbolic of the power of God's word spoken by these two men. Whether literal or symbolic, it will be deadly to their fores.

In verse 6 of Revelation 11, we see that "these men have the power to close the sky so that it does not rain during the days of their prophecy. They also have power over the waters to turn them into blood, and to strike the earth with any plague whenever they want." What kind of power is this? It is the same power that Jesus gave His disciples when He sent them out: "Summoning the Twelve, He gave them power and authority over all the demons, and to heal diseases" (Luke 9:1). And elsewhere, Jesus said, "Look, I have given you the authority to trample on snakes and scorpions and over all the power of the enemy; nothing will ever harm you" (Luke 10:19).

I believe these two prophets will come in the spirit of Elijah and Moses. When we think of Elijah we think of the prophets; when we think of Moses we think of the law. What is the purpose of the law and the prophets? They witness about the Lord Jesus Christ. Luke 24:27 says, "Then beginning with Moses and all the Prophets, He interpreted for them in all the Scriptures the things concerning Himself." We should never make the mistake of thinking that the Old Testament is about Judaism and the New Testament is about Jesus. All of the Bible is about Jesus Christ. The law is about Jesus. The prophets are about Jesus. And these two men represent the law and the prophets.

Why do I say that these men will be sovereignly protected? All the people of God are sovereignly protected if they are in the will of God and speaking the Word of God. I believe they are immortal until their work is finished. When you are in the center of God's will, your work will never lack for God's provision or God's protection.

They Will Be Satanically Persecuted

Revelation 11:7–9 says, "When they finish their testimony, the beast that comes up out of the abyss will make war with them, conquer them, and kill them. Their dead bodies will lie in the public square of the great city, which is called, prophetically, Sodom and Egypt, where also their Lord was crucified. And representatives from the peoples, tribes, languages, and nations will view their bodies for three and a half days and not permit their bodies to be put into a tomb."

Who is this beast? Like many criminals, he has many aliases. He is called the "man of sin" and "son of perdition" (2 Thessalonians 2:3 KJV). He is called the "wicked one" (1 John 2:13–14 KJV). He is called the "little horn" (Daniel 7:8; 8:9 KJV). His name is the Antichrist—the same one who will sit in the temple, declaring himself to be God.

The beast will wage war against the two prophets. Why? Because they preached the Word of God. Most preachers who boldly prearch the Word do not win popularity contests. In fact, Jesus said, "Woe to you when all people speak well of you, because this is the way their forefathers used to treat the false prophets" (Luke 6:26).

As the days grow darker, hatred and persecution against the godly will intensify. "Now wait a minute," you may say. "Just a few paragraphs ago, you said that the man of God is immortal until he has finished the task that God has given him to do." That's my point. Look again at the first part of Revelation 11:7: "When they finish their testimony." Their testimony ends in death. The apostle Paul was one of the greatest missionaries who ever lived. They cut off his head, but not before he said, "I have fought the good fight, I have finished the race, I have kept the faith" (2 Timothy 4:7). What did Jesus say when He bowed His head shortly before His death? "It is finished" (John 19:30). Just because the prophets are silenced doesn't mean the devil has won. No, the story isn't over. The devil will make a great strategic blunder, which we will study in the next chapter.

The communists tried to kill my dear Romanian friend, Joseph Tson, for preaching the Word. They sent a man who said, "Joseph, if you don't knuckle under, we are going to kill you."

Joseph responded, "Before you kill me, I want to say that your chief weapon is killing, but my chief weapon is dying."

They asked him what he meant. He responded, "If you kill me, you will sprinkle every sermon I've ever preached with my blood, every book I've ever written with my blood, and people will know I love the Lord enough to die for Him. So, your chief weapon is killing, but mine is dying. I want to warn you that if you use yours, I will be forced to use mine."

They went away saying, "Leave Joseph alone. He is crazy."

Though the death of these prophets catapults the Antichrist into great fame and popularity, the devil will not ultimately win. Even when their dead bodies are left in the streets without a decent burial and onlookers stand around and gloat, the devil will not have won. The prophets will have finished their testimony. Their work will have been completed.

When Mussolini died, many people took pleasure in his death. When Americans were killed in the 9/11 tragedies of 2001, many people overseas rejoiced. In the same way, when these prophets die, the Bible says that all the world will see them. "But," you ask, "how can the entire world see their dead bodies?" We have satellites that circle the earth to report worldwide news into every home. The world will see it. Things that seem unthinkable before will not be unthinkable in that day.

What is the lesson we need to learn here? If you live for the Lord Jesus Christ, it doesn't mean everybody will love you. Coming events cast their shadows ahead of time, and we can expect increasing persecution.

They Will Be Supernaturally Preserved

Revelation 11:11–12 says, "But after the three and a half days, the breath of life from God entered them, and they stood on their feet. So, great fear fell on those who saw them. Then they heard a loud voice from heaven saying to them, 'Come up here.' They went up to heaven in a cloud, while their enemies watched them."

Could there be anything more supernatural to happen to God's messengers? People had been gloating over them and kicking at them for three and one-half days! Then suddenly the glow of health returned to their lifeless bodies and changed their skin from pallid to rosy. A finger twitched. A hand moved. A limb straightened. They sat up and stretched, then stood before these people. Then another miracle took place. A voice from heaven told them to "'come up here.' They went up to heaven in a cloud" (Revelation 11:12). What a day that will be!

This forthcoming event teaches us that we need not fear ultimate destruction. We are preserved until we finish our task. Satan may be allowed to put us to death, but we are still supernaturally preserved. God has Satan on a leash. If you are persecuted, it will be one of the greatest platforms you will ever have to speak of God's eternal grace. Here is a key passage of Scripture:

> But before all these things, they will lay their hands on you and persecute you. They will hand you over to the synagogues and prisons, and you will be brought before kings and governors because of My name. It will lead to an opportunity for you to witness. Therefore make up your minds not to prepare your defense ahead of time, for I will give you such words and a wisdom that none of your adversaries will be able to resist or contradict. You will even be betrayed by parents, brothers, relatives, and friends; and they will kill some of you. And you will be hated by all because of My name. But not a hair of your head will be lost (Luke 21:12–18).

What if someone said to you, "Deny Christ or I will kill you"? You could say, "Well, kill me. I am going to heaven." But what if they said, "Deny Christ or I'll dismember your wife in front of your eyes"? What if they said, "Deny Christ or we will begin to mutilate your grandchildren"? You may respond, "I don't know; don't ask that question." You don't have to worry about that time in the future, because Jesus said to settle it in your heart (don't worry) about what you will say. God will give you His words and grace to respond in that moment.

"Now wait a minute," you may be saying. "This passage says I will be put in prison and put to death and yet not a hair of my head will perish?" That's exactly right. Jesus is saying in a different way what He was saying earlier: "And I say to you, My friends, don't fear those who kill the body, and after that can do nothing more. But I will show you the One to fear: Fear Him who has authority to throw people into hell after death. Yes, I say to you, this is the One to fear" (Luke 12:4–5).

If you listen to many of the old African-American spirituals, you will hear a recurring theme of resurrection—death is not the end but only the beginning. You will also hear that death is not something to fear, but merely a passageway to enter into a deeper relationship with the Savior. It will be a victorious homegoing! Every man, woman, and child will have a "getting-up morning." And like the spiritual says, "Fare ye well, fare ye well." Will you fare well on that great getting-up morning? When you are no longer afraid to die, then you are ready to live.

There is a God in glory who reigns. And there is nothing the devil can ultimately do to you without His permission. You need to remember that, because if you don't, the devil will pull the wool over your eyes.

They Will Have Successfully Prophesied

Did the prophets fail? No, they succeeded. These prophets witnessed, and God received the glory. Revelation 11:13–14 says, "At that moment a violent earthquake took place, a tenth of the city fell, and 7,000 people were killed in the earthquake. The survivors were terrified and gave glory to the God of heaven. The second woe has passed. Take note: the third woe is coming quickly!"

Those who are left behind will not die in the earthquake; instead, they will give glory to the God of heaven. This doesn't necessarily mean they will be saved. It just means they will recognize that what happened was a "God thing." The same thing happened to Pharaoh and Saul. Indeed, the demons in hell will one day glorify God, and we know they will not be saved.

Years ago I preached at a revival meeting in a south Louisiana town. I fasted, prayed, wept, and examined my heart and my life to make certain that my heart was clean and my motives were pure before I went into the pulpit. I knew the Word was true and preached my best, but revival was not happening. I gave an invitation and a few came forward (maybe it was out of sympathy for me). I got frustrated (you are not supposed to be frustrated if you are a preacher).

One night, we were in the middle of the invitation, and I sat down in one of the chairs on the platform. I told the pastor of the church to take over, and I prayed. I said, "God, I don't understand. I preached Your Word. I prayed. I fasted. Why is this happening? I'm so frustrated. Please give me a word."

I opened my Bible at random and said, Lord, speak to me." My eyes fell upon Ezekiel 2:7, which says, "And thou shalt speak my words unto them, whether they will hear, or whether they will forbear; for they are most rebellious" (KJV).

I saw in a moment the reason that they would not hear me, because they would not hear God. It wasn't that I had not been faithful or had not preached the Word of God. This gave me great confidence. I said, "Lord, that was such a blessing, please give me another verse." And God led my eyes to Ezekiel 2:5, which says, "And they, whether they will hear, or whether they will forbear, (for they are a rebellious house,) yet shall know that there hath been a prophet among them" (KJV).

When I read that, I could hardly contain myself, God seemed to be telling me, "Adrian whether they hear you or whether they don't, you have preached my Word. One day they will know that I sent My messenger." I learned that day anew and afresh that the conversion of souls is not my responsibility. My responsibility is to declare boldly the Word of God, whether people will hear or whether they will not.

Second Timothy 3:12 says, "In fact, all those who want to live a godly life in Christ Jesus will be persecuted." Persecution will come. Is that bad? No, that's good. It is a divine platform to share your testimony about God. When you read what God has said in His Word about the end times, you will see everything fitting into the sockets of prophecy. We are on the winning side.

Why I Love Israel

These are dangerous days in which we live! The storm clouds are gathering. The lightning is flashing—and the lightning rod is Israel. Christians cannot deny or ignore the significance of the nation of Israel. If you read Bible prophecy, you will discover that Israel is someway in 100 percent of all prophecy about the future. Indeed, the eyes of the entire world are upon this tiny state of Israel, and your eyes need to be there too, because the Jews and Israel are the people and the land of destiny. As the Jew goes, so goes the world. Israel is God's yardstick. Israel is God's measuring rod. Israel is God's blueprint. Israel is God's program for what He is doing in the world.

Some may think that God has turned His back on Israel—that perhaps God has abrogated the promises He made to Abraham, Isaac, and Jacob. Absolutely not! Let me explain what God tells us about the nation of Israel from Revelation 12.

Israel's Special Favor

Revelation 12:1–2 says, "And there appeared a great wonder in heaven; a woman clothed with the sun, and the moon under her feet, and upon her head a crown of twelve stars: and she being with child cried, travailing in birth, and pained to be delivered" (KJV).

Who is this wonder woman in heaven? First let me say who she is not. She is not the virgin Mary. She gave birth to the Lord Jesus Christ and is to be honored among all women, but these two verses do not describe her. Second, it is not the church, even though it is spoken of in feminine terms as the bride of Christ. The woman in this passage gives birth to Jesus; Jesus gave birth to the church. It is not the church.

It seems clear that this wonder woman is Israel. Jesus came from the nation of Israel. When God gave Joseph a dream, Israel was described as having "the sun and the moon and the eleven stars" (Genesis 37:9 KJV). Joseph was the *twelfth* star. Elsewhere in the Old Testament, Israel is called the wife of Jehovah. God said to Israel: "For thy Maker is thine husband; the LORD of hosts is his name; and thy Redeemer the Holy One of Israel; the God of the whole earth shall he be called. For the LORD hath called thee as a woman forsaken and grieved in spirit, and a wife of youth, when thou wast refused, saith thy God" (Isaiah 54:5–6 KJV).

Romans 9:4–5 is the key passage of Scripture to explain this woman. Paul spoke about his concern for the nation of Israel. He described the Jews as "Israelites, and to them belong the adoption, the glory, the covenants, the giving of the law, the temple service, and the promises. The forefathers are theirs, and from them, by *physical descent, came the Messiah,* who is God over all, blessed forever. Amen" (emphasis mine).

What is Paul saying? That Israel gave us the Messiah, and thank God for it. Israel is a God-ordained, God-called, God-protected, and God-blessed nation. Did God call and ordain Israel to make them only a blessing? No, He called Israel in order to bless all the world through them. Let's look at another passage of Scripture. God is speaking to Abraham: "And I will bless them that bless thee, and curse him that curseth thee: and in thee shall all families of the earth be blessed" (Genesis 12:3 KJV).

Every Christian is blessed because of Israel. We have a Bible that is a Jewish book. We serve a Jewish Messiah. And God has made Abraham a blessing to all the nations of the world. Here's a word of warning: You would be very foolish and on dangerous ground if you should pronounce a curse on Israel. We are to bless what God has blessed, love what God has loved, and pray for Israel.

God said about Israel: "For thou art an holy people unto the LORD thy God: the LORD thy God hath chosen thee to be a special people unto himself, above all people that are upon the face of the earth" (Deuteronomy 7:6 KJV). Our Jewish friends need to learn that the best friends they have on the face of this earth are Bible-believing Christians. Satan does not want them to know that.

Israel's Satanic Foe

Revelation gives us the symbols of a wonder woman and a dreadful dragon. Revelation 12:3–5 says, "And there appeared another wonder in heaven; and behold a great red dragon, having seven heads and ten horns, and seven crowns upon his heads. And his tail drew the third part of the stars of heaven, and did cast them to the earth: and the dragon stood before the woman which was ready to be delivered, for to devour her child as soon as it was born. And she brought forth a man child, who was to rule all nations with a rod of iron: and her child was caught up unto God, and to his throne" (KJV).

Who is this ferocious dragon? It is Satan himself. He is red because of his lust for blood (see John 8:44). He has seven heads, ten horns, and seven crowns. You may recall that seven means perfection and ten means complete. Horns in the Bible are symbolic of power, so when you put seven and ten together, these things are symbolic of Satan's diabolical earthly power and wisdom.

Satan is the ultimate rebel. Isaiah tells us what happened to him: "How art thou fallen from heaven, O Lucifer, son of the morning! how art thou cut down to the ground, which didst weaken the nations! For thou hast said in thine heart, I will ascend into heaven, I will exalt my throne above the stars of God: I will sit also upon the mount of the congregation, in the sides of the north: I will ascend above the heights of the clouds: I will be like the most High. Yet thou shalt be brought down to hell, to the sides of the pit" (Isaiah 14:12–15 KJV).

Lucifer was a beautiful angel in heaven, but one day he decided he was too wise, strong, glorious, and mighty to be anything less than God. He wanted to exalt himself above the stars of God, so Revelation tells us that his tail swept a third of the stars (angels) from heaven when he led a rebellion and ultimately fell. No sooner had he unsheathed his sword of rebellion than the thunders of Jehovah's wrath rolled through heaven. Does the number of angels who became demons bother you? Then you should remember that two-thirds of the angels did not fall, so there are two angels for every demon.

Hell is the destiny of Satan and his demons. That is what Jesus taught about those who will be judged in the final day: "Then He will also say to those on the left, 'Depart from Me, you who are cursed, into the eternal fire prepared for the Devil and his angels'" (Matthew 25:41). God did not make hell for you. God made hell for the devil and the devil's angels. But if you choose to follow Satan, that will be your destiny. You will go as an intruder.

While Satan wars with Israel, I want you to know that his ultimate war is with the Lord Jesus Christ. Let's look at the second half of Revelation 12:4: "The dragon stood in front of the woman who was about to give birth, so that when she did give birth he might devour her child." Who is her child? The Lord Jesus Christ. What does Satan want to do? He wants to destroy the Lord Jesus Christ. Who do you think influenced Herod to murder all the baby boys who were two years old and under (see Matthew 2:12–18)? Satan was trying to devour the child as soon as the child was born. But he could not stop the plan of God.

Revelation 12:5 says, "But she gave birth to a Son—a male who is going to shepherd all nations with an iron scepter—and her child was caught up to God and to His throne." Jesus Christ was born. He lived a perfect and sinless life, died on the cross, was buried, and rose from the tomb a victorious Savior. Now He has ascended the high hills of glory. Hymn writer John Wilbur Chapman said it best:

> Living, He loved me; dying, He saved me;
> Buried He carried my sins far away;
> Rising, He justified freely forever;
> One day He's coming—O glorious day!

There are two things I want you to learn about Satan: he is anti-Christ, and he is anti-Semitic. Satan hates Jesus, and he hates the Jews. I love Jesus, and I love the Jews, if for no other reason than the fact that Satan hates them. If you were to study the history of God's chosen people, you would discover that they have endured satanic-inspired persecution and atrocities under Pharaoh, Nebuchadnezzar, Alexander the Great, Nero, the Turks, the Ottoman Empire, Russia, Arab nations, and sadly, Christians.

One of the blackest periods in Christian history was the Crusades. How we ought to hang our heads in shame. In modern times, anti-Semitism has reached epidemic proportions. Think of Hitler's death camps and the gas ovens. If the Holocaust doesn't move you to have compassion for Israel, I don't know what will.

Think of the little nation of Israel today. There are four and one-half million Jews surrounded by two hundred million Arabs—most of whom wish Israel did not exist and most of whom would be happy to see the Israelis driven into the sea. If you looked at some maps that have originated in Arab nations, you will not even find Israel on the map, because they do not recognize Israel. How would you like to go into a supermarket and wonder if a bomb will explode while you're inside? How would you like to get on a bus and wonder if you'll make it to your destination?

In a recent issue of *Harper's Magazine*, Stanley Fish shares what a Muslim mother said after she learned of her son's success in a suicide bombing that killed her son and ten Jews. She said, "Because I love my son, I encouraged him to die a martyr's death for the sake of Allah. Jihad is a religious obligation encumbered upon us and we must carry it out. I sacrificed Mohammad [her son's name] as a part of my obligation. I asked Allah to give me ten Israelis for Mohammad, and Allah granted my request, and Mohammad made his dream come true, killing ten Israeli settlers and soldiers. Our God honored him even more in that there were many Israelis wounded."

My heart aches for that mother and her distorted reasoning. Who is the author of all this hatred toward the Jewish nation of Israel? That diabolical dragon named Satan.

Israel's Spiritual Fight

Revelation 12:6–10 says:

And the woman [*Israel*] fled into the wilderness, where she hath a place prepared of God, that they should feed her there a thousand two hundred and threescore days [*three and one-half years*]. And there was war in heaven: Michael and his angels fought against the dragon; and the dragon fought and his angels, and prevailed not; neither was their place found any more in heaven. And the great dragon was cast out, that old serpent, called the Devil, and Satan, which deceiveth the whole world: he was cast out into the earth, and his angels [*stars*] were cast out with him. And I heard a loud voice saying in heaven, Now is come salvation, and strength, and the kingdom of our God, and the power of his Christ: for the accuser of our brethren is cast down, which accused them before our God day and night (KJV, explanatory notes added by the author).

There are two battles taking place in this passage: one in heaven and one on earth, and the purpose of the war is to cast Satan out of heaven. On one side are the dreadful dragon and his demons; on the other side are Michael and his angels.

The War in Heaven

The dragon is described as a serpent because he is so subtle. He is also called the devil, which means "accuser," and Satan, which means "adversary." You may say, "I thought Satan was already cast out of heaven?" Yes, but he still has access to heaven. Job 1:6 says, "Now there was a day when the sons of God came to present themselves before the LORD, and Satan came also among them" (KJV). In the mystery, providence, and plan of God, Satan has been allowed access to heaven. Although Satan has been abolished, God has still allowed him to come and accuse all the saints before God (see Revelation. 12:10). But now Michael and his angels are telling Satan that he does not have access to heaven any longer and will be cast down to earth.

Do you know that Satan is watching everything you do? You know he is if you have felt the sting of his accusations, perhaps of a lustful thought, a bad temper, or selfishness. We can be guilty of these things. But there is a difference between accusing and convicting us of our sin.

Satan comes as a prosecuting attorney and says, "Look at that Adrian Rogers. He's supposed to be a pastor, but did you see what he said? Did you see what he thought? God, how can you honor him? You claim to be so righteous. You claim to be so just. Why don't you cast him into hell?" Night and day he accuses us. But praise God, we have a defense attorney named Jesus. First John 2:1 says, "We have an advocate with the Father— Jesus Christ the righteous One." Jesus turns to the judge and says in our defense: "Yes, Father, Adrian has sinned. But Father, I ask you to look at my wounds. I died for those sins." And God, as judge, rules in our favor because of His Son.

When I was studying this, I thought, *Satan is on his way down.* He was cast down from his lofty place in heaven where he ministered praise to God as an anointed cherub. That limited access to heaven is taken from Satan, and he's cast down to earth. Soon he will be cast into the bottomless pit. And finally, he will be taken out of the abyss and put into the lowest hell where he will spend eternity. The one who said, "I will exalt myself above the stars of God," will be brought down into the lowest hell. And if you're following him, you'll be there with him. Why follow a loser? I'm following the Lord Jesus Christ.

The War on Earth

Revelation 12:11–12 speaks of the saints, and notice what it says about them: "And they overcame [Satan] by the blood of the Lamb, and by the word of their testimony; and they loved not their lives unto the death. Therefore rejoice, ye heavens, and ye that dwell in them. Woe to the inhabiters of the earth and of the sea! for the devil is come down unto you, having great wrath, because he knoweth that he hath but a short time" (KJV).

Satan, who was cast out of heaven, is now upon the earth, and he is filled with violent rage. He is like a cornered animal that knows things are closing in on him. He begins to fight against the saints with an intensity that he's never shown before. And thankfully, there is a threefold formula for victory.

1. *The believers' cleansing.* First, the believers overcame Satan by the blood of the Lamb. Jesus won the victory over Satan on the cross. Facing the cross, Jesus said, "Now is the judgment of this world. Now the ruler of this world will be cast out" (John 12:31). Satan's back was broken at the cross. Ever since then, Satan has been sailing a sinking ship. He rules a doomed domain.

The blood of Jesus Christ conquers and cleanses. Do you believe that? First John 1:7 says, "The blood of Jesus His Son cleanses us from all sin." How are you going to overcome Satan? You will never have victory over Satan as long as there is unconfessed, unrepented sin in your heart. You might as well try to remove Gibraltar by throwing snowballs at it as to get the devil out of your life.

Is there a grudge, lust, or habit in your life that you know is sinful, yet you are withholding it from God's cleansing power? Whatever it is, it is not worth it. You can be as clean as the pure, white snow by repenting of your sin and claiming the blood of Jesus Christ to forgive you.

If you go to war against Satan, you had better make certain your heart is clean. Ephesians 4:27 says, "Don't give the Devil an opportunity." If there is sin in your heart, you have given the devil an unholy place to wage war on the rest of you. Be clean.

2. *The believers' confession.* The believers also overcame Satan by the word of their testimony. Did you know that your testimony is a mighty power to overcome the devil? When you testify who Jesus is in your life, you are throwing water on Satan's fire that is trying to devour you. Revelation 12:17 says, "The dragon was furious with the woman and left to wage war against the rest of her offspring—those who keep the commandments of God and have the testimony about Jesus."

Do you know Jesus? He is Lord. He is the Lamb who died. He is the Lion who rules. When Satan comes against you, testify about what Jesus did at Calvary and the empty tomb. Testify also about who you are. Tell him that when Jesus died, you died. You were co-crucified with Christ. When Jesus was buried, you were buried. When Jesus was raised, you were raised. When Jesus ascended, you ascended. And when Jesus was enthroned and seated in the heavenlies, you were also enthroned in Christ. You are redeemed, accepted, and empowered by the Lord Jesus Christ. You are now a king and a priest.

3. *The believer's courage.* The day of martyrs is not past. More people have died in this century for Jesus than have died in any other century (more than one hundred million persons have given their lives for the Lord Jesus Christ). What is the attitude of a martyr? Revelation 12:11 says, "They did not love their lives in the face of death." They kept on loving Jesus *even if* they died. If their testimony cost their lives, they could say, "I'm going with the Lord Jesus Christ."

"But this sounds like I could get hurt," you say. Yes, but you can't be harmed. There's a difference. Remember how, in the previous chapter, I talked about believers being sovereignly protected? When you are in the center of God's will, your work will never lack for God's provision or God's protection.

Israel's Strategic Flight

Satan realizes what has happened to him. He no longer has access before God, so he turns with intensity to the woman and begins to persecute Israel. Remember, this is the time of the Great Tribulation, and Israel will be persecuted in a tremendous way. This will be a dark time for Israel. Revelation 12:13–16 says:

> And when the dragon saw that he was cast unto the earth,
> he persecuted the woman [*Israel*] which brought forth the man
> child [*Jesus*]. And to the woman were given two wings of a
> great eagle, that she might fly into the wilderness, into her
> place, where she is nourished for a time, and times, and half a
> time [*three and one-half years*], from the face of the serpent.
> And the serpent cast out of his mouth water as a flood after
> the woman, that he might cause her to be carried away of the
> flood. And the earth helped the woman, and the earth opened

her mouth, and swallowed up the flood which the dragon cast out of his mouth (KJV, explanatory notes added by the author).

Let's review what we have learned thus far about the Great Tribulation, which begins after the rapture of the church. In the middle of the seven-year period, the temple will be rebuilt. And when that happens, the Antichrist will move in and declare himself to be God. Then Israel will realize that a false Messiah has betrayed her, and she will refuse to serve him.

During this time, Satan will turn against Israel in a way that he has never done before. Then what happens? Jesus prophesies: "Then those in Judea must flee to the mountains! A man on the housetop must not come down to get things out of his house. And a man in the field must not go back to get his clothes. Woe to pregnant women and nursing mothers in those days! Pray that your escape may not be in winter or on a Sabbath. For at that time there will be great tribulation, the kind that hasn't taken place since the beginning of the world until now, and never will again" (Matthew 24:16–21).

The Jews take flight for three and one-half years as Jesus prophesied above, and as Revelation 12:14 says, "And to the woman were given two wings of a great eagle, that she might fly into the wilderness, into her place, where she is nourished for a time, and times, and half a time [*three and one-half years*], from the face of the serpent" (KJV, explanatory note added by the author).

When the devil sees them flee, he will send a flood of persecution. But Isaiah says, "When the enemy shall come in like a flood, the Spirit of the LORD shall lift up a standard against him" (Isaiah 59:19 KJV).

What does all of this mean? It means that God knows the future. And God is in control. No one could write a book like the Bible, apart from divine inspiration, as you see everything that is happening today fitting into the sockets of prophecy.

Israel's Saving Faith

Revelation 12:17 says, "So the dragon was furious with the woman and left to wage war against the rest of her offspring—those who keep the commandments of God and have the testimony about Jesus." There will come a time when many Jews will come to Jesus Christ as their Messiah.

"And I will pour upon the house of David, and upon the inhabitants of Jerusalem, the spirit of grace and of supplications: and they shall look upon me whom they have pierced, and they shall mourn for him, as one mourneth for his only son, and shall be in bitterness for him, as one that is in bitterness for his firstborn" (Zechariah 12:10 KJV). How can Jehovah God be pierced? The only one way I know is for God to become a man and die on a cross.

"In that day there shall be a fountain opened to the house of David and to the inhabitants of Jerusalem for sin and for uncleanness" (Zechariah 13:1 KJV). That is what the apostle Paul says: "For I do not desire, brethren, that you should be ignorant of his mystery, lest you should be wise in your own opinion, that blindness in part has happened to Israel until the fullness of the Gentiles has come in. And so all Israel will be saved, as it is written: 'The Deliverer will come out of Zion, And He will turn away ungodliness from Jacob'" (Romans 11:25–26 NKJV). What is the fullness of the Gentiles? The church.

Does this bless you? It makes me want to shout with joy to know that God has a plan. God has not forsaken His ancient people. God has blessed Israel so Israel might be a blessing to all the world. There will be a fountain open to them, just like the hymn writer William Cowper said in "There Is a Fountain":

> There is a fountain filled with blood
> Drawn from Emmanuel's veins;
> And sinners plunged beneath that flood
> Lose all their guilty stains.
> Lose all their guilty stains, lose all their guilty stains;
> And sinners plunged beneath that flood
> Lose all their guilty stains.

How can we continue living in these pivotal days without giving everything we have to Jesus Christ? We are to love Him with a burning, blazing, passionate, emotional love. We are to love what God loves—and God loves His Son and His chosen people the Jews.

Thank God, there is coming a day—and it may not be far off—when all of these prophecies will begin to unfold. I am grateful for Revelation. I may not have every jot and tittle correct, because we're dealing with difficult matters to interpret, but I have this much correct—Jesus is Lord and He's coming again. Praise His name!

Biography of the Beast

◄O►

CHAPTER 16

◄O►

People do not know the future. I remind you, God alone knows the future. Isaiah 46:9–10 says, "Remember the former things of old: for I am God, and there is none else; I am God, and there is none like me, declaring the end from the beginning, and from ancient times the things that are not yet done, saying, My counsel shall stand, and I will do all my pleasure" (KJV).

Man has tried to predict the future, but he has failed. In the 1870s, Milton Wright, a bishop of the Church of the United Brethren in Christ was outraged by a college president's suggestion that "within fifty years men will learn to fly through the air like birds." The bishop was shocked by those words, and responded by saying, "Flying is reserved for the angels. I beg you not to mention that again lest you be guilty of blasphemy!" Thirty-three years after the bishop made that statement, his two sons, Wilbur and Orville, launched their powered aircraft at Kitty Hawk.

In 1943, Thomas Watson, who was chairman of IBM, said: "I think there may be a world market for maybe five computers." In 1977, Ken Olson, founder and CEO of Digital Equipment Company, said: "There is no reason anyone would want a computer in their home." In 1876, a Western Union internal memo said: "This telephone has too many short-comings to be seriously considered as a means of communication. The device is inherently of no value to us." Did these men rightly prophesy about the future? Absolutely not. But that didn't stop them from trying.

Do you know who else does not know the future? The devil. Standing in the shadows of history is the Antichrist that we have discussed in brief up to this point. In this chapter, we will look at five things about the beast.

The Social Agitation That Delivers the Beast

Revelation 13:1 says, "And I saw a beast coming up out of the sea. He had 10 horns and seven heads. On his horns were 10 diadems, and on his heads were blasphemous names." Sea and water are symbolic of multitudes of wicked peoples from every tongue and nation. We see this represented elsewhere in God's Word: "But the wicked are like the troubled sea, when it cannot rest, whose waters cast up mire and dirt" (Isaiah 57:20 KJV). Revelation 17:15 says, "He also said to me, 'The waters you saw, where the prostitute was seated, are peoples, multitudes, nations, and languages.'"

The stage is set for the social agitation that will deliver the beast. There is a troubled, growling, seething sea of disturbed and evil people. The Soviet Union has been dissolved, but the former Soviet Republics that were a part of this formidable power are still very dangerous to world peace. Many of them are bastions of Islamic fundamentalism and launching posts for religious jihad. The Russian bear, wounded and hungry, is sniffing out morsels to devour.

What about the People's Republic of China? In Revelation 9 we learn about an army of 200 million along the Euphrates River. China has boasted in previous years that she can fill an army of 200 million. Could that be the army spoken of in chapter 9? At any rate, this red dragon may be getting ready to breathe its fiery breath and scorch the earth. No matter what you may read or hear in the news, China is no friend to the United States of America or to world peace.

Think of what is happening in the spiritual vacuum of Europe that is being filled with New Ageism and occultism. This group of nations is being unified into awesome power. It is a fulfillment of Bible prophecy that predicts the old Roman Empire will be reunified.

Then consider worldwide terrorism. Because of Islamic fundamentalism and its religious jihad we are now being faced with horrendous prospects as biological warfare, chemical warfare, suitcase bombs, hijacking, and who knows what else.

Israel is beleaguered, and the Lion of Judah is sharpening her claws. Israel has the nuclear bomb, and if pushed to the edge will use its resources of destruction.

And we have yet to mention the famines, natural disasters, and political intrigues that are a part of the world events of this day. All of these things tell us that perilous times are here and that the nations of the world are like a seething sea out of which will rise the beast.

Historian and author Arnold Toynbee said, "By forcing on mankind more and more lethal weapons, and at the same time making the world more and more interdependent economically, technology has brought mankind to such a degree of distress that we are ripe for the deifying of any new Caesar who might succeed in giving the world unity and peace." He said in effect, we're in such a mess, technologically and economically, that when a man comes on the scene, we'll deify him. We'll make a god of him.

That sounds like it came right out of the Book of Revelation. A European statesman said, "If the devil could offer a panacea for the problems of the world, I would gladly follow the devil." That is going to happen.

The Satanic Attributes That Describe the Beast

His Father

What will this beast be like? First, let's notice his father: "And I saw a beast coming up out of the sea. He had 10 horns and seven heads. On his horns were 10 diadems, and on his heads were blasphemous names" (Revelation 13:1). Does that remind you of anything you've already read in the Book of Revelation? Just go back to Revelation 12:3, 9: "Then another sign appeared in heaven: There was a great fiery red dragon having seven heads and 10 horns, and on his heads were seven diadems. . . . So the great dragon was thrown out—the ancient serpent, who is called the Devil and Satan, the one who deceives the whole world. He was thrown to earth, and his angels with him." There is a dragon in Revelation 12 and his offspring, the beast, in Revelation 13. Like father, like son. The beast has the attributes of his father.

The Bible teaches that when the beast comes, he will possess all the power of Satan: "The coming of the lawless one is based on Satan's working, with all kinds of miracles, signs, and wonders" (2 Thessalonians 2:9). When Jesus was on earth, He said, "The one who has seen Me has seen the Father" (John 14:9). When the devil enters the Antichrist, the Antichrist will be able to say, "The one who has seen me has seen my father." All the attributes of Satan will be in this man of sin. He will be a consummate liar like his father and will perform the works of his father.

His Family

We know his father; now let's meet the rest of his family—a lion, a bear, and a leopard: "The beast I saw was like a leopard, his feet were like a bear's, and his mouth was like a lion's mouth. The dragon gave him his power, his throne, and great authority" (Revelation 13:2). To understand this, we need to look at Daniel 7, where Daniel described the four great empires of the world as beasts. The first empire the world has ever known was the Babylonian Empire. Daniel described it as a lion (see Daniel 7:4). The lion is the royal king of beasts with a ravenous appetite and incredible strength. He is able to terrify every other animal in the kingdom.

The next world empire was Medo-Persia, and Daniel described it as a bear (see Daniel 7:5). The bear has massive strength and powerful claws to crush its victims—a fitting symbol to describe the way the Medo-Persian kings ruled the world at that time. Next, Daniel characterized the Greek Empire as a leopard because of its rapid movement to conquer the world (see Daniel 7:6). Alexander the Great led the charge and wept because there were no more worlds to conquer.

Daniel saw one more kingdom over which the Antichrist would rule: "After this I saw in the night visions, and behold a fourth beast, dreadful and terrible, and strong exceedingly; and it had great iron teeth: it devoured and brake in pieces, and stamped the residue with the feet of it: and it was diverse from all the beasts that were before it; and it had ten horns" (Daniel 7:7 KJV).

When the Antichrist comes, he will come from this lineage of empires. He will have the royalty of Babylon, the strength of Medo-Persia, and the sophisticated wisdom of Greece. He will be a combination of Alexander the Great, Napoleon, Caesar, Charlemagne, Hitler, and more. This is his family legacy.

His Fortune

Notice the last part of Revelation 13:2: "The dragon gave him his power, his throne, and great authority." This man will receive a throne of authority from Satan in which to rule the world. Does Satan have it to give? Indeed, he does.

In the Gospels, we read that Satan tempted Jesus to follow him and wanted Jesus to bow down to him: "Again, the Devil took Him to a very high mountain and showed Him all the kingdoms of the world and their splendor. And he said to Him, 'I will give You all these things if You will fall down and worship me.' Then Jesus told him, 'Go away, Satan! For it is written: You must worship the Lord your God, and you must serve Him only'" (Matthew 4:8–10).

Notice that Jesus did not tell Satan that he didn't have the kingdoms of the world to give, because He knew that Satan had taken that dominion from Adam.

The devil offered the kingdoms to Jesus; Jesus wouldn't take them. But there's coming a man of sin so diabolically wicked that he will give his heart, mind, soul, and everything to the devil. Satan will enter into him to give him power and authority. This is the man Jesus described: "I have come in My Father's name, yet you don't accept Me. If someone else comes in his own name, you will accept him" (John 5:43). Jesus prophesied that one of these days those who would not receive the Lord Jesus Christ will receive the Antichrist.

The Seductive Appeal That Disguises the Beast

Revelation 13:3–4 says, "One of his heads appeared to be fatally wounded, but his fatal wound was healed. The whole earth was amazed and followed the beast. They worshiped the dragon because he gave authority to the beast. And they worshiped the beast, saying, 'Who is like the beast? Who is able to wage war against him?'" When the Bible describes him as a "beast," it is not describing his appearance; it is describing his character. The beast will be a very appealing person in the eyes of the world. He will be handsome, charming, clever, and intelligent.

The whole world will wonder about the beast (see Revelation 17:8). They will ask, "Who is like him? Who is able to make war against him?" One of the ways he will win their affection is through a counterfeit resurrection. At some time during his world rule, he will be fatally wounded on the head. The whole world will mourn his death; then dramatically he will come back to life. His propaganda machine will churn out the news of his resuscitation. It will be the masterstroke of Satan that causes the world to follow after him as never before.

The devil has always wanted to imitate God. For everything that God has, Satan has a counterfeit. There are counterfeit Christians. We call them hypocrites. There is a counterfeit church. The Bible calls it the synagogue of Satan. There is a counterfeit Trinity—the dragon, the beast, and the false prophet (the anti-Father, anti-Christ, and anti-Holy Spirit). The devil is a counterfeiter. People will be seduced by the devil. First Timothy 4:1 speaks of "seducing spirits" and "doctrines of demons" (KJV). Jesus said, "False messiahs and false prophets will arise and perform great signs and wonders to lead astray, if possible, even the elect" (Matthew 24:24).

The Sinister Ambitions That Drive the Beast

He Is Coming to Deify Satan

The beast wants people to worship Satan. The devil has always wanted to be worshiped. Look again at Revelation 13:4: "They worshiped the dragon because he gave authority to the beast. And they worshiped the beast." Just as God the Father receives worship through God the Son, the devil will receive worship through this Antichrist.

He Is Coming to Defy the Savior

Revelation 13:5–6 says, "A mouth was given to him to speak boasts and blasphemies. He was also given authority to act for 42 months. He began to speak blasphemies against God: to blaspheme His name and His dwelling—those who dwell in heaven." The Antichrist is a blasphemer. He cannot touch God Himself, so he is reduced to name-calling.

Like filthy lava, blasphemy will belch from his mouth as he twists everything good, pure, and holy. With burning eloquence he will turn people away from Jesus Christ and to himself. The ultimate in blasphemy will occur when he sits in the temple of God to proclaim that he is God.

Remember the term *Antichrist?* That word is not found in Revelation; it is found in the first two epistles of John (1 John 2:18, 22; 4:3; 2 John 1:7). The prefix *anti* means "against" and "instead of." He comes *against* Christ by being *instead of* Christ.

He Is Coming to Destroy Saints

Revelation 13:7 says, "And he was permitted to wage war against the saints and to conquer them. He was also given authority over every tribe, people, language, and nation." The Antichrist wants to stamp out every person who believes in the true God. He hates those who love God. During the Great Tribulation, true believers will face torture and terror by dying in firing squads, gas chambers, concentration camps, and the guillotine. Many will be beheaded for the cause of Christ. It will be the devil's last fling. The beast will drink his fill of the blood of the martyrs.

He Is Coming to Dominate Society

Revelation 13:7 tells us there is coming a time when this beast will have global control. How will he do this? He will intimidate and browbeat some people. He will bedazzle others. By persecution or reward, he will eventually have control of the entire world. Even now, the world is moving toward a one-world monetary exchange and global government controls.

He Is Coming to Delude Sinners

Revelation 13:8–10 says, "All those who live on the earth will worship him, everyone whose name was not written from the foundation of the world in the book of life of the Lamb who was slaughtered. If anyone has an ear, he should listen: If anyone is destined for captivity, into captivity he goes. If anyone is to be killed with a sword, with a sword he will be killed. Here is the endurance and the faith of the saints."

God is encouraging faithfulness in His martyrs. Remember that the time is coming when the "table will be turned." The beast himself, who has used the sword, will be taken captive and decimated by the mighty sword that is in the mouth of the conquering Lord Jesus. That blessed blade is His word. Keep believing. He will not fail, because He cannot fail.

The closer we get to the end of time, we will see more and more demonism, occultism, and witchcraft. The Antichrist will be the "christ of the cults." Remember this about the devil: he doesn't want casualties; he wants converts. He wants people to worship him.

The Supporting Agent Who Declares the Beast

This Antichrist will have a propaganda agent who will make him popular and known to the world. Revelation 13:11–12 says, "Then I saw another beast coming up out of the earth; he had two horns like a lamb, but he sounded like a dragon. He exercises all the authority of the first beast on his behalf and compels the earth and those who live on it to worship the first beast, whose fatal wound was healed."

The first beast comes out of the sea, which is considered the Mediterranean because the first beast will come out of the Roman Empire that surrounded the Mediterranean. The second beast will come out of the earth. The word *earth* may be translated "land." When the Bible speaks of the land, most likely it is speaking of Israel. This second beast may look like a lamb, but he has horns. His voice is not the voice of a lamb; it is the voice of a dragon (see Revelation 13:11).

The dragon is the anti-God; the beast is the anti-Christ. This second beast is the anti-Holy Spirit, also known as the false prohet. What is the work of the Holy Spirit? He causes believers to love and worship the Lord Jesus Christ. Knowing that Satan is a counterfeiter, we can then assume that the anti-Holy Spirit will cause people to worship the beast. How will he control the minds and the wills of people to do this?

Deceiving Wonders

Revelation 13:13–14 says, "He also performs great signs, even causing fire to come down from heaven to earth before people. He deceives those who live on the earth because of the signs that he is permitted to perform on behalf of the beast, telling those who live on the earth to make an image of the beast who had the sword wound yet lived."

Does the devil have the power to do miracles? Indeed, he does. Read Revelation 16 about three unclean spirits like frogs. Read Exodus 7, where Pharaoh's magicians caused sticks to become serpents. How did these things happen? There is a dark, devilish, diabolical power at work.

Don't put your eyes on miracles. Put your faith in the Lord Jesus Christ and the Word of God. If you find some charlatan who is able to perform miracles, he may be anointed and appointed by the devil to do these miracles.

Our text tells us that the anti-Holy Spirit will set the heavens ablaze. I don't know what he will do, but somehow he will bring fire down from heaven so the world will see it. It may be an atomic explosion in the atmosphere.

Enforced Worship

The Bible says that the anti-Holy Spirit will make an image to the beast: "He deceives those who live on the earth because of the signs that he is permitted to perform on behalf of the beast, telling those who live on the earth to make an image of the beast who had the sword wound yet lived. He was permitted to give a spirit to the image of the beast, so that the image of the beast could both speak and cause whoever would not worship the image of the beast to be killed" (Revelation 13:14–15).

Is the image of the beast a talking statue driven by animatronics? Perhaps. But I think the simplest explanation of the image of the beast is television. When John wrote Revelation, television did not exist. Today you can tune to any channel you want and see someone talking. If the beast is resurrected, he could appear on television via satellite, and his image could be fed into every home around the world. It could also be a computer image. Or by then, the technology of virtual reality could be the medium.

Controlled Wealth

There is coming a time when this false prophet will control the wealth and commerce of the world. If you do not have the seal of the Holy Spirit and you go into the Great Tribulation, you will be branded by this beast: "And he requires everyone—small and great, rich and poor, free and slave—to be given a mark on his right hand or on his forehead, so that no one can buy or sell unless he has the mark: the beast's name or the number of his name. Here is wisdom: The one who has understanding must calculate the number of the beast, because it is the number of a man. His number is 666" (Revelation 13:16–18).

During this time, the only way you will be able to purchase food is to show a mark. The only way you will be able to get medicine is to show a mark. The only way you will make your house payment is to show a mark. The only way you will fill your car up with gas is to show the mark. We are moving toward a cashless society and a regimentation of society by the computer. When this time comes, it will seem so reasonable, so quick, so necessary. There won't be any cheating or books to balance.

What is this mark? The number 666. As you may recall, six is the number of a man (Adam was created on the sixth day). The number cannot be 777, because seven is the number of perfection and man is a sinner. There are three numbers of "man" in 666. What is the divine number? Three. This number is man showing himself that he is God. Many people get offended when someone says there is only one way to heaven and that way is the Lord Jesus Christ. The world wants to homogenize society by putting everyone into one big world church and world system.

You have a choice. You can choose the Lamb of God, who says, "Come to Me, all you who are weary and burdened, and I will give you rest" (Matthew 11:28). Or you can choose the beast that will come out of the boiling, writhing sea of humanity. If the rapture is near, then the beast is alive today and waiting in the shadows to step on the stage. Would you be ready if the trumpet blew and you heard a voice from heaven saying, "Come up here"? Are you ready for the second coming of Jesus Christ?

The Mark of the Beast

-◄o►-
CHAPTER 17
-◄o►-

The devil has always wanted to exalt himself above the stars to be like the Most High God. Martin Luther called him "God's ape." In fact, this desire is what caused this angelic being to fall from heaven and become the devil in the first place. Because of his ambition, he thinks that by imitating God he can be equal to Him. In the previous chapter we discussed this counterfeit mentality.

For instance, we serve a holy Trinity: God the Father, God the Son, and God the Holy Spirit. The devil has his holy trinity as well: the dragon (the anti-Father), the beast (the anti-Christ), and the second beast that is the false prophet (the anti-Holy Spirit). Just as the Holy Spirit causes us to worship the Lord Jesus and give glory to God the Father, the unholy spirit causes people to worship the Antichrist and give glory to the devil. John mentions these three in one verse: "Then I saw three unclean spirits like frogs coming from the dragon's mouth, from the beast's mouth, and from the mouth of the false prophet" (Revelation 16:13).

Revelation 13 refers to the false prophet as the second beast. I want us to learn four things about this false prophet (the anti-Holy Spirit) who will cause the world to worship the Antichrist in the last days.

He Will Be a Servant of Satan

Revelation 13:11–12 says, "Then I saw another beast coming up out of the earth; he had two horns like a lamb, but he sounded like a dragon. He exercises all the authority of the first beast on his behalf and compels the earth and those who live on it to worship the first beast, whose fatal wound was healed."

The beast is not a harmless lamb. His lamb disguise is just a camouflage of deception, because his horns are sticking out and his dragon breath gives him away. He is a devilish, diabolical, powerful individual who will receive his power from Satan—the master deceiver. Jesus Christ said of the

Pharisees, "You are of your father the Devil, and you want to carry out your father's desires. He was a murderer from the beginning and has not stood in the truth, because there is no truth in him. When he tells a lie, he speaks from his own nature, because he is a liar and the father of liars" (John 8:44).

The devil is a liar. So, if this lamb speaks as the dragon and the dragon is the devil, then you can be certain that this anti-Holy Spirit will be a liar. And don't think that you will be clever or wise enough to see through his lies (see Mark 13:22). Unless you have the protection of Almighty God, he *will* deceive you. The best lies sound the most like the truth. And every good lie has some truth in it.

Not only will he be a liar, but he will also be a great communicator and have commanding executive ability. He will be sensible and persuasively articulate. He will tell people what wicked hearts want to hear and what depraved minds will believe. He will be the CEO of Satan & Sons, Inc. He will be to the Antichrist what the Holy Spirit is to the true Christ.

He Will Be a Worker of Worship

Satan's unholy desire is to be like God. God's Word tells us that Satan said: "I will ascend above the heights of the clouds; I will be like the most High" (Isaiah 14:14 KJV). Don't get the idea that the devil is against worship. Satan's burning ambition is to be worshiped. He wants to divert your worship from God to him! Revelation 13:12 says, "He exercises all the authority of the first beast on his behalf and compels the earth and those who live on it to worship the first beast, whose fatal wound was healed."

Satan will seek worldwide worship by trying to establish a one-world religion, economy, and government. I believe he will seek to accomplish this by cutting off people who are on the extreme ends of their beliefs. His team of public relations people will spin their lie: "We want to invite everyone to come together and agree in the middle—sort of like a big homogenization of all religions. And everything will be peaches and cream, because we will be one big happy family." If you don't believe what I am saying is true, just read the newspapers. It is happening today as journalists and others take subtle digs at Bible-believing Christians. We are being compared to extremist organizations—those terrorists are the ugly fundamentalists in Islam and those fanatics are the ugly fundamentalists of Christianity.

When I played football, we had to learn the fundamentals of the game—blocking, passing, and kicking. Now the term *fundamentalist* is being applied to someone who believes in Christianity. He believes the Bible is the Word of God. Jesus Christ is the Savior of the World. He was born of a virgin, lived a sinless life, died on the cross, was buried, and literally walked out of the tomb. He ascended the high hills of glory and is coming again in power and glory. We believe that. We make no apology for that. Those are the fundamentals of the faith. If you take those things out of Christianity, it is like taking the water out of a well, like taking the keys out of a piano, like taking the blue out of the sky.

But now notice what the spin doctors do with that truth. They call Bible-believing Christians fundamentalists, and then they tell the world that we are in the same gene pool as every extremist organization. They say, "We must get rid of all of these extremist groups, and those of us who are left will come together into one great, big, cozy religion." The false prophet will be a unifier of the world's religion.

The people of this world are very clever when they frame the issues. Think of the following phrases: "Women's rights," "death with dignity," "sexual freedom," and "religious tolerance." They sound fine. Who would be against women having rights? Who would be against dying with dignity? Who would be against having sexual freedom? Who would be against tolerating other religions?

But what they don't tell you is what is behind those labels. "Women's rights" means that women have the right to murder their unborn children. "Death with dignity" means the euthanasia of the elderly. "Sexual freedom" means sodomy and perversion. "Religious tolerance" means you need to tolerate every religion but the one that says the only way to heaven is through Jesus Christ. You are labeled a hate monger if you tell others about the exclusiveness of Jesus Christ. We are quickly moving toward a one-world religion.

Remember Mikhail Gorbachev, the former president of the former Soviet Union? At a news conference in Madrid, Spain, he said, "The victims of the September 11 attack on the United States will not have died in vain if world leaders use the crisis to create a new world order. These victims will not have died in vain if the world reflects and looks at itself in the mirror. . . . If we act as we did after September 11 uniting efforts of fighting against terrorism, if we maintain the coalition, we will not only prevent a new cold war, but we could get a new world order that is so desirable for all of us."

Such a world order is not desirable to me, but it is desirable to the Antichrist, because he is the one who will rule over this new world order. Until that time, the false prophet is working toward this goal.

Artist and philosopher Benjamin Crème is a leading proponent of the one-world idea. Perhaps you have seen full-page ads signed by Crème in your local newspaper. According to the organization Share International, Crème "has become the principal source of information about the emergence of Maitreya, the World Teacher." Share International gives this information about Maitreya, whom they call simply "The Teacher": "He will launch a call to action to save the millions of people who starve to death every year in a world of plenty. Among Maitreya's recommendations will be a shift in social priorities so that adequate food, housing, clothing, education, and medical care become universal rights. Under Maitreya's inspiration, humanity itself will make the required changes and create a saner and more just world for all."

Here is how Maitreya describes his emergence into the world: "Without disturbing anyone, I will choose my moment. Even when you see me, do not run after me. If you run after me, you will lose me. If you parade me, you do not know who I am. I cannot be monopolized— I belong to everyone. I have not come to create followers. Each of you should continue to develop within your own religious tradition. Respect your own religions, your own ideologies—in brief, your own thought form, and you will experience the Master. I do not want you to believe in me. I want you to experience me. If you take one step towards me, I will take two steps towards you. I will lend you my strength. I am always with you."

Crème says of Maitreya: "To the Christians, he will be the second-coming of Christ; to the Jews, the Messiah; the Imam Maude, to the Muslims; Krishna to the Hindus; and the fifth Buddha to the Buddhists." In December 2002, the following question-and-answer exchange was attributed to Maitreya: "If your Master or the Christ could today address directly the United Nations Security Council and the world's leaders, what would they advise in order to cement a real and permanent rapprochement in the Middle East, and with the Muslim world in general? The creation of justice and freedom through the sharing of essential resources throughout the world. Sharing is inevitable, and the sooner understood and implemented, the sooner peace and security for all will be achieved. This is true for the Middle East and the world in general."[6]

The world is looking for this kind of a leader who will blend together the religions of the world. At that time, Christians will face great persecution when they tell others that Jesus Christ is the one and only Savior of the world. We will be made to look like religious fools, fanatics, bigots, and more.

A booklet entitled *Muslim-Christian Alliance* makes a case for an alliance between Christians and Muslims:

> Moreover, the saying of the prophet Mohammed states that in the end of time, true, pious, devout Christians will unite with Muslims and put a great fight together against the common threat, atheism. For the time being, true devout Muslims must unite, not only with their fellow co-religionists, colleagues, and fellow brothers, but with true Christian believers by skipping any dispute, since they will have to unite urgently against the common enemy. . . . Eventually, Christianity will be purified and get rid of all superstitions and misbeliefs and will unite with the true Islamic religion and will be, in a way, transformed into Islam. . . . And by adopting guidance to the Koran, the Christian community will become a follower of Islam, and Islam religion will be in the leader position. The true religion of Islam will gain great power as a result of that unification.

Basically, this booklet is saying that we need to get Muslims and Christians together so we can be co-belligerents against atheism. Their goal is for Christians to stop believing in Jesus and believe in Islam instead as the world religion. "That is far-fetched," you say. You would think so, but this kind of movement is very strong, not only in America but also in the entire world.

He Will Be a Master of Miracles

Revelation 13:13–15 says about the beast:

> He also performs great signs, even causing fire to come down from heaven to earth before people. He deceives those who live on the earth because of the signs that he is permitted to perform on behalf of the beast, telling those who live on the earth to make an image of the beast who had the sword wound

yet lived. He was permitted to give a spirit [*breath*] to the image of the beast, so that the image of the beast could both speak and cause whoever would not worship the image of the beast to be killed (explanatory note added by the author).

We have learned in the Bible that Satan has the power to do miracles. Second Thessalonians 2:9 says, "Even him, whose coming is after the working of Satan with all power and signs and lying wonders" (KJV). Lying wonders means that these miracles will be deceitful and deceptive in their purpose. The devil has a number of tricks in his bag, and they are devilish and diabolical.

One of these wonders will be a celestial fire out of heaven. Second Kings 1:10 tells us that Elijah called down fire from heaven. Since the Bible teaches the Jewish tradition that Elijah will precede the Messiah, this fire could be Satan's counterfeit to tempt our Jewish friends to worship the false messiah. Another wonder will be that he will give an image the ability to speak. All of us watch images speak every day on the television and computer. "But if the devil has the power to work miracles," you ask, "how can we tell whether a miracle is of God or whether it is from Satan?" Let me give you three ways to know.

1. *Does the miracle worker confess that Jesus Christ has come in the flesh?* Second John 1:7 says, "Many deceivers have gone out into the world; they do not confess the coming of Jesus Christ in the flesh. This is the deceiver and the antichrist." Anybody who does not believe that Jesus Christ has come in the flesh is of the devil.

2. *Does the miracle worker glorify the Lord Jesus Christ?* What is the ministry of the Holy Spirit of God? John 16:13–14 says, "When the Spirit of truth comes, He will guide you into all the truth. For He will not speak on His own, but He will speak whatever He hears. He will also declare to you what is to come. He will glorify Me, because He will take from what is Mine and declare it to you." Any miracle worker who does not glorify the Lord Jesus Christ is of the devil.

3. *Does the miracle worker say or do anything that contradicts the clear teaching of God's Word?* Deuteronomy 13:1–5 says:

> If there arise among you a prophet, or a dreamer of dreams, and giveth thee a sign or a wonder, and the sign or the wonder come to pass, whereof he spake unto thee, saying, Let us go after other gods, which thou hast not known, and let us serve them; thou shalt not hearken unto the words of that prophet, or

that dreamer of dreams: for the LORD your God proveth you, to know whether ye love the LORD your God with all your heart and with all your soul. Ye shall walk after the LORD your God, and fear him, and keep his commandments, and obey his voice, and ye shall serve him, and cleave unto him. And that prophet, or that dreamer of dreams, shall be put to death; because he hath spoken to turn you away from the LORD your God, which brought you out of the land of Egypt, and redeemed you out of the house of bondage, to thrust thee out of the way which the LORD thy God commanded thee to walk in. So shalt thou put the evil away from the midst of thee (KJV).

If you see a miracle with your own eyes, it is an undisputable miracle, but if that teacher leads you away from God, don't go. The devil has the power to do miracles.

He Will Be a Controller of Commerce

When you control religion, miracles, and money, you have a grip on this world. Revelation 13:16–18 says, "And he [anti-Holy Spirit] requires everyone—small and great, rich and poor, free and slave—to be given a mark on his right hand or on his forehead, so that no one can buy or sell unless he has the mark: the beast's name or the number of his name. Here is wisdom: The one who has understanding must calculate the number of the beast, because it is the number of a man. His number is 666" (explanatory note added by the author).

As we saw in the last chapter, 666 is the number ascribed to man pretending to be God, for that is exactly what the Antichrist will do. How is the Antichrist going to control the world? With the help of his agent, the anti-Holy Spirit. He will take this world and turn it into a vast concentration camp with all of the inmates numbered. Everybody will be encoded.

The reason to do this is very simple—increased control of commerce. It will be perfect control. No mark, no merchandise. No seal, no sale. It is just that simple. It will be the most ironclad form of control that you can possibly imagine. We are already headed toward a cashless society, with or without Bible prophecy.

When people are required to receive the mark, they will be able to walk out of any store and simply wave their hand to debit their account. At that moment, the store will know how much money you have in the bank and whether or not you will be accepted. There will not be checks or need to show any identification. There won't be any cheating. And there won't be any books to balance.

There is an organization today that has already perfected this whole scheme of things. It is listed on the American Stock Exchange. It is called Digital Angel. Here is what their press releases say about the company:

> Digital Angel™ technology represents the first-ever combination of advanced sensors and Web-enabled wireless telecommunications linked to Global Positioning Systems (GPS). By utilizing advanced sensor capabilities, Digital Angel is able to monitor key functions—such as ambient temperature and physical movement—and transmit that data, along with accurate emergency location information, to a ground station or monitoring facility. The company also invented, manufactures and markets implantable identification microchips the size of a grain of rice for use in humans, companion pets, fish, and livestock. Digital Angel Corp. owns the patents for its inventions in all applications of the implantable microchip technology for humans and animals.[7]

The most important development in recent years from Digital Angel is one that is still in the development stages, but on the verge of introduction. It is a medical recording device for real-time monitoring of patients. It will integrate biosensors and envirosensors, wireless communications, and Global Positioning Systems (GPS) technology. The biosensor will be inserted under your skin, and it will be able to read your heart rate, temperature, blood pressure, pulse, and blood chemistry. Because this technology is networked by the Internet and GPS, your information will be sent instantly to your doctor wherever you are. There will be no escape from this thing.

Another company to watch is called VeriChip. Similar to the biosensor chip technology, the VeriChip will be implanted beneath your skin. The chip has been approved by the FDA with this caveat: as long as "no medical information" of any kind is encoded on the chip, and as long as the chip is not linked to any kind of medical database. The company describes the VeriChip this way:

> VeriChip is a miniaturized, implantable radio frequency identification device (RFID) that has the potential to be used in a variety of security, financial, and other applications. About

the size of a grain of rice, each VeriChip product contains a unique verification number and will be available in several formats. The verification number is captured by briefly passing a proprietary scanner over the VeriChip. A small amount of radio frequency energy passes from the scanner energizing the dormant VeriChip, which then emits a radio frequency signal transmitting the verification number.[8]

An instrument smaller than an insulin syringe will inject it under your skin. You won't need a watch or a credit card. *You* will be the card. *Business Week Online* said:

> Strictly voluntary? So far so good. But now imagine that same chip being used by a totalitarian government to keep track of or round up political activists or others who are considered enemies of the state. In the wrong hands, VeriChip could empower the wrong people.
>
> ADS [Applied Digital Solutions] Vice-President Keith Bolton insists that VeriChips will be used only in voluntary situations. But the company gives up control of how devices are used when they're sold to customers. The U.S. government might consider regulating the international sale of the VeriChip tracking device in much the same way it regulates the sale of arms to rogue states.[9]

Could this chip empower the wrong people? Absolutely! A wise person said, "The more machines act like people, the more people will act like machines." We will be controlled when the beast comes into power.

What kind of application can we make for our lives today, knowing the truth that the anti-Holy Spirit will become a servant of Satan? We need to ask the Holy Spirit to make us a servant of Jesus. Will you do that right now? Will you pray this prayer of commitment to Him?

> *Father, I want these truths to make a present-day impact in my life. I want to recommit my life to you. If the anti-Holy Spirit will be a worker of worship, teach me to worship you. If the anti-Holy Spirit will be a master of miracles, make my life a true living miracle. If the anti-Holy Spirit will control the commerce of this world, take control of all my possessions, I want my work, my worship, my wonder, and my wealth all to belong to you. In Jesus' name. Amen.*

The Decisions of the Living and the Destiny of the Dead

<o>

CHAPTER 18

<o>

Revelation 14 contrasts the Lamb and the beast, earth and heaven, the harvest of the doomed and the harvest of the saved. One day you are going to die; I am going to die. The only intervening factor that might keep that from happening is the second coming of the Lord Jesus Christ. And before we die, there is a choice to be made.

I was witnessing on the streets of Pensacola, Florida, and I stopped to talk to two girls whom I knew, but they didn't know me. I shared the gospel with them and could tell that the Holy Spirit had them under conviction. I asked each girl if she would pray and receive Christ. The first girl gave her heart to Christ.

I turned to the second girl, expecting her to make the same decision, but she said, "I need to, but I don't want to do it right now."

"If you know what you need to do and the Lord stands ready to save you," I asked her, "is there any reason why you should not do it right now?"

"I am just not ready," she replied.

I said, "Behold, now is the accepted time; today is the day of salvation" (see 2 Corinthians 6:2). "You can give your heart to Jesus."

She said again that she was not ready. I knew I should not press beyond that point because I would be manipulating, so I said, "All right, then I pray that you will do it. Before I go, would you shake my hand?"

She said she would.

I told her, "If you will take Christ and eternal life, would you take my right hand? If you take the devil and eternal hell, would you take my left hand?"

She asked, "What?"

"You said you would shake hands."

She stepped back and said, "I am not going to shake hands with you."

"But you said you would."

"Well," she replied, "I am not going to choose the devil and eternal hell."

I told her, "Well, you are either going to say yes to Jesus or no to Jesus. He said, 'He that is not with me is against me; and he that gathereth not with me scattereth abroad' (Matthew 12:30 KJV). Now, will you shake hands with me?"

She said, "I'm not going to shake hands with you. I just don't want to decide."

The point is, if a person decides *not* to decide, that is a decision. We are free to choose; we are *not* free *not* to choose. We are also not free to choose the consequences of our choices.

Our lives are only a vapor. We are here today and gone tomorrow. James 4:14 says, "Whereas ye know not what shall be on the morrow. For what is your life? It is even a vapour, that appeareth for a little time, and then vanisheth away" (KJV).

Amelia Lynch was walking down a street in New York City when lightning struck a flowerpot causing it to fall off a ledge on the eighth floor of a building. The pot hit Amelia on the head. She died instantly. Can you imagine that? Walking down a street in New York City and struck on the head by a flowerpot!

I read about a man who was mowing his grass while his children and wife were watching. Suddenly he grabbed his side and fell to the ground. His mower had picked up a half-inch piece of wire no bigger than a pencil lead and driven it into his heart, killing him instantly.

In the Philippines, a man named Carlos Umbos was fishing. He opened his mouth to yawn, and a fish jumped into his mouth. They were not able to remove the fish from his mouth, and he strangled to death.

People die in many strange ways, but in reality there are only two ways to die. Revelation 14:13 says: "Then I heard a voice from heaven saying, 'Write: Blessed are the dead who die in the Lord from now on.' 'Yes,' says the Spirit, 'let them rest from their labors, for their works follow them!'" If you died today, where would you be—in the Lord or outside of the Lord? If you get to where you are headed, where will you be?

Five minutes from now you may be in heaven, or you may be in hell. There are three things I want you to consider about the decisions of the living and the destiny of the dead.

The Character of Those Who Are Led by the Lamb

Revelation 14:2–4 says:

> I heard a sound from heaven like the sound of cascading waters and like the rumbling of loud thunder. The sound I heard was also like harpists playing on their harps. They sang a new song before the throne and before the four living creatures and the elders, but no one could learn the song except the 144,000 who had been redeemed from the earth. These are the ones not defiled with women, for they have kept their virginity. These are the ones who follow the Lamb wherever He goes. They were redeemed from the human race as the firstfruits for God and the Lamb.

Revelation 7:3 calls the 144,000 tribulation saints the "servants of our God" (KJV). I want you to see their character, because in many ways they represent those of us today who believe in the Lamb of God.

They Are Secure in Their Protection

Revelation 14:1 says, "Then I looked, and there on Mount Zion stood the Lamb, and with Him were 144,000 who had His name and His Father's name written on their foreheads." This tells us that the tribulation saints are saved and sealed with the Father's name on their foreheads (this seal stands for protection, possession, and preservation).

I am glad it doesn't say there were 143,999. Not one is lost. Nowhere in the Bible will you find a truly saved person losing his or her salvation. Why? Because saints are sealed by the Spirit. And the King's seal cannot be broken by any person.

You may say, "It would be wonderful if I were sealed that way." Guess what? You are! Ephesians 1:13 says, "In Him [Jesus] you also, when you heard the word of truth, the gospel of your salvation—in Him when you believed—were sealed with the promised Holy Spirit." Whether you are a saint in the Great Tribulation or a saint in this present age, you are sealed!

They Are Singular in Their Praise

Revelation 14:2–3 says, "And I heard a voice from heaven, as the voice of many waters, and as the voice of a great thunder: and I heard the voice of harpers harping with their harps: and they sung as it were a new song before the throne, and before the four beasts, and the elders: and no man could learn that song but the hundred and forty and four thousand, which were redeemed from the earth" (KJV).

The four beasts represent the attributes of God; the elders represent the saved of all the ages. The 144,000 are the saved Jews who will fill heaven with their song as they rejoice before the Lamb, the Lord Jesus Christ. And the Bible says it is a new song. There are two Greek words translated "new." One has to do with time; the other has to do with character. The word *new* in Revelation 14:3 means new in character. Because of their own special experience, the saved Jews have a song that nobody else can sing.

How does this apply to us? I have a song that you can't sing, and you have a song that I can't sing. Jesus is unique to every person. I cannot put into words what Jesus means to me. "For who among men knows the concerns of a man except the spirit of the man that is in him? In the same way, no one knows the concerns of God except the Spirit of God" (1 Corinthians 2:11).

They Are Separated in Their Purity

Revelation 14:4 says, "These are they which were not defiled with women; for they are virgins" (KJV). What does the phrase "they which were not defiled" mean? First, it does not mean that these people are against marriage (and I'm glad for that). Instead, John is using symbolism to mean that these people are *spiritually* undefiled. Remember that Satan's false church is called a harlot (later in Revelation, we will learn about a scarlet woman who represents false religion). Revelation 14:8 says, "A second angel followed, saying: 'It has fallen, Babylon the Great has fallen, who made all nations drink the wine of her sexual [*spiritual*] immorality, which brings wrath'" (explanatory note added by the author).

These people are virgins who are true to the Lamb, the Lord Jesus Christ. They have not defiled themselves. James used this same symbolism when he said, "Adulteresses! Do you not know that friendship with the world is hostility toward God? So whoever wants to be the world's friend becomes God's enemy" (James 4:4). In the same way, Paul said to the church, "For I am jealous over you with a godly jealousy, because I have promised you in marriage to one husband—to present a pure virgin to Christ" (2 Corinthians 11:2).

Are you spiritually pure? Do you have an undefiled love for the Lord Jesus Christ? Would you disgrace the Lord Jesus? I would rather die by torture than be unfaithful to my darling wife. And I know I would rather die by torture than be unfaithful to my heavenly bridegroom, the Lord Jesus Christ.

They Are Steadfast in Their Purpose

Revelation 14:4 says, "These are the ones who follow the Lamb wherever He goes." They are marked by their loyalty to the Lamb. They have no rival, no refusal, and no restraint. Do you have that kind of loyalty to the Lamb? Are you steadfast in your purpose? These people are.

They Are Symbolic in Their Prophecy

Revelation 14:4 says, "They were redeemed from the human race as the firstfruits for God and the Lamb." In Israel there was a feast during harvest time called the Feast of Firstfruits (see Exodus 23:14–19). God instructed His people to harvest the first ripened grain and take it to the temple for a ceremony, because the firstfruits signify the harvest that is to come.

There will be 144,000 saved Jews who will preach the gospel like the apostle Paul around the world. Revelation 7:9 tells us that millions and millions will come to Christ during the Great Tribulation: "After this I looked, and there was a vast multitude from every nation, tribe, people, and language, which no one could number, standing before the throne and before the Lamb. They were robed in white with palm branches in their hands." Why are these saved? Because they are protected and sealed for the Lord Jesus Christ.

They Are Sincere in Their Profession

Revelation 14:5 says, "No lie [hypocrisy] was found in their mouths; they are blameless" (explanatory note added by the author). These people will know the truth, believe the truth, tell the truth, speak the truth, and live the truth. They will not be hypocrites who speak the slogans of the beast during the Great Tribulation. If you faced the Lord today, would your words condemn you or justify you?

The Corruption of Those Who Are Bossed by the Beast

In the Great Tribulation, you will either be led by the Lamb or bossed by the beast. Revelation 14:6–7 says, "Then I saw another angel flying in mid-heaven, having the eternal gospel to announce to the inhabitants of the earth—to every nation, tribe, language, and people. He spoke with a loud voice: 'Fear God and give Him glory, because the hour of His judgment has come. Worship the Maker of heaven and earth, the sea and springs of water.'"

If the gospel is preached in this dispensation, then it is preached by me, you, and others like us, or it is not preached. In the Great Tribulation, however, God in His mercy gives one final call to the Gentiles by sending angels to preach the gospel. Some people say this is a different gospel, but it cannot be, according to Galatians 1:6–9: "I am amazed that you are so quickly turning away from Him who called you by the grace of Christ, and are turning to a different gospel—not that there is another gospel, but there are some who are troubling you and want to change the gospel of Christ. But even if we or an angel from heaven should preach to you a gospel other than what we have preached to you, a curse be on him!"

If an angel appears in the heavens and preaches any other gospel than that which Paul preached, the curse of God is on him. It is the saving gospel of God's grace. "For by grace are ye saved through faith; and that not of yourselves: it is the gift of God: not of works, lest any man should boast" (Ephesians 2:8–9 KJV).

When the angel ceases his message, another angel begins to speak: "It has fallen, Babylon the Great has fallen, who made all nations drink the wine of her sexual immorality, which brings wrath" (Revelation. 14:8). This is the first time in Revelation that Babylon is mentioned. We will discover in Revelation 17 and 18 that there is a great emphasis upon Babylon, which is the cradle and the grave of all idolatry and false worship.

In Genesis 10 and 11, we learn about a man name Nimrod (his name means "rebel") who built a city called Babel. Originally, he wanted to build a city with a tower that reached into the heavens. From this tower, he would create a one-world government and religion. This ultimately became Babylon, which is the fountainhead of all false religion and, therefore, is the quintessential symbol of evil and sin.

Here is an interesting thing. The early Christians in the first century called Rome the Babylon of its day because Rome epitomized Babylon. For all we know, Rome could be the place where the Antichrist will rule. Or it could be ancient Babylon rebuilt. We will see. For now, we know that Babylon is destined for destruction and that it is the capital city of the Antichrist. Babylon will corrupt the entire world and bring in a one-world government and a one-world religion. For further information, consult any modern newspaper.

The Consequences of Those Destined by Decision

The Destiny of Those Who Are Branded by the Beast

It is decision that determines destiny. Think of those who have been branded by the beast. Revelation 14:9–12 says:

> And a third angel followed them and spoke with a loud voice: "If anyone worships the beast and his image and receives a mark on his forehead or on his hand, he will also drink the wine of God's wrath, which is mixed full strength in the cup of His anger. He will be tormented with fire and sulfur in the sight of the holy angels and in the sight of the Lamb, and the smoke of their torment will go up forever and ever. There is no rest day or night for those who worship the beast and his image, or anyone who receives the mark of his name. Here is the endurance of the saints, who keep the commandments of God and the faith in Jesus."

As I told you before, the Antichrist will have a minister of propaganda who will cause everyone to receive a mark on the right hand or forehead. He will also be a controller of commerce. You will not be able to buy or sell without the mark of the beast, and if you do take the mark of the beast, you will commit an unpardonable sin. There will be no hope for you whatsoever—you will be forever damned.

But if you do not receive his mark, you will be persecuted by the beast and put to death. You can anticipate torture and death. Either way, you do not want to be here during the Great Tribulation. You will either defy the beast or deify the beast. Those will be your choices. If you do take the mark of the beast, then you will drink from the cup of the indignation of Almighty God (see Revelation 14:10). (In ancient times, capital punishment was often carried out by causing a person to drink a cup of poison.)

In case you did not know, there is an eternal hell of fire and brimstone. Have you ever heard of a fire-and-brimstone preacher? That is a person who preaches about the eternal damnation that awaits souls who have rejected Jesus Christ. Somebody may say, "Well, this is all just symbolic, isn't it?" For your sake, I hope it is not symbolic if you die and go to hell; the symbolism is always weaker than the reality. For instance, what is more beautiful—a painting of a sunset or the sunset itself? The painting is the symbol of the reality. Whatever it is, you don't want to experience what the Bible describes as fire and brimstone.

You may say, "If I go there, I won't stay very long." Oh no? Look at Revelation 14:11: "And the smoke of their torment ascendeth up *for ever and ever*: and they have no rest day nor night, who worship the beast and his image, and whosoever receiveth the mark of his name" (KJV). There is no hope once you go to hell. The Bible says in Proverbs 11:7: "When a wicked man dieth, his expectation shall perish: and the hope of unjust men perisheth" (KJV). Hopelessness is the destiny of the damned. Bernard M. Baruch said, "The saddest word in the English language is the word *hopeless.*"

Jesus Christ had more to say about hell than any other preacher in the Bible. He also talked more about hell than about heaven. He said, "And if your hand causes your downfall, cut it off. It is better for you to enter life maimed than to have two hands and go to hell—the unquenchable fire" (Mark 9:43). In essence, Jesus said it would be better to be a crippled saint than a healthy sinner on the way to hell.

The Destiny of Those Who Are Sealed by the Spirit

Revelation 14:13 says, "Then I heard a voice from heaven saying, 'Write: Blessed are the dead who die in the Lord from now on.' 'Yes,' says the Spirit, 'let them rest from their labors, for their works follow them.'" What a great verse! The beast may put these tribulation saints to death, but the Bible says, "Yet we are confident and satisfied to be out of the body and at home with the Lord" (2 Corinthians 5:8). The minute a child of God dies, he goes immediately into the presence of the Lord.

Stephen was stoned, "but Stephen, filled by the Holy Spirit, gazed into heaven. He saw God's glory, with Jesus standing at the right hand of God, and he said, 'Look! I see the heavens opened and the Son of Man standing at the right hand of God'" (Acts 7:55–56). I know Jesus is normally seated in heaven, but He stood up for Stephen, didn't He? And He lovingly said, "Welcome home, my son!"

Do you have a mother or father, brother or sister, perhaps a child in heaven? Here are three things from Revelation 14:13 that can give you comfort:

1. *They are rejoicing* ("Blessed are the dead"). In the Greek, the word *blessed* is *makarios,* which means "rejoicing." Saints who have died are now leaping, dancing, and praising God. Heaven is all that the loving heart of God can desire, the omniscient mind of God can conceive, and the omnipotent hand of God can perform. That is what heaven is. Consider the artistry that God has put into heaven. The God who sculpted the wings of the butterfly, blended the hues of the rainbow, and painted the meadows with daffodils is the same One who made heaven. Blessed are the dead in Christ, for they are rejoicing.

2. *They are resting* ("Let them rest from their labors"). This type of resting does not mean that the saints are sitting around on a fluffy cloud wearing a robe and halo and plucking a harp. It also does not mean that they are passively listening to music for all eternity. Revelation 22:3 says, "And there shall be no more curse: but the throne of God and of the Lamb shall be in it; *and his servants shall serve him*" (KJV). In heaven, the saints will rule kingdoms and universes in service to God.

3. *They are rewarded* ("For their works follow them"). If you are trying to work your way to heaven, you will never be able to do it. It would be like running up the "down" escalator. You will not get there by your works, but your works will follow you to heaven. Jesus said, "Whoever gives just a cup of cold water to one of these little ones because he is a disciple—I assure you: He will never lose his reward" (Matthew 10:42).

There is a God to serve. There is a hell to shun. There is heaven to gain. There is an eternity to live. There are the decisions of the living and the destiny of the dead, whether you are in this age or the age to come.

How to Gain and Celebrate Victory

◄O►
CHAPTER 19
◄O►

The greatest celebration that I can remember took place when I was a boy in my early teens. The year was 1945. America was in a world war and as the Allies advanced, Hitler saw the tide turning and committed suicide. We had won the victory in Europe, but we were still fighting the Japanese in the Pacific. On August 6, 1945, I remember hearing the news that America had dropped the atomic bomb on Hiroshima and the Japanese still fought on. Three days later, we dropped another bomb on Nagasaki. Then the Japanese declared that they would surrender unconditionally. There in Tokyo Bay, aboard the battleship *Missouri*, they signed an unconditional surrender. It was September 2 in Japan and September 1 in the United States.

We didn't have television, but I remember people filling the streets shouting, "Victory! Victory!" Soon the newsboys came out with the papers and began shouting, "Extra! Extra! Read all about it! The war has ended!" Our family was living in West Palm Beach, Florida, at the time, so we drove downtown to Clematis Street. It was crowded with people shouting and hugging and laughing. All the boys except me were making the most of this moment by kissing all the girls. They called it V-J Day. There is coming a day that will make V-J Day pale in significance. In fact, it's another V-J Day—Victory in Jesus! What a day that will be when our Lord returns!

David Jeremiah, preacher, author, and founder of *Turning Point* radio and television ministry, gives the following anecdote about the composer and musical genius Johann Sebastian Bach: "Sometimes he would sleep more than he ought to sleep. His children had a way of waking him up. They would go to the piano, and they would begin to play a composition. When they would get to the last note they would stop. They wouldn't play the last note. It would always wake him up. He would get up from his sleep, go to the piano, and play the final chord."

I think all of us are waiting for that last note on the final page of God's song of victory, aren't we? In this chapter, I want to give you three principles of victory that God has given us from Revelation 15 and 16: the reliant Word of God, the redeeming works of God, and the righteous wrath of God.

The Reliant Word of God

As I have mentioned in previous chapters, a beast is coming to regiment everybody and everything during the Great Tribulation. Is this just Bible prophecy? No, things are happening today to ready the Antichrist's entrance. Here's what one newspaper reporter said:

> Big Brother is scanning you. Photo IDs may become a thing of the past, replaced by biometric identifiers—things like fingerprints and scans of the eyes. Privacy experts fear access to such personal information invites abuse by scam artists or over-zealous civil servants. Nonetheless, the following advances are likely to gain wider use. There is no more punching the time clock at some companies, including a New York City supermarket. Instead, a hand reader scans the image and logs the time. The system eliminates buddy punching, when one employee punches the card for another who is late or absent, and streamlines payroll and accounting. Forget your credit card. Some Seattle supermarkets and a McDonald's in Fresno, California, are testing a system in which a participant's fingerprint is scanned, retrieving his or her credit card information. Congress is debating switching to a national identification card system instead of driver's licenses, all linked to one database.

Revelation 15:1–2 says, "Then I saw another great and awe-inspiring sign in heaven: seven angels with the seven last plagues, for with them, God's wrath will be completed. I also saw something like a sea of glass mixed with fire, and those who had won the victory from the beast, his image, and the number of his name, were standing on the sea of glass with harps from God."

This passage tells us that there will be a group of people in heaven who will praise God because they have gained the victory. How did they get the victory? The key is in verse 2: They stand on a "sea of glass." This sea is not an ocean. Instead, John sees a great basin or laver similar to the one in Solomon's temple. First Kings 7:23 says, "And he [Solomon] made a molten sea, ten cubits from the one brim to the other: it was round all about, and his height was five cubits: and a line of thirty cubits did compass it round about" (KJV).

Before the priest would go into the temple to worship, he washed in a laver. It symbolized the Word of God that cleanses man from sin. Ephesians 5:26 tells us how Jesus Christ (the Word made flesh) cleanses and sanctifies the church: "To make her holy, cleansing her in the washing of water by the word." In that day, people washed in the sea. In the Book of Revelation, these people do not wash in it because it has become crystallized. They stand upon it. In Revelation 4:6 it is called the crystal sea: "Also before the throne was something like a sea of glass, similar to crystal. In the middle and around the throne were four living creatures covered with eyes in front and in back." The saints who have come out of the Great Tribulation are now standing on the Word of God.

When Joshua was going into Canaan, God gave him a formula for victory. It is older than the Dead Sea Scrolls, but as fresh as tomorrow's newspaper. Here is what God told Joshua (and what He is telling us today): "This book of the law shall not depart out of thy mouth; but thou shalt meditate therein day and night, that thou mayest observe to do according to all that is written therein: for then thou shalt make thy way prosperous, and then thou shalt have good success" (Joshua 1:8 KJV).

Victory comes by the Word of God, which according to Joshua, is to be in our *mouths*. The New Testament affirms this: "No rotten talk should come from your mouth, but only what is good for the building up of someone in need, in order to give grace to those who hear" (Ephesians 4:29). Do you want victory? Learn to quote the Word of God, not just in your head but out loud. And when you verbalize it, you vitalize it.

John Bunyan, who wrote *Pilgrim's Progress*, was convicted and converted by listening to a conversation between some women about the Word of God. If someone were to eavesdrop on one of your conversations, would it lead him to Christ? Not only is the Word of God to be in your mouth, but it is also to be in your *mind*. Joshua said we are to meditate on it day and night.

Meditation is like a song that you can't get out of your mind. When you meditate on the Word of God, you think God's thoughts after Him. And when you do that, you will find out that you have incredible wisdom. As problems come (and they will) the Word of God will give you the wisdom you need.

Finally, you and I need to have the Word of God in our *manner of life*. God told Joshua that he was to do all that is commanded in the Word of God. Reading and meditating upon the Word of God is important, but it is obeying the Word of God that causes the Bible to burst into flame in your life. When God speaks to you through His Word and gives you a command to obey, you need to stop right there if you are not obeying that command. Don't read any further. Jesus said, "The one who has My commandments and keeps them is the one who loves Me. And the one who loves Me will be loved by My Father. I also will love him and will reveal Myself to him" (John 14:21).

All the rest is just religious talk. You can read and write all manner of notes in your Bible, but when you hear God's Word and obey it, Jesus said, "You love me." Reading the Bible gives you knowledge *about* God; obeying the Bible gives you knowledge *of* God. God will become real to you.

Would you like to live in victory *today?* I don't mean in the "sweet by and by"; I mean in the "nasty now and now." You will live in victory as you learn to plant your feet firmly upon the solid Word of God.

The Redeeming Works of God

Revelation 15:3 says, "They sang the song of God's servant Moses, and the song of the Lamb: 'Great and awe-inspiring are Your works, Lord God, the Almighty; righteous and true are Your ways, King of the Nations.'" When the Israelites were in Egypt they weren't singing; they were groaning. But God brought them out of Egypt and redeemed them by the blood of the Passover Lamb. Their song is found in Exodus 15 after they crossed through the parted Red Sea. It is the first recorded song in the Bible. The last recorded song in the Bible is the song of the Lamb. Both of these songs speak of redemption.

Thank God for singing! Thank God for music! The way that you celebrate the Lord Jesus is to sing of His works. You can tell a lot about people when you listen to their songs. Do you know why people sing rock and roll? Because they have rocks rolling around in their hearts. Do you know why the Russians sing in a minor key? Because that is the way they live. Only in Jesus can we sing a redemption song.

If you are standing like a wooden Indian in a song service, don't call yourself spiritual. May God have mercy upon you if you don't offer praise to God with a joyful noise during a song service. The Scottish-born evangelist John Linton said, "There are as many commands in the Bible to sing as there are to pray." We are to praise our mighty God. Isaac Watts wrote the hymn "Marching to Zion." This song has a stanza that fits well here:

> *Let those refuse to sing,*
> *Who never knew our God;*
> *But children of the heavenly King*
> *May speak their joys abroad.*

When the Israelites were going into the Promised Land, they asked God which tribe should go first. Judah was chosen because the name Judah means praise. It is praise that *precedes* every victory; it is praise that *follows* every victory.

You may say, "I have problems. I don't feel like singing." That is all the more reason you ought to sing. When Paul and Silas were arrested for preaching the gospel, they were thrown into jail. Acts 16:25–26 says, "About midnight Paul and Silas were praying and singing hymns to God, and the prisoners were listening to them. Suddenly there was such a violent earthquake that the foundations of the jail were shaken, and immediately all the doors were opened, and everyone's chains came loose." Talk about jailhouse rock!

If Paul and Silas had not been filled with the Spirit, I wonder if the following might have happened.

Paul: "Silas, you awake?"

Silas: "Of course, I am awake. How could anybody sleep in this filth?"

Paul: "Well, you don't have to get huffy about it."

Silas: "I have a headache."

Paul: "So do I."

Silas: "Well, Paul, you got us into this mess."

Paul: "Wait a minute. I want you to know that I could have a position teaching in the University of Tarsus. I sold the Damascus Tent and Awning Company for almost nothing to get into this preaching thing. What have you done?"

Silas: "I have been following you, and I think you are one of the poorest leaders I have ever known."

Jailer: "Just as I thought. These are a bunch of phonies. What they have is not real. It is no different from what I have."

Praise God, they didn't react that way. When Paul and Silas began to sing and praise God, God sent the earthquake angel. The conversation may have gone like this:

Paul: "Silas, are you awake?"

Silas: "Hallelujah, brother, I'm awake. How do you feel?"

Paul: "I'm having victory in Jesus."

Silas: "You mean with those stripes on your back?"

Paul: "Yes, sir."

Silas: "In this prison?"

Paul: "Yes, sir! I feel like singing. Why don't we sing, 'What a Friend We Have in Jesus, all our sins and griefs to bear'? Why don't we sing, 'Everyday with Jesus Is Sweeter Than the Day Before'?"

Jailer: "Wow! They must believe the stuff they're singing about!"

If you've got problems, pull some of the groans out of your prayers and shove in some hallelujahs. And if God gives you a victory, praise Him! Praise Him! Praise Him! God forbid that your church should fail to be a praising church. Evangelism is as much caught as it is taught. When visitors come into your church and you're praising the Lord, those visitors will look around like the jailer and they will say, "These folks believe that stuff." And before long, they will be believing it, too. What is victory's song? It is not singing about what we have done, but it is singing about the redemptive work of Almighty God.

The Righteous Wrath of God

Many people ask where is God when there is so much sin in the world—wickedness, rape, arson, pillage, child abuse, blasphemy, war. Where is God? He is on His throne! And you can be certain that every sin will be punished. Yours will be punished. Mine will be punished. The only question is: Who will bear that punishment? Every sin will be pardoned by Christ or punished in hell, but it will never be overlooked. Nobody's sin is ever overlooked. All sin is dealt with.

These people who are standing on the sea of glass understand that there is coming a day when God will put the final period on the final paragraph, on the final chapter, on the final book of history. Our God is a mighty God! Revelation 15:4–8 says,

> "Lord, who will not fear and glorify Your name? Because You alone are holy, because all the nations will come and worship before You, because Your righteous acts have been revealed." After this I looked, and the heavenly sanctuary—the tabernacle of testimony—was opened. Out of the sanctuary came the seven angels with the seven plagues, dressed in clean, bright linen, with gold sashes wrapped around their chests. One of the four living creatures gave the seven angels seven gold bowls filled with the wrath of God who lives forever and ever. Then the sanctuary was filled with smoke from God's glory and from His power, and no one could enter the sanctuary until the seven plagues of the seven angels were completed.

Seven angels will come from the temple to give four judgments: (1) a righteous judgment because they are wearing white robes; (2) a sovereign judgment because they are wearing golden sashes, which represent the priests and king; (3) a solemn judgment because they have bowls of wrath; and (4) a sure judgment because the Bible says no man can enter into the temple until God is finished. The place will be filled with smoke (which speaks of the judgment of God consuming the sacrifice), and the Bible says that no man could approach. It is almost as if God were saying, "Stay out. I am busy. Don't interrupt me. I am going to judge this world."

Now we come to the period of time in Revelation known as the seven bowls of wrath. Revelation 16:1–2 says, "Then I heard a loud voice from the sanctuary saying to the seven angels, 'Go and pour out the seven bowls of God's wrath on the earth.' The first went and poured out his bowl on the earth, and severely painful sores broke out on the people who had the mark of the beast and who worshiped his image."

Do you see the irony here? The mark turns into a cankerous, contagious sore that is putrefying and incurable. Then as the judgment continues, we see corrupted seas.

Corrupted Seas

Revelation 16:3 says, "And the second angel poured out his vial upon the sea; and it became as the blood of a dead man; and every living soul died in the sea" (KJV). Here is a dead world lying in its own gore. The sea becomes not blood but *as* blood. God could turn it to blood if He wished, but His Word says "*as* blood."

Occasionally the ocean is infected with something called the red tide. This is caused by microorganisms called dinoflagellates or *Karenia brevis*. By some strange alchemy, this one-cell organism turns the water red, poisons the sea life, and produces potent chemical neurotoxins. These toxins cause extensive fish kills, contaminate shellfish, and create severe respiratory irritation to humans along the shore. As the organisms approach the shoreline, you can begin to see and feel the obvious effects: dead fish, the characteristic burning sensation of the eyes and nose, and a dry, choking cough.[10]

Could this be what John is talking about? I don't know, but the seas will become contaminated and the streams will become corrupted. Revelation 16:4–7 says, "The third poured out his bowl into the rivers and the springs of water, and they became blood. I heard the angel of the waters say: 'You are righteous, who is and who was, the Holy One, for You have decided these things. Because they poured out the blood of the saints and the prophets, You also gave them blood to drink; they deserve it!' Then I heard someone from the altar say: 'Yes, Lord God, the Almighty, true and righteous are Your judgments.'"

Consuming Sun

Global warming is coming! Revelation 16:8–9 says, "The fourth poured out his bowl on the sun. He was given the power to burn people with fire, and people were burned by the intense heat. So they blasphemed the name of God who had the power over these plagues, and they did not repent and give Him glory."

When Jesus died, the sun hid its face and refused to shine. When He is manifest in all His glory, there will be erupting flames of fire and judgment. Scientists may even refer to this as solar flares. But whatever they are, the heat will be intense. Will it cause people to repent? No, it won't cause them to repent. According to this passage of Scripture, it will only cause them to blaspheme God. If the love of God does not bring you to repentance, then the judgment of God will not bring you to repentance.

Confounded Sinners

Their beloved beast will not be able to help them now. Revelation 16:10–11 says, "The fifth poured out his bowl on the throne of the beast, and his kingdom was plunged into darkness. People gnawed their tongues from pain and blasphemed the God of heaven because of their pains and their sores, yet they did not repent of their actions."

There will be a cascade of hurt that will culminate in a crescendo of hate, as these confounded sinners lurch forward in their hatred against God. The darkness described here doesn't speak necessarily of physical darkness, but of moral and spiritual darkness that will engulf the world.

Controlling Spirits

Revelation 16:12–16 says:

> The sixth poured out his bowl on the great river Euphrates, and its water was dried up to prepare the way for the kings from the east. Then I saw three unclean spirits [*demons*] like frogs coming from the dragon's mouth, from the beast's mouth, and from the mouth of the false prophet. For they are spirits of demons performing signs, who travel to the kings of the whole world to assemble them for the battle [*of Armageddon*] of the great day of God, the Almighty. "Look, I am coming like a thief. Blessed is the one who is alert and remains clothed so that he may not go naked, and they see his shame." So they assembled them at the place called in Hebrew Armagedon (explanatory notes added by the author).

These demon spirits are already working to draw the nations to the final decisive battle of mankind. How are they doing that? They are going into the hearts and minds of people. Do you ever wonder how people can follow through with suicide bombings? They are pawns in the hands of the evil one that is driving men to a cataclysm of wickedness. And if you think it is bad now, just wait until the church is taken out of the world.

The Euphrates River is the dividing line between the Near East and the Far East. It is 1,800 miles long, 3,600 feet wide, and an average of 30 feet deep. On the eastern side of the Euphrates are the multitudes from Asia, India, and Japan. The Euphrates actually flows past modern-day Iraq, which is biblical Babylon. Special demon spirits reside there.

Cataclysmic Shaking

All of these things climax in Revelation 16:17: "Then the seventh poured out his bowl into the air, and a loud voice came out of the sanctuary, from the throne, saying, 'It is done!'" Correspondingly, Jesus poured out His blood for our sin, then bowed His head and said, "It is finished" (John 19:30). At Calvary, redemption was completed. In Revelation, retribution will be completed.

Revelation 16:18–19 continues: "There were lightnings, rumblings, and thunders. And a severe earthquake occurred like no other since man has been on the earth—so great was the quake. The great city split into three parts, and the cities of the nations fell. Babylon the Great was remembered in God's presence; He gave her the cup filled with the wine of His fierce anger."

Don't forget that one of the secrets of our victory is the wrath of God. Apart from the wrath and righteous judgment of God, there can be no ultimate victory. Sin must be dealt with. Revelation 16:20–21 concludes: "And every island fled away, and the mountains were not found. And there fell upon men a great hail out of heaven, every stone about the weight of a talent: and men blasphemed God because of the plague of the hail; for the plague thereof was exceeding great" (KJV).

A talent is about all that a man can carry. During this period of time, men will have crushing missiles of ice falling upon them.

This chapter ends by talking about people drinking from the cup of God's wrath. When Jesus was in the Garden of Gethsemane, He drank a cup. Do you remember what it was? He took the sin of mankind upon Himself and carried it to the cross. Thank God that He drank that bitter cup! There is another cup. The psalmist said, "I will take the cup of salvation, and call upon the name of the LORD" (Psalm 116:13 KJV). Because Jesus drank the bitter cup of God's wrath, you can drink the loving cup of God's grace and mercy. If you fail to drink the cup of salvation, you will drink the cup of the wrath of God. God will never overlook sin!

There is a way that you can have victory and stand on the reliant Word of God, sing of the redeeming works of God, and see the righteous wrath of God executed upon His enemies. That way is yours if you will trust Him.

Beauty and the Beast

◄O►

CHAPTER 20

◄O►

Let me give you a classic example of the beauty and the beast. A while ago, one of my granddaughters got married. She asked if I would take her and her new husband from the church to their car in the rumble seat of my 1929 black-and-yellow Model A Ford. Like any good Papa, I said yes. To make the experience complete, someone hung a sign saying "Just Married" on the back bumper, along with tin cans. We had a grand time.

When I had to take my car home, I asked another of my granddaughters if she wanted to ride with me. As we were driving down the Interstate highway, truck drivers were blowing their horns and pointing at me and clapping their hands. It took me by complete surprise until I realized what was happening. People were thinking, *What is that old geezer doing with that young twenty-something girl? How on earth did he ever talk her into marrying him?*

The difference between that episode and this episode about a Babylonian mother and a Babylonian monster is that my granddaughter who was riding with me is beautiful *without* and *within*. The beauty we will be talking about was beautiful outside, but ugly within.

Prophecy, such as the one we will learn about in this chapter, is in the news. In fact, *Time* magazine devoted its front page one week to prophecy and the second coming of Jesus Christ. Man has always wanted to look into the future, but sometimes he makes awful mistakes. I heard about a weatherman who had to leave one city and go to another because the weather didn't agree with him. People make prognostications about all kinds of things, but they fail. The Bible is the only book that has a batting average of one thousand.

No Christian can afford to be ignorant of prophecy in these days in which we live, because the things that are prophesied in God's Word are imminent. I believe that the shadows of the end of the age are lengthening, the sands of time are running low, and we are standing on the threshold of the second coming of Jesus Christ and the rapture of the church.

Every child of God needs to know that there is a beast called the Antichrist, who is lurking in the shadows and getting ready to take over. Why? (1) Because of the *intercession factor*. We need to pray like we have never prayed before. (2) Because of the *soul-winning factor*. We need to get our loved ones into the ark of safety. (3) Because of the *family instruction factor*. We need to prepare our loved ones for the things that are coming. We cannot afford to be ignorant. (4) Because of the *comfort factor*. You may think that things are coming apart, but everything is fitting into the sockets of prophecy.

I want to remind you that Revelation 17 is about the period of time called the Great Tribulation. The church, the blood-bought body of the Lord Jesus Christ, has been taken out and now the false bride shows herself. We will call her "beauty," while the Antichrist is called the "beast."

The Woman and Her Mysterious Character
Revelation 17:1–4 says:

> And there came one of the seven angels which had the seven vials, and talked with me, saying unto me, Come hither; I will show unto thee the judgment of the great whore that sitteth upon many waters: with whom the kings of the earth have committed fornication, and the inhabitants of the earth have been made drunk with the wine of her fornication. So he carried me away in the spirit into the wilderness: and I saw a woman sit upon a scarlet colored beast, full of names of blasphemy, having seven heads and ten horns. And the woman was arrayed in purple and scarlet colour, and decked with gold and precious stones and pearls, having a golden cup in her hand full of abominations and filthiness of her fornication (KJV).

The Scarlet Harlot

Women in Bible prophecy are always considered a symbol of religion, whether good or bad. For example, the church of the Lord Jesus Christ is called "the bride of Christ." This "mother of harlots" in Revelation 17:5 (KJV) represents an apostate worldwide religion—the anti-church, if you will. This woman is one who will seduce the nations.

God's Word is very clear: If we flirt with this harlot world, we will become an enemy of the bridegroom. James warns about this: "Adulteresses! Do you not know that friendship with the world is hostility toward God? So whoever wants to be the world's friend becomes God's enemy" (James 4:4). Paul put it very clearly when he said, "For I am jealous over you with a godly jealousy, because I have promised you in marriage to one husband—to present a pure virgin to Christ" (2 Corinthians 11:2). The church is the virgin who will be presented to the Lord Jesus Christ, the bridegroom.

Babylon also stands for false religion. Actually, the word *Babylon* is a code word. It's like when someone says "Wall Street." We don't think about the literal street; we think about the economic business of Wall Street. When people say "Madison Avenue," are they talking about an avenue named Madison? No, they are talking about more than that. They are talking about a system of merchandising.

When the Bible uses the term *Babylon,* it is talking about more than a city. Babylon is great in antiquity and iniquity. Every false religion has its roots in Babylon. When Daniel was in Babylon, Nebuchadnezzar the king of Babylon had a dream, and he wanted it interpreted. Did he call religious, godly men to interpret the dream? No. Daniel 2:2 says, "Then the king commanded to call the *magicians,* and the *astrologers,* and the *sorcerers,* and the *Chaldeans,* for to show the king his dreams. So they came and stood before the king" (KJV). These were men and women of false religions. Throughout history, Babylon has been a den of demons. And today, the ghosts of Babylon haunt the world.

Another phrase I want you to consider is "the wine of her fornication." This wine was bottled centuries ago, and yet men are still getting drunk on that wine today. What is that wine? Astrology. One billion people in the world today practice astrology. Many of them are Americans. Do you have a horoscope in your home? If you do, get it out! Don't fool with it. You say, "I know it's not real; I'm just having fun with it." That is akin to a married man flirting with somebody who is not his wife. Get it out.

The Woman and Her Mischievous Children

Revelation 17:5 tells us that the mother of harlots, whose origin is in Babylon, has given birth to all the false religions of the world: "And upon her forehead was a name written, MYSTERY, BABYLON THE GREAT, THE MOTHER OF HARLOTS AND ABOMINATIONS OF THE EARTH" (KJV). This scarlet woman has taught her daughters how to prostitute themselves. Who are some of these harlots? New Age religion, Satan worship, mother earth worship, globalism, Hinduism, Islam, apostate Christianity. All of these are daughters of this false religion.

Daughters of the New Age movement—holistic health professionals, ecologists, political activists, educators, human potential advocates, goddess worshipers, reincarnationists, astrologers, and more—are engulfing the world today. It is a syncretism of all of the world's religions. A leader in the New Age movement said: "We honor the truth and beauty of all the world religions, believing that each has a seed of God, a kernel of the spirit that unites us." Doesn't that sound beautiful? Another leader in the same movement said, "New Agers believe that God revealed Himself in Jesus, but he also revealed Himself in Buddha, Krishna, and a host of others." The followers of New Age do not believe that the Bible alone is the guide.

There is a new religion to which they espouse called "monism," which comes from the Greek word *monos*, meaning "single." The *Internet Encyclopedia of Philosophy* defines monism like this: "The meaning applies to any doctrine or theory that claims that all things, no matter how many or of what variety, can be reduced to one unified thing in time, space, or quality."[11] Everything is together. Any apparent or perceived differences are not real.

If you combine monism and pantheism (*pan* meaning "all" and *theism* meaning "God"), you get the belief that everything is God. That is the fundamental philosophy behind most New Age thinkers. For instance, you may have heard about Mother Earth—this is a philosophy to which they hold rather than Father God. These people want to unify the religions of the world. As a matter of fact, a charter has been formed for an organization in the United Nations for united religions. Here is the declaration on a global ethic: "We affirm that there is an irrevocable, unconditional norm for all areas of life: for families and communities, for races, nations, and religions. There already exist ancient guidelines for human behavior which are found in the teachings of the religions of the world and which are the condition for a sustainable world order."

You ask, "Will anybody buy into that?" Pope Paul II, the Dalai Lama, and the leaders of the World Council of Churches have endorsed religious unity. A worldwide religion is coming!

The Woman and Her Murderous Conduct

This hideous woman is not only a prostitute, but she is a murderess. Revelation 17:6 says, "Then I saw that the woman was drunk on the blood of the saints and on the blood of the witnesses to Jesus. When I saw her, I was utterly astounded."

During the Great Tribulation, many thousands will be coerced to convert. The false prophet said, "He was permitted to give a spirit to the image of the beast, so that the image of the beast could both speak and cause whoever would not worship the image of the beast to be killed" (Revelation 13:15). If you are alive during this time, you will be forced to believe and bow the knee to the beast or you will die.

I believe forced conversion is a contradiction in terms. One of the blackest mistakes in Christian history was the Crusades. We are still today reaping the bitter fruit of the time when "knights in shining armor" tried to enforce Christianity and conquered the Holy Land with the sword. Islam even today is into forced conversion. I want the right to try to persuade anybody to believe in the Lord Jesus Christ, but with all of my heart and soul I resist any kind of forced conversion.

During the Great Tribulation, the soil of planet earth will be drenched with blood by this harlot. False religion has always produced much bloodshed. That is why I say that Christianity is not truly a religion. Instead, it is a vital *relationship* with Jesus Christ.

The Woman and Her Monstrous Consort

The woman has a friend named the beast. I would refer to her as the bride of the beast, but I don't believe they get married. Revelation 17:3 reveals him: "So he carried me away in the Spirit to a desert. I saw a woman sitting on a scarlet beast that was covered with blasphemous names, having seven heads and 10 horns." Here is the ultimate alliance of church and state. John writes:

> And the angel said unto me, Wherefore didst thou marvel?
> I will tell thee the mystery of the woman, and of the beast that
> carrieth her, which hath the seven heads and ten horns. The
> beast that thou sawest was, and is not; and shall ascend out of

the bottomless pit, and go into perdition: and they that dwell on the earth shall wonder, whose names were not written in the book of life from the foundation of the world, when they behold the beast that was, and is not, and yet is. And here is the mind which hath wisdom. The seven heads are seven mountains, on which the woman sitteth. And there are seven kings: five are fallen, and one is, and the other is not yet come; and when he cometh, he must continue a short space. And the beast that was, and is not, even he is the eighth, and is of the seven, and goeth into perdition. And the ten horns which thou sawest are ten kings, which have received no kingdom as yet; but receive power as kings one hour with the beast. These have one mind, and shall give their power and strength unto the beast (Revelation 17:7–13 KJV).

This passage tells us that the beast has died and is going to come out of the bottomless pit. How will he do that? I talked about this in chapter 16. The devil will have a false resurrection. He will be mortally wounded, and then he will arise out of the abyss. This will cause the world to wonder and will prove to be the beast's stamp of authenticity. His purpose is to deceive.

I have seen the body of Lenin in that crystal sarcophagus in the middle of Red Square. What would have happened if Lenin were resurrected from the dead in such a public area? It would make news, wouldn't it? The entire world would wonder about it. Perhaps everyone would jump on the communism bandwagon.

Notice the *power* with which the beast comes. Revelation 17:9 says, "Here is the mind with wisdom: the seven heads are seven mountains on which the woman is seated." What city is built on seven hills? Rome. Will this power will be concentrated in Rome?

In 1957, half a dozen European countries wrote a very important treaty called the Treaty of Rome. The European Common Market, the reunification of Europe, came out of this treaty. The Roman Empire will be reestablished in the last days, so the beast will consort with religious leaders in Rome, and he will rule over the United States of Europe.

When will he come? Revelation 17:10 says, "They are also seven kings: five have fallen, one is, the other has not yet come." When John wrote Revelation, there had already been five great kings or emperors that ruled over the Roman Empire: Caesar Augustus, Claudius, Caligula,

Tiberius, and Nero. "One who is yet to come" speaks of the Antichrist who will rule over a revived Roman Empire during the Great Trbulation. John continues: "And when he comes, he must remain for a little while. The beast that was and is not, is himself the eighth, yet is of the seven and goes to destruction" (Revelation 17:10–11). This seventh beast is the one that will go into the grave, and when he comes out he will be the eighth. He will enter the grave as a human, but he will arise a super human. This is the Antichrist.

Now think about the *people* with whom he will come. Revelation 17:12–13 says, "The 10 horns you saw are 10 kings who have not yet received a kingdom, but they will receive authority as kings with the beast for one hour. These have one purpose, and they give their power and authority to the beast." We learned earlier that a horn in Bible prophecy speaks of power. The ten horns on this beast are puppet kings out of the unified Roman Empire.

Notice the *passion* with which he comes. Revelation 17:14 says, "These will make war against the Lamb, but the Lamb will conquer them because he is Lord of lords and King of kings. Those with him are called and elect and faithful." The battle of Armageddon will be against the King of kings and Lord of lords. In his deranged mind, the devil will think he can overthrow the Lamb of God. It is planned insanity.

The beast has one passion—to defy the Lamb. The beast will strut across the stage of history and will meet his demise at Armageddon. Those who follow their beloved beast will discover they have made a poor choice.

The Woman and Her Momentous Calamity

What will happen to this scarlet woman and her apostate religion? Revelation 17:14–18 speaks of the beast and his armies:

> These will make war against the Lamb, but the Lamb will conquer them because he is Lord of lords and King of kings. Those with him are called and elect and faithful." He also said to me, "The waters you saw, where the prostitute was seated, are peoples, multitudes, nations, and languages. The 10 horns you saw, and the beast, will hate the prostitute. They will make her desolate and naked, devour her flesh, and burn her up with fire. For God has put it into their hearts to carry out His plan by having one purpose, and to give their kingdom to the beast

until God's words are accomplished. And the woman you saw is the great city that has an empire over the kings of the earth.

The Babylonian monster will turn around and destroy the Babylonian mother. The scenario reminds me of a song I sang as a child called "The Crocodile":

She sailed away, on a lovely summer's day
On the back of a crocodile.
"You see," said she, "he's as tame as tame can be,
I'll ride him down the Nile."
The croc winked his eye, and the lady waved "goodbye,"
Wearing a happy smile.
At the end of the ride, the lady was inside,
And the smile on the crocodile!

The writing is on the wall for this consort of friends. The honeymoon is over, and the beast in his rage will desolate her. Why does he hate her so much? Envy. He is jealous of all her riches and wants them for himself. After he desolates her, he will disgrace her by stripping her naked to expose her moral vileness. Next, he will devour her by eating her flesh. Then he will destroy her by burning what is left of her body.

Why is the Antichrist going to do this? He wants to be the ruler of the world, and he does not want any competition. He also will destroy the harlot for providential reasons. Revelation 17:17 says that God will put it in their hearts. Did you know that the devil is really God's servant, and that the beast doesn't rule? God rules. The devil is on a leash. Finally, the devil will destroy the harlot for political reasons. He wants to rule the world.

What is our application from this chapter? We are the bride of Christ. And we need to take the covenant we have made with God seriously by not flirting with false religions. I know that some of you will rationalize and say that you need to know about other religions and perhaps you have even started studying the religions of the world. Do you know what I think of when I hear people wanting to study other religions? I think of the married man who says, "I want to see what all the other women in the world are like." You be true to Jesus Christ and get a bulldog grip on the truth. You don't have to flirt with all these other religions. Make it your life ambition to know the Lord Jesus Christ.

$\mathscr{G}$ood-bye to Babylon

--◄◦►--
CHAPTER 21
--◄◦►--

The Bible has a lot to say about Babylon. As a matter of fact, Babylon is mentioned more than any other city in the Bible except Jerusalem. Perhaps you have heard of the Hanging Gardens of Babylon built by Nebuchadnezzar. They were considered one of the seven wonders of the ancient world. Then they disappeared.

In this chapter, we will learn that there is coming a time when the entire world will wonder at Babylon once again. Babylon will rise to meet her doom at the hand of Almighty God. Revelation 18:1–2 says, "After this I saw another angel with great authority coming down from heaven, and the earth was illuminated by his splendor. He cried in a mighty voice: 'It has fallen, Babylon the Great has fallen! She has become a dwelling for demons, a haunt for every unclean spirit, a haunt for every unclean bird, and a haunt for every unclean and despi-cable beast.'"

Again we need to ask, was the angel speaking symbolically or literally about Babylon? In the previous chapter we learned that names of places sometimes speak of something more than geographical location. For example, Wall Street and Madison Avenue have become code words for commerce and merchandising. Likewise when Scripture speaks of "the world," it may be referring to the planet or be referring to the world's ungodly system.

Some think that the ancient city of Babylon itself will be rebuilt and become the headquarters of the Beast. That seems unlikely to me.

Saddam Hussein imagined himself to be an incarnation of the former tyrant of Babylon, Nebuchadnezzar. He admired Nebuchadnezzar for destroying and subjecting Israel. He endeavored to rebuild the ancient city and imprinted his name on every brick; but all of that has come to a piti-ful failure. Jeremiah 51:64 says, "Then you shall say, Thus Babylon shall sink and not rise from the catastrophe that I will bring upon her. And they shall be weary. Thus far are the words of Jeremiah (KJV)."

Chapters seventeen and eighteen of Revelation speak of "mystery" Babylon. (Revelation 17:5). A mysterious connection links ancient Babylon with its false religion and powerful dominion to today's world.

Doubtless the beast will have a headquarters city somewhere. It may be Rome. In his first epistle, Peter seems to refer to Rome as Babylon (1 Peter 5:13). Rome and its religion may be a good fit, but the system appears to be larger than any one city.

How should we interpret the phrase "Babylon the Great has fallen"? It is a double fall. There is the fall of the ecclesiastical Babylon (see Revelation 17) and the fall of the political and commercial Babylon (see Revelation 18). In Revelation 17:5, God calls Babylon "the mother of harlots" (KJV) who is devoured and destroyed in judgment by the rulers of political Babylon. In Revelation 18, God judges these kings, and we will learn four things about Babylon.

Babylon Is Dominated by Demons

Revelation 18:1–6 says:

> After this [*after the judgment of ecclesiastical Babylon*]
> I saw another angel with great authority coming down from
> heaven, and the earth was illuminated by his splendor. He cried
> in a mighty voice: "It has fallen, Babylon the Great has fallen!
> She has become a dwelling for demons, a haunt for every
> unclean spirit, a haunt for every unclean bird, and a haunt for
> every unclean and despicable beast. For all the nations have
> drunk the wine of her sexual immorality, which brings wrath.
> The kings of the earth have committed sexual immorality with
> her, and the merchants of the earth have grown wealthy from
> her excessive luxury." Then I heard another voice from heaven:
> "Come out of her, My people, so that you will not share in her
> sins, or receive any of her plagues. For her sins are piled up to
> heaven, and God has remembered her crimes. Pay her back the
> way she also paid, and double it according to her works. In the
> cup in which she mixed, mix a double portion for her"
> (explanatory note added by the author).

These demons are the devil's "dirty birds" that defile the landscape.

Babylon will rise from the dust and become Babylon the Great when the Antichrist takes his throne. During the Great Tribulation, the world will be infested and led by demonic spirits that have nested in ancient Babylon. Satan has been building a Babylonian system of iniquity in this world. And God has not forgotten. Revelation 18:6 says that she will be paid back double for the evil she has done.

What does this mean to us? As we get closer to the second coming of Jesus Christ, the rapture of the church, and the rule of the beast, we can expect to see a tidal wave of sin, debauchery, and demonism. Beyond the shadow of any doubt, the Babylonian system is in the world today.

Babylon Is Defiant in Depravity

Remember Suddam Hussein? In arrogance and defiance, Saddam had leveled a brazen challenge: "Stop me if you can." Though just about as evil as a man can become, he is only a faint picture of the defiance of the beast that will come and rule over Babylon. Why will he be so defiant in this day?

Babylon has its own system of government, and the beast doesn't want to compete. He confiscates its wealth and becomes immensely wealthy. Every luxury known to man will pour into Babylon. The beast will become a law unto himself as the eastern powers subjugate themselves to him. Global corporations will make their headquarters in Babylon, and the beast will rule over the system. He will seem absolutely invincible.

Have you ever noticed how arrogant Satan has become in these days because he thinks he actually is going to win? If you haven't, you have been asleep. Sin that used to slink down back alleys now struts down Main Street. But we must remember that this will come to an end.

Babylon Is Destined for Destruction

God's Word reminds us that in spite of all the defiance of the beast, he cannot hold back the judgment of Almighty God: "Therefore her plagues will come in one day—death, and grief, and famine. She will be burned up with fire, because the Lord God who judges her is mighty. The kings of the earth who have committed sexual immorality and lived luxuriously with her will weep and mourn over her when they see the smoke of her burning. They stand far off in fear of her torment, saying: 'Woe, woe, the great city, Babylon, the mighty city! For in a single hour your judgment has come'" (Revelation 18:8–10).

From Cash to Crash

Satan sails a sinking ship. His doom is announced and will be carried out. Sin cannot win, and faith cannot fail. If you are a lover of Babylon, you are following a lost cause. Babylon will be destroyed by a devastating collapse. It will happen cataclysmically fast. And its destruction will be utterly complete.

Revelation 18:10 tells us that its destruction will come in one hour. I believe Babylon could be destroyed by an atomic blast, and the people who stand afar off will see the mushroom cloud and fear the radiation. An angel illustrates this destruction in Revelation 18:21: "Then a mighty angel picked up a stone like a large millstone and threw it into the sea, saying: 'In this way, Babylon the great city will be thrown down violently and never be found again.'" If you could throw a huge stone into the ocean, you would see shock waves emanating from the point of entry and sweeping everything away in its path.

No one knows what will happen because this is symbolism, and many things we simply will not know until they are literally fulfilled. But whatever happens, it will be absolutely devastating. In an hour, God will judge the sin of Babylon that has been piling up for centuries. His vengeance will come howling through the streets of Babylon.

Babylon Is Depressing in Desolation

Revelation 18:10–23 says:

> They stand far off in fear of her torment, saying: "Woe, woe, the great city, Babylon, the mighty city! For in a single hour your judgment has come." The merchants of the earth will also weep and mourn over her, because no one buys their merchandise any longer—merchandise of gold, silver, precious stones, and pearls; fine fabrics of linen, purple, silk, and scarlet; all kinds of fragrant wood products; objects of ivory; objects of expensive wood, brass, iron, and marble; cinnamon, spice, incense, myrrh, and frankincense; wine, olive oil, fine wheat flour, and grain; cattle and sheep; horses and carriages; and human bodies and souls.

"The fruit you craved has left you. All your splendid and glamorous things are gone; they will never find them again." The merchants of these things, who became rich from her, will stand far off in fear of her torment, weeping and mourning, saying: "Woe, woe, the great city, clothed in fine linen, purple, and scarlet, adorned with gold, precious stones, and pearls; because in a single hour such fabulous wealth was destroyed!"

And every shipmaster, seafarer, the sailors, and all who do business by sea, stood far off as they watched the smoke from her burning and kept crying out: "Who is like the great city?" They threw dust on their heads and kept crying out, weeping, and mourning: "Woe, woe, the great city, where all those who have ships on the sea became rich from her wealth; because in a single hour she was destroyed. Rejoice over her, heaven, and you saints, apostles, and prophets, because God has executed your judgment on her!"

Then a mighty angel picked up a stone like a large millstone and threw it into the sea, saying: "In this way, Babylon the great city will be thrown down violently and never be found again. The sound of harpists, musicians, flutists, and trumpeters will never be heard in you again; no craftsman of any trade will ever be found in you again; the sound of a mill will never be heard in you again; the light of a lamp will never shine in you again; and the voice of a groom and bride will never be heard in you again. All this will happen because your merchants were the nobility of the earth, because all the nations were deceived by your sorcery."

The wealth of former ecclesiastical Babylon will belong to the beast, because no one will be able to buy or sell without his mark upon him or her. He will get his cut on every transaction and will control the world economy. Money, like a mighty Niagara, will flow into Babylon. But notice that a part of the merchandise will be the souls of men. There will be a great trade in iniquity and sin.

U.S. News and World Report recently produced an investing guide. Inside was an article entitled "Stock Up on Sin," which contained an article for those who are worried about their investments: "A portfolio that panders to humankind's moral weaknesses might redeem investors' fortunes. Unseemly perhaps, but the fact is that in a year of exploding corporate scandal and retribution it has been good to be bad. Not legally bad, just a little sinful. Profit, so fleeting on much of Wall Street, has come easily to firms catering to humanity's weakness for fatty foods, strong drinks, wastrel ways, and carnal passions."

And it goes on to encourage investors to buy shares in cable companies, which make millions of dollars from pay-per-view adult movies. The article goes on to talk about the liquor and tobacco industries. Basically, what it was saying was: "Do you want to get rich? Invest in sin." Whether it is cable networks that bring pornography into so-called family entertainment or politicians who promote state lotteries, they do it for one reason—money! They don't care about the families that spend their grocery money on lottery tickets. They say, "Just show us the money!"

Gamblers sit in their fine homes built by dishonest gain. Doctors rake in millions by killing babies. Liquor barons climb the ladder of success on the backs of broken homes. All of this is driven by a love of money. First Timothy 6:10 says, "For the love of money is a root of all kinds of evil, and by craving it, some have wandered away from the faith and pierced themselves with many pains." This is the kingdom of the Antichrist.

How the rulers of this world are going to weep! All of their resources and wealth will not be able to stay the judgment of Almighty God. They will stand in their executive suites and watch as the market craters and the controllers of the world's commerce dive into pools of panic. The after-effects will make the Great Depression seem like a Sunday school picnic.

The bundle of "no mores" in this passage sound almost like a funeral bell tolling. There will be no more music, no more merchandising, no more manufacturing, and no more marriage. I believe all of this is a trigger for Armageddon.

What can we learn from Revelation 18? It is not enough to say what may or may not happen in the future. I want to give you three principles about Babylon which I pray God will use to stir your heart into action.

Come Out of Her

Revelation 18:4 says, "Then I heard another voice from heaven: 'Come out of her, My people, so that you will not share in her sins, or receive any of her plagues.'" The spirit of Babylon is already in the world. Second Corinthians 6:17 says, "Therefore, come out from among them and be separate, says the Lord; do not touch any unclean thing, and I will welcome you."

We hear so much today about the separation of the church and the state. We need to preach more about the separation of the church and the world. If you dance with the devil, you are going to be burned. When God's judgment falls, you will not escape, although you may be a child of God. If you don't want to feel the judgments of Babylon, don't keep company with Babylon.

Don't Envy Her

Perhaps you see people wheeling and dealing and getting rich. And you want some of it, too. Don't envy Babylon. Only a fool envies fools. Gene McCombs, a mighty preacher of the Word of God, shared this story with me.

> I was getting off an airplane one time and reached up to get my things from the overhead when my hand fell on a stack of paper. I pulled it out and discovered it was a stack of hundred dollar bills. I put my hand up there again and found another stack of one hundred dollar bills. There was twenty thousand dollars in cold cash.
>
> I had never held that much money in my hands. I waited until everybody got off the plane and went to the pilot and said, "I found a substantial amount of money on this plane. What should I do?" The pilot directed me to a certain office in the airport. I went to the office and put the money on the desk of a man and said, "Here is the money." The man was filling out a report. I said, "What is going to happen to this money?" He said, "Well, if nobody comes to claim it, it will be yours."
>
> About that time a man came into the office. He was shabbily dressed with disheveled hair. He said, "I lost some money on that airplane. Has it been reported?" The man behind the desk said, "Describe it exactly." He said, "Twenty thousand dollars. Two packets." He described it perfectly, so the man gave him the two stacks of bills. That man picked up that money and left. He never said thanks, just turned around and walked out.
>
> I was at least expecting a thank-you, but not a word. I got in a cab to go to my meeting and the devil got in the cab with me. I was sitting in the back seat and the devil began whispering, "Sir, you are a fool. You know that was drug money. You

know that man was no good. That money could have been used for good or for your family. You are a fool to have given it back. He didn't even say thank you."

The devil was working on me, and I got to thinking about what I have in the Lord Jesus Christ: how He called me, saved me, bought me, keeps me, gives me joy day by day, and there is laid up for me a crown of glory. I began to talk back to the devil, and I spoke out loud. I said, "But look what I've got."

The cab driver knew no one else was in the back seat, and he said, "What is that, buddy? What did you say?" And I said, "Never mind, I was just talking to the devil." The cab driver never took his eye off that rear view mirror from that time on.

That's what you need to tell the devil: "Look what I've got!" Don't envy Babylon.

Rejoice Over Her

The Bible teaches that the world is headed toward a climax. Revelation 18:20 says, "Rejoice over her, heaven, and you saints, apostles, and prophets, because God has executed your judgment on her." Never let the devil get you to thinking negatively about God. We are on the winning side.

Those in heaven will see God's righteous judgment on sin and Satan's system. At last, at last! Hallelujah! The hearts of all true saints have been bowed with sorrow and bruised by Satan. Now this sinful system has met its doom. It is gone forever. The saints are on the side that wins, and that calls for celebration. I think we can start this celebration early.

The Marriage of the Lamb

I remember the day I married Joyce, my childhood sweetheart. What an exciting, long-awaited day that was! Weddings are meant to be beautiful and full of joy. And the marriage of the Lamb will be such an event. No one knows when this will happen. The Father has set the wedding date, and He has not whispered it to anyone. Anyone who tries to set a date for His return is bordering on heresy.

In Revelation 19, the Great Tribulation comes to a close and the church comes to the most climactic time in all of its history. God chooses the picture of a marriage to illustrate that glorious moment when we become one with our Lord: "Let us be glad, rejoice, and give Him glory, because the marriage of the Lamb has come, and His wife has prepared herself" (Revelation 19:7). The bride, which is the church of the Lord Jesus Christ, has made herself ready for the marriage to the Lamb.

One day Jesus told a parable about the marriage of the Lamb and gave this admonition: "'I assure you [unbelievers]: I do not know you!' Therefore be alert, because you don't know either the day or the hour" (Matthew 25:12–13, explanatory note added by the author). Jesus may come at any moment. We are not waiting on any prophecies to be fulfilled. At any moment we could hear the shout, "Here's the groom! Come out to meet him" (Matthew 25:6). Let us consider several truths about the marriage of the Lamb as we anticipate this wonderful time.

The Music Will Be Magnificent

Revelation 19:1–6 says:

> After this I heard something like the loud voice of a vast multitude in heaven, saying: "*Hallelujah!* Salvation, glory, and power belong to our God, because His judgments are true and righteous, because He has judged the notorious prostitute who corrupted the earth with her sexual immorality; and He has avenged the blood of His servants that was on her hands." A second time they said: "*Hallelujah!* Her smoke ascends forever and ever!" Then the 24 elders and the four living creatures fell down and worshiped God, who is seated on the throne, saying: "Amen! *Hallelujah!*" A voice came from the throne, saying: "Praise our God, all you His servants, you who fear Him, both small and great!" Then I heard something like the voice of a vast multitude, like the sound of cascading waters, and like the rumbling of loud thunder, saying: "*Hallelujah*—because our Lord God, the Almighty, has begun to reign!"

What do you think the wedding music is going to be? The "Hallelujah Chorus"! Revelation 19 is the basis of Handel's great composition that is known around the world. The world *hallelujah* is used four times in these six verses. What does the word *hallelujah* mean? It comes from two Hebrew words—*halal* meaning "praise" and *Yahweh* meaning "Jehovah." Praise the Lord! As a side note, this word *hallelujah* is not used in any other place in the entire Bible!

In Revelation 19, we also find the word *amen,* which means "let it be." It is true, praise the Lord, let it be! Did you know that the words *hallelujah* and *amen* are the same in every language? I have preached in many places around the world, and those words are the same everywhere. That gives me comfort. I may not understand a word the people are singing or saying until they say "hallelujah" and I say "amen."

Two Christian men from two different countries were on a ship and decided they needed to get away from the crowd to meditate for a little while. Each man took his Bible and was walking on the deck. They saw each other and then saw the Word of God each held. At that moment, they knew they were comrades in Christ. They didn't know how to communicate until one brother said, "Hallelujah," and the other said, "Amen." They embraced and knew that in the Lord Jesus Christ they were brethren.

Let's look at the stanzas of this "Hallelujah Chorus":

Stanza One: Hallelujah for the Redemption of the Saints

In Revelation 19:1, the people are saying "hallelujah" because that which was begun at Calvary has now come to full consummation. As Philippians 1:6 says, "I am sure of this, that He who started a good work in you will carry it on to completion until the day of Christ Jesus." Also, we notice that there is a great multitude giving praise to the Lamb. There will be millions and billions of people in heaven. Don't you be in hell when this "Hallelujah Chorus" is being sung.

Stanza Two: Hallelujah for the Retribution of the Sinner

Revelation 19:2–3 tells us that the multitudes are praising God because He has made things right, His justice has prevailed, and He has avenged those who have persecuted the church through the ages. If you look for judgment in this world, you will not find it. If you look for justice in the courtrooms of America or any other tribunal on earth, you will not find it. But one of these days we will say "Hallelujah!" There is a God who will make everything right.

Stanza Three: Relationship of the Saved

Revelation 19:4–5 explains that God is *our* God, not just *the* God. Psalm 23:1 says, "The LORD is my shepherd; I shall not want" (KJV). It doesn't say He is a "good" shepherd or a "great" shepherd. He says He is "my" shepherd. What a song we can sing when we believe: I am His and He is mine! He is my God and I am His servant. I am His and He is mine. Why shouldn't I shout hallelujah? In 1905, Charles H. Gabriel wrote:

> *What a Savior Jesus is!*
> *He is mine, and I am His;*
> *He the price of sin has paid,*
> *And for me atonement made.*
>
> *What a Savior, what a Savior,*
> *What a Savior Jesus is!*
> *I will praise Him, ever praise Him,*
> *He is mine, and I am His!*

Stanza Four: Reign of the Savior

Revelation 19:6 tells us there was "the voice of a vast multitude." What do you picture when you think of that sound? Perhaps a football stadium filled with cheering fans when a winning touchdown is made in the last few seconds? In some stadiums, that is a deafening roar—like the next descriptive phrase: "The sound of cascading waters." Have you ever been to Niagara Falls? The first time I saw it I said, "I wonder if they turn it off at night." It just keeps coming and coming. And there is a tumultuous sound as more than six million cubic feet of water rushes over the falls every minute.[12]

Add lightning and thunder rolling up and down the heavens to the noise of the multitude and the falling waters—and one can only imagine what that will sound like. Our God reigns! Every knee will bow to the One who was despised and rejected by men. And the shouts of His praise will ring through heaven. It will be wonderful!

The Bride Will Be Beautiful

The bride has prepared herself for the wedding. Revelation 19:7–8 says, "Let us be glad, rejoice, and give Him glory, because the marriage of the Lamb has come, and His wife has prepared herself. She was permitted to wear fine linen, bright and pure. For the fine linen represents the righteous acts of the saints."

We have learned that God will judge the false church, and now the true church will be presented to the Lord Jesus Christ. Right now, the church is only *betrothed* to Jesus; we are not yet married to Him. The best is yet to come.

The apostle Paul said, "For I am jealous over you with a godly jealousy, because I have promised you in marriage to one husband—to present a pure virgin to Christ" (2 Corinthians 11:2). The true church is the dearest object in all the universe to our Lord and Savior. How do I know that? Because the dearest thing on this earth to me, other than my relationship with God, is my darling wife. She is my bride, and I love her with all of my heart. And that is only a faint representation of the love that Jesus Christ has for us.

When I asked Joyce to marry me, I was working my way through college. I left my football scholarship and was preaching in a little church. Now that was a get-rich-quick experience! The church paid me twenty-five dollars a week, and I had to drive three hundred miles with no car allowance. I did other odd jobs as well and was finally able to buy Joyce a little diamond engagement ring. I paid a dollar or two every week until I paid for it. They called it a "lay-away" plan. I called it a "lay-awake" plan. But the size of the diamond didn't matter. The size of our commitment far exceeded the cost of the ring.

Since you are a part of the bride of Christ, how are you getting ready? There are three steps each of us must take.

1. Redemption

If we are not saved, we are not a part of the bride of Christ. When God saves us, we call that redemption. This is the first part of our beauty treatment as we receive the inner nature of the Lord Jesus Christ. We become partakers of the divine nature.

2. Rapture

When the rapture comes, we will be changed in a moment into the likeness of the Lord Jesus Christ. All the sinful tendencies of our old sinful flesh will be left behind. Thank God for that!

3. Reward

We have been to the judgment seat of Christ, and we will receive according to the deeds that we have done. The Bible says the white linen is the righteous acts of the saints. This is a threefold beauty treatment.

The Guests Will Be Glad

More people than the bride will be present at the wedding of the Lamb. Revelation 19:9 says, "Then he said to me, 'Write: Blessed are those invited to the marriage feast of the Lamb!' He also said to me, 'These words of God are true.'" Who are these guests? The redeemed of all the ages who were saved before or after the church age. The Old Testament saints will be there as guests.

John the Baptist called himself a friend of the bridegroom. He was a friend; he was not the bride. Jesus said, "I assure you: Among those born of women no one greater than John the Baptist has appeared, but the least in the kingdom of heaven is greater than he" (Matthew 11:11).

There is a sense in which the church is especially privileged. What a celebration it will be. At the wedding feast of Cana, Jesus performed His first miracle by turning water into wine. The master of ceremonies said, "Everybody sets out the fine wine first, then, after people have drunk freely, the inferior. But you have kept the fine wine until now" (John 2:10).

If you think that is something, wait until the marriage of the Lamb, when Christ is both the bridegroom and the host. What a table He will set! What a celebration that will be! The evangelist Paul Rader said, "We are living so close to the second coming of Jesus Christ that I can hear the tinkling of the silverware as the angels are setting the table for the marriage supper of the Lamb." All of this is perhaps just a heartbeat or a trumpet sound away.

The Groom Will Be Glorified

This wedding doesn't center around the bride but on the groom. Revelation 19:10 says, "Then I fell at his feet to worship him, but he said to me, 'Don't do that! I am a fellow slave with you and your brothers who have the testimony about Jesus. Worship God, because the testimony about Jesus is the spirit of prophecy.'" John is not talking about Jesus; he is talking about an angel who is sent out to welcome the guests. If an angel appeared to you today, you would probably fall on your face because his appearance would be so glorious and majestic.

But did John do the right thing? No. The angel let John know that he had made a breach of etiquette. It was as if the angel said, "Hey buddy, get up off your face, or we will both be in trouble. I will be in trouble for letting you worship me. You will be in trouble for doing it." The Bible tells us plainly that there is one God, and no one else is to be worshiped other than Jehovah God. If Jesus is not God, Jesus is guilty of aiding and abetting idolatry. This angel knew that. So the angel said, "Get up; worship God and Him only."

Do you know what the spirit of prophecy is? Jesus Christ. So many people get overly concerned about the meaning of the "third toe on the left foot of some beast." Every detail is inspired and important, but don't miss the spirit of prophecy. If you read Revelation and don't come to know and love Jesus more, you have missed it all. This is the revelation of Jesus Christ; it is the unveiling of Jesus Christ.

How do we learn about Jesus Christ? The Holy Spirit persuades us. In Genesis 24, we read the story of Abraham's plan to get a bride for his son Isaac. Abraham sent his chief servant to get a bride for Isaac. Abraham was immensely wealthy, so he also gave his servant jewels and gold and silver to give to the bride.

But the servant said, "How will I know who is the right one?" The Holy Spirit brought Rebekah to him and confirmed that she was the one. This servant had to persuade Rebekah to leave her family and home to marry a man she had never met. That took some persuasion! And she went. Why? Genesis 24:50–51 says, "Then Laban and Bethuel answered and said, The thing proceedeth from the LORD: we cannot speak unto thee bad or good. Behold, Rebekah is before thee, take her, and go, and let her be thy master's son's wife, as the LORD hath spoken" (KJV). There was no denying that God was in this.

When Rebekah made her decision, Abraham's servant gave her the trinkets and gifts. Imagine the scene. Abraham's entourage of travelers are on their way back to Canaan, and the servant looks over at Rebekah and sees her chin quivering a little and tears in her eyes. Maybe she is having second thoughts. The servant stops the train of travelers and opens the box of jewels to place a necklace around her neck. "This is from Isaac," he says. "You will love him. He is wonderful." After a while, the scene perhaps repeats itself. The servant puts a ring on her finger and says, "Isaac wants you to have this. Isaac is so great and so wonderful. You will love him."

Isaac is a picture of Jesus, Abraham is a picture of God the Father, and the chief servant is a picture of the Holy Spirit sent to bring the bride to the Lord Jesus Christ. When you give your heart to Christ, doubts, fears, and anxiety will inevitably come. But when they do, the Holy Spirit will take a jewel from Jesus and give it to you. "You are going to love Jesus," He will say. "He died for you to have an inheritance with Him in glory." First Peter 1:8 says, "You love Him, though you have not seen Him. And though not seeing Him now, you believe in Him and rejoice with inexpressible and glorious joy."

Do you know why I love Jesus? Because of the Holy Spirit of God. "Isaac went out to meditate in the field at the eventide: and he lifted up his eyes, and saw, and, behold, the camels were coming. And Rebekah lifted up her eyes, and when she saw Isaac, she lighted off the camel" (Genesis 24:63–64 KJV). When Rebecca finally arrived in Canaan, she had no difficulty recognizing her groom. And when Jesus comes, every child of His will have no difficulty recognizing Him. In 1873, Horatio Gates Spafford wrote these timeless words in the hymn "It Is Well with My Soul":

And Lord, haste the day when my faith shall be sight,
The clouds be rolled back as a scroll;

The trump shall resound, and the Lord shall descend,
Even so, it is well with my soul.

We are not talking about fantasy here. Words and illustrations cannot sufficiently explain or begin to describe what will happen when Jesus comes for His bride. Are you ready?

Our Coming King

◄○►

CHAPTER 23

◄○►

At the end of a long, hard day, a salesman came back to his hotel room. It was late, and he was tired. He sat down on the edge of his bed and began to take off one of his shoes. It fell to the floor with a thud, and he thought to himself, *That was so thoughtless of me. It is late at night, and my shoe probably disturbed the person in the room below.* When he took the second shoe off, he put it down very gently on the floor and went to bed. About thirty minutes later, there was knock at the door. He answered the door, and there stood a man with dark circles under his eyes. The man said, "Would you please drop the other shoe, so I can get some sleep?" The world is waiting for the other shoe to drop.

The Christ who was born at Bethlehem, walked the dusty shores of Galilee, hung naked on a cross, was buried, and has ascended the high hills of glory—He is coming again. The incarnation without the coronation would be like east without west. It would be like an engagement without a marriage. This is another "shoe" to fall.

We are on a collision course with destiny. Soon and very soon the King will come, and we cannot afford to be ignorant or indifferent. Many people all around us are perplexed, and they need to hear the Good News. Sorrow looks backward, worry looks around, but faith looks upward. Are you setting the example for the world to see—hopeful and faithful to look for His return? The King, the Lord Jesus Christ, is coming.

In this chapter, we will look at three things about the return of Jesus that we discover from Revelation 19:11–15:

> Then I saw heaven opened, and there was a white horse! Its
> rider is called Faithful and True, and in righteousness He

judges and makes war. His eyes were like a fiery flame, and on His head were many crowns. He had a name written that no one knows except Himself. He wore a robe stained with blood, and His name is called the Word of God. The armies that were in heaven followed Him on white horses, wearing pure white linen. From His mouth came a sharp sword, so that with it He might strike the nations. He will shepherd them with an iron scepter. He will also trample the winepress of the fierce anger of God, the Almighty.

Jesus Is Coming Visibly

Some people try to spiritualize the second coming of Jesus Christ instead of understanding that it will be a real event in history. Jesus ascended into heaven literally and visibly. And He is coming back literally and visibly. On the Mount of Transfiguration the disciples heard the angels say, "Men of Galilee, why do you stand looking up into heaven? This Jesus, who has been taken from you into heaven, will come in the same way that you have seen Him going into heaven" (Acts 1:11).

John saw Him: "Then I saw heaven opened, and there was a white horse! Its rider is called Faithful and True" (Revelation 19:11). If John saw Jesus, will you see Him, too? Revelation 1:7 says, "'Look! He is coming with the clouds,' and 'every eye will see Him, including those who pierced Him. And all the families of the earth will mourn over Him.' This is certain. Amen." Yes! You, along with every other soul on earth, will see Him. Don't believe what you may have heard (and most probably will continue to hear) from different cults, asserting that past events in history were the second coming of Christ. You will see Him! Jesus is coming back visibly in power, glory, and majesty.

A lot of people get confused at this point about Christ's second coming because 1 Thessalonians 5:2 and 2 Peter 3:10 teach us that Jesus' coming is mysterious—like a thief in the night. But when the Bible uses the word *mystery*, it doesn't mean like a mystery novel. It means a truth previously unknown that is now revealed.

So is Christ coming in *mystery*, or is He coming in *majesty?* There are two phases to the coming of our Lord Jesus Christ. First, there will be the rapture when He comes *for His bride* and we are taken out before the Great Tribulation. And then after the tribulation, we have the revelation when the Lord will come *with His bride* in power and great glory. The rapture will be a great mystery. The revelation will be gloriously majestic.

Second Thessalonians 2:1 teaches us about the rapture: "Now concerning the coming of our Lord Jesus Christ and our being gathered to Him: we ask you, brothers." Jesus will return and rapture the church. Jesus is also coming with His church, as we see in Revelation 19:14: "The armies that were in heaven followed Him on white horses, wearing pure white linen." Who are these armies? They are the saints who make up the bride of Christ. White linen represents the righteousness of the saints.

The Old Testament prophets didn't know anything about the rapture, so we don't find the rapture in the Old Testament. It was a mystery revealed in the New Testament. Paul said, "Listen! I am telling you a mystery: We will not all fall asleep, but we will all be changed, in a moment, in the twinkling of an eye, at the last trumpet. For the trumpet will sound, and the dead will be raised incorruptible, and we will be changed" (1 Corinthians 15:51–52). I understand that the twinkling of an eye is the fastest movement of the human body.

He will return sweetly like a bridegroom. Matthew 25:6 says, "In the middle of the night there was a shout: 'Here's the groom! Come out to meet him.'"

Not only is He coming sweetly as a bridegroom, but He is also coming sovereignly as a King. Second Thessalonians 1:7–10 says:

> And to reward with rest you who are afflicted, along with us.
> This will take place at the revelation of the Lord Jesus from
> heaven with His powerful angels, taking vengeance with flaming fire on those who don't know God and on those who don't
> obey the gospel of our Lord Jesus. These will pay the penalty of
> everlasting destruction, away from the Lord's presence and
> from His glorious strength, in that day when He comes to be
> glorified by His saints and to be admired by all those who have
> believed, because our testimony among you was believed.

What a day that will be! We are not waiting on any signs to be fulfilled for the rapture. Jesus may come at any moment for His church. To deny that fact is heresy. Here is what the greatest prophecy preacher of all time had to say about Jesus' eminent and imminent coming. Jesus Himself said:

Now concerning that day and hour no one knows—neither the angels in heaven, nor the Son—except the Father only. As the days of Noah were, so the coming of the Son of Man will be. For in those days before the flood they were eating and drinking, marrying and giving in marriage, until the day Noah boarded the ark. They didn't know until the flood came and swept them all away. So this is the way the coming of the Son of Man will be: Then two men will be in the field: one will be taken and one left. Two women will be grinding at the mill: one will be taken and one left. Therefore be alert, since you don't know what day your Lord is coming. But know this: If the homeowner had known what time the thief was coming, he would have stayed alert and not let his house be broken into. This is why you also should get ready, because the Son of Man is coming at an hour you do not expect (Matthew 24:36–44).

Christians should not be waiting for the tribulation; we should be looking for Jesus. First Thessalonians 5:9–11 says, "For God did not appoint us to wrath, but to obtain salvation through our Lord Jesus Christ, who died for us, so that whether we are awake or asleep, we will live together with Him. Therefore encourage one another and build each other up as you are already doing." The Great Tribulation will be a time when God will pour out His wrath on the unsaved.

God promises that He will keep you from this terrible time: "Because you have kept My command to endure, I will also keep you from the hour of testing that is going to come over the whole world to test those who live on the earth" (Revelation 3:10). "But," you may say, "that was God speaking to the church in Philadelphia two thousand years ago." Yes, you're right, but look at verse 13 of that same chapter: "Anyone who has an ear should listen to what the Spirit says to the churches." What God said to the church at Philadelphia, He is saying to us.

In the Old Testament, we see examples of when God poured out His wrath upon the earth, but He spared a remnant of His people. God put Noah in the ark before the flood came (see Genesis 6). God took Lot out of Sodom before the fire and brimstone fell (see Genesis 19). Jesus will not beat up His bride in wrath.

Jesus is coming like a thief in the night to take the church out of this world.

Jesus Is Coming Victoriously

Revelation 19:11–13 says, "Then I saw heaven opened, and there was a white horse! Its rider is called Faithful and True, and in righteousness He judges and makes war. His eyes were like a fiery flame, and on His head were many crowns. He had a name written that no one knows except Himself. He wore a robe stained with blood, and His name is called the Word of God."

The Mastery of His Conquest

Jesus will be riding on a white horse when He comes with His raptured bride in victory. When Jesus entered Jerusalem just before His crucifixion, the crowds threw palm branches in front of Him and bowed down shouting, "Hail Him! Hail Him!" And yet, in a few days this same crowd would yell, "Nail Him! Nail Him!" Do you remember what Jesus was riding through the streets of Jerusalem? A lowly donkey. But when He comes the second time, He will be riding a white charger, which is a symbol of victory, honor, and conquest.

The Mystery of His Character

Philippians 2:9 says, "For this reason God also highly exalted Him and gave Him the name that is above every name." What is that name? We know Him as Jesus, but there is mystery about Him that we will never fathom, even in heaven. He is beyond our understanding. He is the highest of the high. And we will be *like Him* one of these days, but we will never be *as Him.*

The Majesty of His Coronation

He is wearing many crowns, which are not *stephanos*, the Greek word for a victor's crown. But it is the Greek word *diadema*, which means a regal crown that kings wear. And He doesn't have just one; He has many, because He is King of kings and Lord of lords. No longer does He wear a crown formed from the briars of this world, but instead He wears the jewels of heaven. I am looking forward to seeing my Savior wear that crown and to singing "Crown Him with Many Crowns."

The Ministry of His Crucifixion

Revelation 19:13 says, "He wore a robe stained with blood, and His name is called the Word of God." Some Bible scholars think this is the blood from His enemies. Instead, I think this is a reminder of His precious blood spilled at Calvary that He will wear forever as an emblem of His sacrifice. Thank God for the ministry of His crucifixion and His blood that gives us the victory. Revelation 12:11 says, "They conquered him by the blood of the Lamb and by the word of their testimony, for they did not love their lives in the face of death." The victory that Jesus will win over the Antichrist is based on His blood.

Where is our hope? Not in science that has made the world a neighborhood instead of a brotherhood. Scientifically, we are in graduate school; morally, we are in kindergarten.

Hope is also not found in politics. No president or politician can deliver us. We win the wars and lose the peace. And these days it seems we can't even win the wars. What about social reform? That is not the answer either. All that social reform accomplishes, if it works at all, is to make the world a better place from which to go to hell. Social reform will not save this world.

It may sound like I am a pessimist, but I am not. I am a glowing optimist because I know the only One who can save the world. I am waiting for the Lord Jesus Christ to come again. The answer to this world's problems, beyond a shadow of any doubt, is the coming of our Lord Jesus Christ. He is coming visibly. He is coming victoriously.

The Lord Jesus Is Coming Vengefully

Some people don't like the idea of vengeance or judgment, because they think that would be unloving of God. I hear people say that God is too good to punish sin. No! God is too good *not* to punish sin. God is a holy God. God said, "Friends, do not avenge yourselves; instead, leave room for His wrath. For it is written: 'Vengeance belongs to Me; I will repay,' says the Lord" (Romans 12:19). Revelation 19:14–16 says, "The armies that were in heaven followed Him on white horses, wearing pure white linen. From His mouth came a sharp sword, so that with it He might strike the nations. He will shepherd them with an iron scepter. He will also trample the winepress of the fierce anger of God, the Almighty. And on His robe and on His thigh He has a name written: KING OF KINGS AND LORD OF LORDS."

God is a God of love. But if you preach the love of God to the exclusion of the wrath of God, you don't have the whole gospel. If you preach the wrath of God to the exclusion of the love of God, you don't have the whole gospel.

So many times things are not made right in this world. Justice is not done. Wrong seems to prevail. Wrong is on the throne, and truth is on the scaffold. It will not always be that way. Let me repeat an earlier verse: "Taking vengeance with flaming fire on those who don't know God and on those who don't obey the gospel of our Lord Jesus" (2 Thessalonians 1:8). Jesus is coming vengefully to make things right.

What does this mean to us today? First, we need to *learn of His coming*. We cannot afford to be ignorant of these things, and we need to teach others what we know about His second coming. Second, we should *look for His coming*. If I thought I was going to go through the Great Tribulation, I wouldn't be looking for the Lord Jesus Christ. Instead, I would be looking around waiting for something to happen. But we are to live every day as if Jesus might come at any moment.

Third, we are to *long for His coming*. The last prayer in the Bible is this: "Even so, come, Lord Jesus" (Revelation 22:20 KJV). Have you prayed, "Thy kingdom come. Thy will be done in earth, as it is in heaven" (Matthew 6:10 KJV)? What a day that will be when we see Jesus! Fourth, we need to *live for His coming*. The Bible says we are to occupy. Jesus said, "Occupy till I come" (Luke 19:13 KJV). John Corts of the Billy Graham Evangelistic Association told the following story:

> When I was a sixteen-year-old boy, I went with about eight of my cousins out to our grandfather's farm for a big celebration. The kids wanted to go out and work in the fields, but grandfather said that it was not a good idea. We said, "Please, Grandpa, please. We want to go out and work in the fields. Please let us go." My grandfather said, "All right. But you will not come in till the end of the day. John, don't bring them back until the end of the day."
>
> My cousins were so happy. They were on the tractor pitching hay, and for about an hour it was wonderful. Then the sun came up, the hay went down their collars, and they began to get all gritty and grimy, and they asked me to take them in. But I told them, "Papa said we are going to stay out here all day."
>
> "But it's hot," they whined.
>
> At noontime they were hot, miserable, tired, and whining, "We want to go in."

I said, "Nope, we are going to stay out here the whole day. Papa said we are staying out here the whole day." About three o'clock, there came an incredible thunderstorm and the lightning streaked across the sky. They asked to go in again, but I told them we were staying out there the whole day.

At the end of the day, about five o'clock, I said, "All right, we are going in." They got in the wagon and we left. When we got to the house, they got their baths and had their supper. They were so proud that they had stayed in the field all day long. And then grandfather gathered us at the supper table and said, "Children, I want to tell you something. God has blessed us. We have a fine farm here. We've got a good heritage. Let me tell you why God has blessed us. There have been times when we were hot, tired, and grimy, and we wanted to come in, but we didn't. We stayed in the fields. All that you see is because we learned the lesson of work. We learned what it means to stay in the field."

Do you know why some churches are thriving today? Because men and women have stayed in the field. It has not been easy, but they have been faithful to occupy until He comes. When He comes, will you be found faithfully serving Him?

The Signposts on the Road to Armageddon

◄○►

CHAPTER 24

◄○►

A young man was learning to fly a single-engine airplane, and it was time to do the landing phase of his instruction. The instructor said, "Are you ready to go down?" He said, "Let's do it." So the plane began to descend. The instructor looked over at the young man, and he was cool and calm. There wasn't a sign of nervousness about him—no sweaty palms or biting of his lip. The instructor thought this boy would make a great pilot.

The plane descended, and suddenly it hit the ground with a thud, bounced fifty feet in the air, hit the ground again and bounced off the runway where it finally stopped. The instructor said, "Son, I have been teaching for a long time, and I believe that is the worst landing ever done by a student pilot." He replied, "Me? I thought *you* were landing the airplane!"

I think a lot of times we wonder who is in control of this crazy world. God is in control, no matter what is happening or what we think.

If you look around and read the newspaper, you can see the storm clouds gathering. The dynamite is laid, the fuse is in place, and the match is ready to be struck. And we are running out of time. The battle of Armageddon is rushing upon us.

Armageddon, which literally means "Mount of Megiddo," includes a valley called the Valley of Jezreel and three mountains called Mount Carmel, Mount Tabor, and Mount Gilboa. Many leaders have fought battles here, including Napoleon, who said, "This is the world's greatest natural battlefield." Other leaders who have fought here include Titus, Pompey, Richard the Lionhearted, Nebuchadnezzar, and Rameses.

The Mount of Megiddo is soaked and drenched with blood. Why? Because it was an ancient crossroads where trade caravans traveled back and forth. Whoever controlled Megiddo controlled the land, the trade, and the commerce of that day. The Bible says that the last great war will be fought there. And this war will end all wars.

The apostle John wrote about this war in Revelation 19:11–15:

> Then I saw heaven opened, and there was a white horse! Its rider is called Faithful and True, and in righteousness He judges and makes war. His eyes were like a fiery flame, and on His head were many crowns. He had a name written that no one knows except Himself. He wore a robe stained with blood, and His name is called the Word of God. The armies that were in heaven followed Him on white horses, wearing pure white linen. From His mouth came a sharp sword, so that with it He might strike the nations. He will shepherd them with an iron scepter. He will also trample the winepress of the fierce anger of God, the Almighty.

Revelation 19 is only a snapshot of a panoramic drama that began earlier in our study of Revelation. Now we will get a look at the big picture of this drama with these signposts on the road to Armageddon.

Detailed Prophecies That Predict Armageddon

Many prophecies detail the future and our inevitable journey toward Armageddon. For instance, Revelation 16:16 says, "So they assembled them at the place called in Hebrew Armagedon." Let me mention several signposts that tell us we may be living in the last days.

Israel Has Reoccupied Their Land

The Republic of Israel was formed on May 14, 1948. After eighteen centuries, Israel returned to her land. Now we see the hostilities of many nations being turned against her. It is a fulfillment of the end-time prophecies.

There Is a Reunified Europe

These days, you can travel throughout Europe without a passport and there is one common currency—the euro. World influence is moving gradually, but inexorably, toward Europe as it becomes more dominant in commerce, military superiority, and politics. It is a fulfillment of Bible prophecy that the old Roman Empire would be reconstituted and that out of Europe the Antichrist would come. The signs are everywhere that many people want a one-world government. Their voices will not be silenced as we will hear more and more as the end nears.

Here are the words to a song that children are being taught in classrooms:

> Come young citizens of the world,
> We are one,
> We are one.
> Come young citizens of the world,
> We are one,
> We are one.
> We have one hope,
> We have one dream,
> And with one voice we sing;
> Peace, prosperity and love for all mankind.

Doesn't that sound sweet? But let me tell you it is quite ominous if you will go back to Genesis 11:6 and the song the people sang at the Tower of Babel. "And the LORD said, Behold, *the people is one, and they have all one language;* and this they begin to do: and now nothing will be restrained from them, which they have imagined to do" (KJV). The Tower of Babel was the beginning of the Babylonian Empire and religion.

The same move toward globalism is happening right now because of terrorism. People say the world needs to come together as one force to overcome terrorism. This movement is so strong that there is an effort underway to replace the phrase "A.D." that precedes the years after the birth of Jesus Christ with C.E., meaning "Common Era." *Anno Domini* means "the year of our Lord." Why do world officials want to do this? So we will have all things in common. They don't want the era since Christ's birth to be called "the Christian era." They want it to be "the Common Era."

The Former Soviet Republics and Arab Nations Are Coalescing Against Israel

Ezekiel 37–39 prophesies that the kings of the East will gather strength. In the Book of Revelation, the apostle John saw an army of two hundred million coming across the Euphrates River. Signs will intensify as the Lord Jesus Christ readies for His return. But when you see these events, does that only mean that Armageddon may be near? No, it also may mean that the rapture is coming, when Jesus comes for His church.

Demonic Passions That Provoke Armageddon

Revelation 16:13–16 says, "Then I saw three unclean spirits like frogs coming from the dragon's mouth, from the beast's mouth, and from the mouth of the false prophet. For they are spirits of demons performing signs, who travel to the kings of the whole world to assemble them for the battle of the great day of God, the Almighty. 'Look, I am coming like a thief. Blessed is the one who is alert and remains clothed so that he may not go naked, and they see his shame.' So they assembled them at the place called in Hebrew Armagedon."

Did you know that Satan is itching for a fight with God? How could Satan be so stupid? You have to know this about Satan: his wisdom is warped and corrupted. He is thinking that he will have a showdown at Megiddo with the Son of God. He is sending out his envoys to get the nations ready, mesmerize the monarchs, manipulate the kings, and bring them to Armageddon. In that day we will find out who has the ultimate power.

There are dark, devilish, demonic, malevolent powers working in the world today. And behind them and standing in the shadows is Satan. People say to me, "Do you believe in the conspiratorial theory of history?" I do, but the little conspiracies that many people talk about are lightweight. I am talking about a devilish conspiracy that goes beyond anything you may have imagined. Let me cite some Scriptures.

- "False messiahs and false prophets will arise and perform great signs and wonders to lead astray, if possible, even the elect" (Matthew 24:24). I have said it before, but I'll say it again: Satan has such unbelievable persuasive power he will make you think up is down, good is bad, and white is black.
- "But there were also false prophets among the people, just as there will be false teachers among you. They will secretly bring in destructive heresies, even denying the Master who bought them, and will bring swift destruction on themselves" (2 Peter 2:1). Peter is talking about Armageddon.

- "Now the Spirit explicitly says that in the latter times some will depart from the faith, paying attention to deceitful spirits and the teachings of demons" (1 Timothy 4:1). Satan will have a heyday in the last days deceiving people.

- "For false messiahs and false prophets will rise up and will perform signs and wonders to lead astray, if possible, the elect" (Mark 13:22). One day, Satan may perform a miracle before your eyes and you may say, "I saw with my own eyes a glorious sign and wonder. No one could do this but God." You'd better get a lock on the Word of God. Don't bring your intellect or intuition to this matter. Bring the Word of God.

- "For this reason God sends them a strong delusion so that they will believe what is false" (2 Thessalonians 2:11). The demon forces of this world will work with Satan's new religion of neopaganism, which is the amalgamation of the corrupt sons of old Adam. And they will come together with demonic power to deceive the nations of the world.

Determined People That Plot Armageddon

Who will come against the Lord? Revelation 17:12–14 says, "And the ten horns [*symbols of power*] which thou sawest are ten kings, which have received no kingdom as yet; but receive power as kings one hour with the beast [*the Antichrist*]. These have one mind, and shall give their power and strength unto the beast. These shall make war with the Lamb [*battle of Armageddon*], and the Lamb shall overcome them: for he is Lord of lords, and King of kings: and they that are with him are called, and chosen, and faithful" (KJV, explanatory notes added by the author).

The phrase "one hour" doesn't mean sixty minutes. Instead, it means the same kind of hour to which Jesus referred when He said to His mother, "My hour has not yet come" (John 2:4). He meant His special time.

Who are "these" to whom Revelation 17 refers? They form a confederacy of ten kings or kingdoms that will be seduced by the beast and come against Christ at Armageddon. They have one mind and will give their power and strength to the beast. Why will they do that? Because they will be drunk with the pride and power of the mighty beast.

Devilish Pride That Precipitates Armageddon

In the Book of Revelation the devil is called the dragon, and his ambition has always been to be like the Most High. In the Great Tribulation, he gains this worship. Revelation 13:4–6 says, "And they worshipped the dragon which gave power unto the beast: and they worshipped the beast, saying, Who is like unto the beast? who is able to make war with him? And there was given unto him a mouth speaking great things and blasphemies; and power was given unto him to continue forty and two months. And he opened his mouth in blasphemy against God, to blaspheme his name, and his tabernacle, and them that dwell in heaven" (KJV).

In essence, the dragon (the devil) says to the Antichrist, "I will pour my power into you if you get the world to worship me." Do you see how arrogant he is? The beast will be an incredible orator. He will have such persuasion that little children will speak his name with reverence, men will gladly die for him, and women will worship at his shrine.

The forty and two months are three and one-half years, which form the second half of the Great Tribulation. At this point, the beast will give the ultimate blasphemy. During the first part of the tribulation, he will be carefully gathering strength and unifying the world. When the temple is rebuilt in Jerusalem, his golden moment will arrive and he will stride into the temple saying, "You built this temple in anticipation of worshiping God. Do you want to see God? I am God." He will declare himself to be God.

The scales will be removed from the eyes of the Jews, and they will wake up and say, "You two-legged devil; you are not God." They will see the arrogant pride that made Lucifer the devil. Notice Revelation 13:7: "And he was permitted to wage war against the saints and to conquer them. He was also given authority over every tribe, people, language, and nation." Why would he make war with the saints? Because they will no longer worship him. Daniel prophesied it, and Jesus talked about it:

> So when you see "the abomination that causes desolation,"
> spoken of by the prophet Daniel, standing in the holy place
> (let the reader understand), then those in Judea must flee to
> the mountains! A man on the housetop must not come down
> to get things out of his house. And a man in the field must not
> go back to get his clothes. Woe to pregnant women and nursing
> mothers in those days! Pray that your escape may not be in

winter or on a Sabbath. For at that time there will be great tribulation, the kind that hasn't taken place since the beginning of the world until now, and never will again (Matthew 24:15–21).

The honeymoon will be over when this happens. No longer will the sons and daughters of Abraham be deceived. Satan's pride will be wounded, and his rage will intensify. He will say, "I am going to solve this problem once and for all." Armageddon will be his vengeance on those who have refused to bow and worship him.

Devastating Plagues That Precede Armageddon

Revelation 16:8–11 says, "The fourth poured out his bowl on the sun. He was given the power to burn people with fire, and people were burned by the intense heat. So they blasphemed the name of God who had the power over these plagues, and they did not repent and give Him glory. The fifth poured out his bowl on the throne of the beast, and his kingdom was plunged into darkness. People gnawed their tongues from pain and blasphemed the God of heaven because of their pains and their sores, yet they did not repent of their actions."

The party is over. The kingdom of the beast is unraveling before his eyes. Everything is going upside down. The beast who was sitting on the throne learns that he cannot control the forces of nature. Revelation 18:8 says, "Therefore her [Babylon the Great] plagues will come in one day— death, and grief, and famine. She will be burned up with fire, because the Lord God who judges her is mighty."

If you say that a calamity is a judgment of God, people will get angry with you. They don't like the idea of a God of judgment. If the Supreme Court of the United States could vote on it, they would outlaw hell as cruel and unusual punishment. Proverbs 28:5 says, "Evil men understand not judgment: but they that seek the LORD understand all things" (KJV).

Do you think that pain and judgment and plagues will bring people to God? It will not. Do you think they are crying out for mercy in hell? No. Do you know what they are doing in hell? They are cursing God. They are gnashing their teeth against God. They hate God. In perpetuity they will hate God. If the love of God does not bring you to your knees, His punishment will not accomplish it either. Punishment is coming, because God is righteous and just. The same sun that melts the ice hardens the clay. These hearts will be hardened.

Divine Power That Prevails at Armageddon

Revelation 19:11–16 says:

Then I saw heaven opened, and there was a white horse! Its rider is called Faithful and True, and in righteousness He judges and makes war. His eyes were like a fiery flame, and on His head were many crowns. He had a name written that no one knows except Himself. He wore a robe stained with blood, and His name is called the Word of God. The armies that were in heaven followed Him on white horses, wearing pure white linen. From His mouth came a sharp sword, so that with it He might strike the nations. He will shepherd them with an iron scepter. He will also trample the winepress of the fierce anger of God, the Almighty. And on His robe and on His thigh He has a name written: KING OF KINGS AND LORD OF LORDS.

Here is the scene that will prevail at the battle of Armageddon. The Antichrist will be gnawing his tongue and blaspheming God because his pride will be wounded and his power challenged. The demonic spirits will organize a confederacy of ten nations that will move against Jerusalem once and for all to solve the "Jewish problem." In the great valley of Jezreel, between these three mountains, this confederacy will get ready to move against Jerusalem with their tanks, guns, napalm, lasers, jets, rockets, poisonous gas, and whatever else is in the mind of this insane man. It is going to look dark.

Suddenly, there will be an invasion from outer space. Here comes Jesus riding a snow-white horse (a symbol of a conquering general). He is followed by wave after wave of armies—not dressed in battle fatigue or carrying weapons, but robed in white (the righteousness of the saints). In His mouth will be a sharp two-edged sword (the Word of God) to strike the nations. The Antichrist may have all of his weapons of war, but 2 Corinthians 10:4 says, "The weapons of our warfare are not fleshly, but are powerful through God for the demolition of strongholds."

All Jesus has to do is speak, and the battle is won. Have you ever thought of the power of the voice of our Lord? He spoke, and the universe came into existence. Hebrews 11:3 says, "By faith we understand that the universe was created by *the word of God,* so that what is seen has been made from things that are not visible." He spoke everything into existence. What power resides in His Word!

The disciples were with Jesus in a boat when a storm arose on the Sea of Galilee. What was Jesus doing? He was asleep! Matthew 8:25–27 tells us what happened: "The disciples came and woke Him up, saying, 'Lord, save us! We're going to die!' But He said to them, 'Why are you fearful, you of little faith?' Then He got up and *rebuked the winds and the sea. And there was a great calm.* The men were amazed and said, 'What kind of man is this?—even the winds and the sea obey Him!'"

Jesus spoke, and that raging sea became as calm as a millpond on a moonlit night. Those waves lay down at His feet like whipped puppies. The night before Jesus was crucified, He went to the Garden of Gethesmane with His disciples to pray. Within a few hours, Judas arrived with a band of chief priests, officers, and Pharisees. Here is what happened next, according to John's Gospel: "Then Jesus, knowing everything that was about to happen to Him, went out and said to them, 'Who is it you're looking for?' 'Jesus the Nazarene,' they answered. 'I am He,' Jesus told them. Judas, who betrayed Him, was also standing with them. When He told them, 'I am He,' *they stepped back and fell to the ground* (John 18:4–6).

Jesus literally used the word "I AM," which is one of the most holy words for God in the Bible. This band of men collapsed from the sound of His voice. Would they have stayed on the ground? Absolutely. But Jesus allowed them to get up, because He knew His capture by these men was part of His Father's plan.

When Jesus comes in power and great glory at the battle of Armageddon, how will the battle be won? Not by guns or weapons, but by the sword that goes out of His mouth. The One who spoke this army into existence will speak them into oblivion. What is the lesson for us today? Never be at war with God. A preacher once said: "Your arms are too short to box with God." Soon and very soon, 777 will take care of 666, and the kingdoms of this world will become the kingdoms of our Lord and His Christ.

Are you at peace with God, or are you at war with God? Paul said, "For God was pleased to have all His fullness dwell in Him, and through Him to reconcile everything to Himself by making peace through the blood of His cross—whether things on earth or things in heaven. And you were once alienated and hostile in mind because of your evil actions. But now He has reconciled you" (Colossians 1:19–22). You can sign a peace treaty with the Prince of Peace if you will say yes to Calvary.

The Final Judgment of the Unsaved Dead

◄o►

CHAPTER 25

◄o►

On the day of the final judgment the unsaved dead will rise from their graves to stand and be judged before Almighty God. All that men have dreamed, schemed, and sold their souls for will turn to rust, dust, mold, and corruption. John described that day:

> Then I saw a great white throne and One seated on it. Earth and heaven fled from His presence, and no place was found for them. I also saw the dead, the great and the small, standing before the throne, and books were opened. Another book was opened, which is the book of life, and the dead were judged according to their works by what was written in the books. Then the sea gave up its dead, and Death and Hades gave up their dead; all were judged according to their works. Death and Hades were thrown into the lake of fire. This is the second death, the lake of fire. And anyone not found written in the book of life was thrown into the lake of fire (Revelation 20:11–15).

We come now to the Great White Throne Judgment, where God settles the score and once and for all adjudicates the world with righteousness and justice. There are four things we learn from this day of holy judgment.

The Fearful Setting Described

Notice the setting of this judgment in Revelation 20:11: "Then I saw a great white throne and One seated on it. Earth and heaven fled from His presence, and no place was found for them." The white throne is called "great" because of its awesome power and ultimate purpose, which is judgment. It is called "white" because of its unsullied purity.

The earth and heaven will flee. Everything that we have known and depended on will be gone. There will be no place to run and no place to hide. Adam and Eve ran into the trees to hide themselves from the presence of the Lord, but there will be nowhere to hide when the unsaved stand before the Lord on judgment day.

Perhaps you have heard someone pray: "Lord, grant that some day we might stand before Thy great white throne." Please don't pray that prayer for me, and don't pray it for yourself. Those who stand before the great white throne will stand to be judged by the Lord Jesus Christ. John 5:22 says, "The Father, in fact, judges no one but has given all judgment to the Son." Jesus Christ is not only Savior, but He is also judge. The Lamb will become the Lion.

You are going to meet Jesus Christ. Every person who has ever lived is going to meet Jesus Christ. He is inescapable and unavoidable. And if you don't meet Him as Savior, you will meet Him as Judge. It doesn't matter how you treated Him when you were alive. In fact, you may have ignored Him, denied Him, and even cursed Him, but one day you will stand before Him.

What will He be like when we meet Him face to face? We were introduced to the Judge in Revelation 1:13–16: "And among the lampstands was One like the Son of Man, dressed in a long robe, and with a gold sash wrapped around His chest. His head and hair were white like wool—white as snow, His eyes like a fiery flame, His feet like fine bronze fired in a furnace, and His voice like the sound of cascading waters. In His right hand He had seven stars; from His mouth came a sharp two-edged sword; and His face was shining like the sun at midday."

Jesus will be wearing the regal robes of a king and judge, and His white hair will speak of His unsullied purity. His eyes will be like a flame of fire, which tell us that He sees all and knows all. Hebrews 4:13 says, "No creature is hidden from Him, but all things are naked and exposed to the eyes of Him to whom we must give an account." He cannot be deceived. He cannot be disputed. He cannot be discredited. The Bible says His feet will be like bronze ("brass," KJV), which is a symbol of judgment. His voice will be like the sound of cascading waters. Can you imagine talking back to Niagara Falls? Judgment day will be a fearful setting.

The Forceful Summons Delivered

The People Who Are Called

Notice the people who are brought before the great white throne of judgment—the dead, the small, and the great. Revelation 20:12 says, "I also saw the dead, the great and the small, standing before the throne, and books were opened. Another book was opened, which is the book of life, and the dead were judged according to their works by what was written in the books."

People from five categories of life will be there. See if you are in any of these categories.

1. *Out-and-out sinners.* These are the ones who hate God and His church. They boldly, braggingly, brazenly shake their fists in the face of Almighty God and say, "If there is a God, You are not big enough to make me serve You." They have denied Him and are unrepentant.

2. *Self-righteous people.* These people think they are too good to be damned. They think the gospel is for the drunkard, murderer, pervert, harlot, child abuser, or blasphemer. They are nice people who live in nice homes and have nice manners. They are members of the PTA, give money to worthy causes, help the poor, teach the illiterate to read, volunteer at the local soup kitchen, and perhaps attend church every now and then.

This describes most of the egomaniacs in the world who are strutting to hell—thinking they are too good to be damned. What they don't realize is that there is no one so bad that he cannot be saved and no one so good that he need not be saved. They fail to see that the worst form of badness is human goodness when human goodness becomes a substitute for the new birth.

3. *Procrastinators.* This group intended to be saved. They knew they were sinners. They weren't antagonistic to the gospel, but they just didn't intend to give their hearts to Jesus, at least not when they had the chance. Do you fit in this category? Proverbs 27:1 says, "Boast not thyself of tomorrow; for thou knowest not what a day may bring forth" (KJV).

If you are procrastinating, in the name of Jesus I beg you not to put away this day of salvation. Second Corinthians 6:2 says, "Look, now is the acceptable time; look, now is the day of salvation." Psalm 95:7–8 says, "For he is our God; and we are the people of his pasture, and the sheep of his hand. Today if ye will hear his voice, harden not your heart, as in the provocation, and as in the day of temptation in the wilderness" (KJV).

Can you feel your heart beat? That small beat is all that is between you and hell. Someone has called the heartbeat of an unsaved person "a muffled drum beating a funeral march to the grave." Your heart will stop beating one day; and when it does, if you don't know Jesus, you are going to hell. You may respond, "You are trying to frighten me." I would to God I could! I would rather frighten you into heaven than lull you into hell.

4. *Unsaved church members.* These people are religious, but they have not crowned Jesus Christ as Lord of their lives. They are not anti-God; they have simply been deceived. Somehow they are counting on their church attendance, service to the church, tithes, baptism, or the faith of their family to be saved. But religion never saved anybody. It is Jesus who saves. It will be a great day when people stop enduring religion and start enjoying salvation.

The devil had just as soon send you to hell from the pew as from the gutter. Many people are going to hell surrounded by baptismal certificates, receipts for tithes and offerings, and Sunday school attendance pins. That's the reason the Bible says, "Test yourselves to see if you are in the faith. Examine yourselves. Or do you not recognize for yourselves that Jesus Christ is in you?—unless you fail the test" (2 Corinthians 13:5).

Are you a Christian? I am not asking if you know the plan of salvation. I am not asking if you are religious. I am not asking if you are Baptist, Methodist, Presbyterian, Lutheran, Church of Christ, or Pentecostal. I am asking if you know you are truly saved. Are you?

5. *Those who have never heard the gospel.* Some people may say, "Wait a minute. If a person has never heard the gospel, how can he be condemned?" He may not have enough light to save him, but he has enough sin to condemn him. Romans 3:23 says, "For all have sinned and fall short of the glory of God."

The judgment, however, will not be as severe for those who have never heard as it will be for those who stubbornly refused the gospel.

If anyone hears the gospel and willfully and knowingly refuses the Lord Jesus Christ, he will stand before the great white throne in judgment. I would not want to be in his shoes on that day. When Jesus sent out the disciples to preach the Good News, He said, "If anyone will not welcome you or listen to your words, shake the dust off your feet when you leave that house or town. I assure you: It will be more tolerable on the day of judgment for the land of Sodom and Gomorrah than for that town" (Matthew 10:14–15).

Those who have heard, yet did not repent and believe, may stand before Christ and plead for mercy, saying they didn't have a chance. But God will say, "Angel, bring Exhibit A." What is this? It will be the dust on the shoes of the man or woman who shared the gospel with you. You had your opportunity.

Some people have never heard the gospel of Jesus Christ. God deals with them in a unique way. There will be degrees of judgment. Hell will not be the same for everybody. How do I know this? Read Luke 12:47–48: "And that slave who knew his master's will, and didn't prepare himself or do it, will be severely beaten. But the one who did not know [*he did not have the light*], and did things deserving of blows [*he sinned*], will be beaten lightly. Much will be required of everyone who has been given much. And even more will be expected of the one who has been entrusted with more" (explanatory notes added by the author).

The Places from Which They Are Called

Revelation 20:13 says, "Then the sea gave up its dead, and Death and Hades gave up their dead." Death and hades will deliver up the dead people who are in them. Earth will open its graves to give up the dead. Out of tombs the dead will rise. The depths of the sea will heave its bosom and swell to give up the dead. From the Arctic waste they will come; from the desert sands they will come; from the tropical jungles they will come. Wherever people have died, they will be raised.

We need to understand at this point that death has the body, but hades has the soul. When a child of God dies, he or she goes immediately to paradise. "Therefore, though we are always confident and know that while we are at home in the body we are away from the Lord" (2 Corinthians 5:6). Jesus said to the thief on the cross who repented and believed, "I assure you: Today you will be with Me in paradise" (Luke 23:43).

When a person dies without Jesus Christ as his Savior, his soul goes immediately to hades. He will not be judged at that moment. In Luke 16, Christ gives us a picture of this when He describes what happened to the rich man and the beggar man named Lazarus who both died. The rich man went to hades; Lazarus went to paradise.

"And being in torment in hades, *[the rich man]* he looked up and saw Abraham a long way off, with Lazarus at his side. 'Father Abraham!' he called out, 'Have mercy on me and send Lazarus to dip the tip of his finger in water and cool my tongue, because I am in agony in this flame!'" (Luke 16:23–24). In this passage, the Greek word *hadēs* is different from the word that is translated "lake of fire." Hades is more like a jail where the indicted criminal is retained until judgment. The lake of fire is the penitentiary.

The Power with Which They are Called

Sometimes when a judge issues a summons, the criminal refuses to come. He may disguise himself, flee to another country seeking asylum, or he may even commit suicide to keep from coming to judgment. But on this judgment day, there will be no refusal and no escape. The resurrection of Jesus Christ guarantees the judgment of the unsaved dead. Acts 17:31 says, "Because He has set a day on which He is going to judge the world in righteousness by the Man He has appointed. He has provided proof of this to everyone by raising Him from the dead." This man whom God has ordained is Jesus Christ. And He has been raised from the dead.

Jesus Christ walked out of the grave. You can't hold court if the judge is dead or the defendant is dead. The God who raised Jesus from the dead is the God who will raise the unsaved dead. No person will be able to pull the dirt over his face and hide from God. A forceful summons is coming.

The Fatal Secrets Displayed

At this judgment there will come an indictment. Let's read Revelation 20:12 again: "I also saw the dead, the great and the small, standing before the throne, and books were opened. Another book was opened, which is the book of life, and the dead were judged according to their works by what was written in the books."

Did you know that God has your life recorded in His book? Not a thing about your life has escaped His knowledge. And one of these days you will face His accounting of your life. Ecclesiastes 12:14 says, "For God shall bring every work into judgment, *with every secret thing*, whether it be good, or whether it be evil" (KJV). Romans 2:16 says, "On the day when God judges what people have kept secret, according to my gospel through Christ Jesus."

God knows the secret things in your life that nobody else knows. If there were a glass window on our hearts, most of us would want that to be a stained-glass window with a heavy glaze on it. A preacher friend of mine, Peter Lord, said, "It never bothers me when anybody says anything bad about me. I just say, 'Thank God, they don't know any more.'"

The other day I found some tapes of sermons that I had preached almost half a century ago. I said, "I'll put one on and listen to what this fool has to say." It was odd to recall all those words I said so long ago. Something Jesus said came to mind: "I tell you that on the day of judgment people will have to account for every careless word they speak. For by your words you will be acquitted, and by your words you will be condemned" (Matthew 12:36–37). God's candid camera is moving. God's tape recorder is playing.

Have you ever taken God's name in vain? Maybe you've forgotten it, but God hasn't forgotten. You say, "I didn't mean anything by it." Then you are twice condemned that you could take His name in vain and not mean anything by it. God says, "Thou shalt not take the name of the LORD thy God in vain; for the LORD will not hold him guiltless that taketh his name in vain" (Exodus 20:7 KJV).

Luke 12:2 says, "There is nothing covered that won't be uncovered; nothing hidden that won't be made known." On judgment day, skeletons will come out of closets. And things that your mother didn't know, your father didn't know, your wife didn't know, your husband didn't know, your child didn't know will be shouted from the rooftop. Think about it.

One day I called my son David and his wife Kelly, who serve as missionaries in Spain. Kelly told me that their sewer had backed up, and she had called the plumber. He went out in the street and took the manhole cover off. My daughter-in-law said, "Papa, thousands of roaches came out and ran all over the streets!" One roach would drive me up the wall! When God takes the lid off our lives on judgment day, thousands of roaches will come out: things in your heart and mind that you have repressed and thought you had covered up.

The Final Sentence Determined

The Sureness of the Judgment

Revelation 20:14–15 says, "Death and Hades were thrown into the lake of fire. This is the second death, the lake of fire. And anyone not found written in the book of life was thrown into the lake of fire." No one will be able to bribe the judge. No shrewd lawyer will be able to put a spin on your case. Romans 14:11–12 says, "For it is written: 'As I live, says the Lord, every knee will bow to Me, and every tongue will give praise to

God.' So then, each of us will give an account of himself to God." God swears by Himself that judgment is coming.

The Severity of the Judgment

God will judge according to our works, not according to His grace or mercy. If you want grace, you may have it. If you want mercy, you may have it. But you must have it in *this day* and in *this life*. You will not have it *then*.

As I said before, don't get the idea that you are going to throw yourself on the mercy of the court on judgment day. There is no room for mercy in the courtroom of God on judgment day. Romans 10:13 says, "Everyone who calls on the name of the Lord will be saved."

There are three parts to every trial. First, *the evidence is presented*. The books are opened. Everything will be known—every idle word, thought, and deed. Every dishonest thing you did, every nickel you stole from your mother's dresser, every gray hair you gave your father, every wrinkle you pinched into the brow of your wife—all this evidence will be known. And not only will this evidence be things that you have said, done, or thought, but these will be things that you have left unsaid, unthought, and undone. James 4:17 says, "So, for the person who knows to do good and doesn't do it, it is a sin."

Next, you have a chance to *make your defense*. What will you say? I can hear people saying, "Wait a minute, Lord, don't judge my sin. I didn't know which church to join. There was a Baptist Church, Methodist Church, Presbyterian Church, Church of God, Church of Christ, Church of God in Christ, Episcopalian Church, Catholic Church, and Church of Jesus Christ of Latter Day Saints." God will respond, "I didn't say believe on the church. I said believe on the Lord Jesus Christ and you will be saved."

And they might say, "Wait a minute, God. I didn't respond to your call to be saved, because I didn't want to be like those hypocrites in the church. And I wasn't going to call myself a Christian in front of other people and not be able to live like one." God will respond, "I didn't say believe on yourself. I said believe on the Lord Jesus Christ and you will be saved."

What defense will you give if you are not saved? What can you possibly say in defense of your trampling beneath your feet the precious blood of the Lord Jesus and despising His spirit of grace? What can you say on that judgment day when you know that you rejected His outstretched nail-pierced hands and His voice that invited you: "Come to Me, all you who are weary and burdened, and I will give you rest. Take My yoke upon you and learn from Me, because I am gentle and humble in heart, and you will find rest for your souls. For My yoke is easy and My burden is light" (Matthew 11:28–30)?

Finally, *the verdict of the court is handed down*. The brokenhearted Judge will say, "But whoever denies Me before men, I will also deny him before My Father in heaven" (Matthew 10:33). Jesus also said: "Not everyone who says to Me, 'Lord, Lord!' will enter the kingdom of heaven, but the one who does the will of My Father in heaven. On that day many will say to Me, 'Lord, Lord, didn't we prophesy in Your name, drive out demons in Your name, and do many miracles in Your name?' Then I will announce to them, 'I never knew you! Depart from Me, you lawbreakers!'" (Matthew 7:21–23).

If you are not saved, your soul will drop down into hell at that moment. "And anyone not found written in the book of life was thrown into the lake of fire" (Revelation 20:15). You may say, "I don't believe in hell fire." Five minutes after you get there, you will believe in it. Either the Bible is true, or it is not true. There is a lake of liquid fire, and the sadness of it is this: You don't have to go.

C. S. Lewis said that everybody in the world is in two categories. One group is like Satan. They say to God the Father, "Not Your will, but mine be done." The second group is like God the Son. They say to God the Father, "Not my will, but Thine be done." Those in the first category will have lived a self-concerned, self-controlled life, and they will drop into hell as a brokenhearted God will say, "Not My will, but thine be done." God doesn't want you to go to hell.

Someone asked a preacher, "Do you really believe in hell? If so, tell me where it is." The wise pastor said, "Hell is at the end of a Christless life." If you die outside the Lord, you will come to a judgment, and then you will know that the Bible is indeed true.

I am not going to stand before the great white throne, and I will tell you why. I settled out of court. Jesus became my Savior when He died on the cross in agony and blood, and with His blood He paid the debt of my sin. Romans 8:33–34 says, "Who can bring an accusation against God's elect? God is the One who justifies. Who is the one who condemns? Christ Jesus is the One who died, but even more, has been raised; He also is at the right hand of God and intercedes for us." Isn't that wonderful? Your sin can be buried in the grave of God's forgetfulness, never to be brought up against you again.

The Golden Age

◄O►

CHAPTER 26

◄O►

Did you know that there is coming a day when the Garden of Eden will
be restored? I'll let the prophet Isaiah explain what I mean: "The
wilderness and the solitary place shall be glad for them; and the desert
shall rejoice, and blossom as the rose. It shall blossom abundantly, and
rejoice even with joy and singing: the glory of Lebanon shall be given
unto it, the excellency of Carmel and Sharon, they shall see the glory of
the LORD, and the excellency of our God" (Isaiah 35:1–2 KJV).

Can you imagine what the Garden of Eden must have been like?
I heard that one day Cain and Abel found a wall and they climbed it and
looked over. They went back to Adam and said, "Daddy, you will never
believe what we saw." Then they described the luxurious foliage, fruit, and
flowers. They said, "Daddy, do you think we could ever live in a place like
that?"

Adam said, "We did once. That was before your mother ate us out of
house and home!"

Of course, that is not true—it's just a story. And we certainly can't
blame Eve any more than we can blame Adam. But seriously, I want to say
that there is coming a time when we will live in a place like that.

Imagine a time when there will be no more poverty and every person
will have all that his heart desires. Imagine that, and more. There will be
no prisons, no hospitals, no mental institutions, no army bases, no gam-
bling dens, and no houses of prostitution. The bloom of youth will be on
everyone's cheek. The wolf and the lamb, the calf and the lion, and the
little child and the serpent will all play together. The implements of war
will be relics of the past. Israel will be restored to her land. Jerusalem will

be the world's capital. The resurrected saints will rule and reign with the Lord Jesus Christ. The desert will blossom like a rose, and the earth will be filled with the knowledge of the glory of the Lord as waters that cover the sea.

This time will be called the Golden Age (or the millennium of Christ's reign on earth). The word *millennium* means "one thousand years." *Mille* means "thousand"; *annum* means "year." Just look at all the references to this thousand-year period in Revelation 20: The latter part of verse 2 says, "and bound him a *thousand years*." The middle part of verse 3 says, "till the *thousand years* should be fulfilled." The last part of verse 4 says, "they lived and reigned with Christ a *thousand years*." The first part of verse 5 says, "But the rest of the dead lived not again until the *thousand years* were finished." The second half of verse 6 says, "But they shall be priests of God and of Christ, and shall reign with him a *thousand years*." Verse 7 says, "And when the *thousand years* are expired, Satan shall be loosed out of his prison" (Revelation 20:2–7 KJV).

Theologians are divided on whether there will be a thousand-year Golden Age. There are basically three interpretations about the millennium: amillennialism, postmillennialism, and premillennialism. An amillennialist believes there will not be a literal millennium. If you put the alpha prefix in front of a word, it simply negates the meaning of the word. For instance, the word *amuse* means "not to think." If you want to think, you go to a museum.

Amillennialists interpret Revelation's prophecies about the millennium as pure symbolism. They do not look for a literal fulfillment of a Golden Age. Also, amillennialists take all the promises given by God to Israel in the Old Testament and apply them to the New Testament church. Generally, moderate theologians hold this view. I am not an amillennialist.

Next is the postmillennialist view. The prefix *post* means "after." These theologians believe that Jesus is coming *after* the thousand years of peace on earth. The Golden Age to the postmillennialist is the age when the church fulfills its God-given mandate to evangelize the world with the gospel of Jesus Christ.

There aren't many postmillennialists around today, because their theory that the world is getting better and better is rapidly being disproved by the reality that our world is going deeper and deeper into sin (which is what the Bible teaches). If you are a postmillennialist, you do not believe in the imminent return of Jesus. Instead, you believe that you need to wait a thousand years for Jesus to come again. I am not a postmillennialist.

I am a premillennialist, and that is what I hope you are (or will be before I finish this chapter). The premillennialist believes that Jesus must come before the church can enjoy a thousand years of peace on earth. We believe that Jesus will come in power and great glory and He will rule and reign from Jerusalem. We also believe that God will give His nation Israel a second chance to repent and rise to political greatness. In this day and age, the premillennialist's goal is to prepare people for the second coming of Jesus Christ by preaching His glorious saving gospel.

Having laid that foundation, let's look at four basic things about the Golden Age that will usher in the rule and reign of Jesus Christ on earth.

The Forceful Restraint of Satan

John has a revelation: "Then I saw an angel coming down from heaven with the key to the abyss and a great chain in his hand. He seized the dragon, that ancient serpent who is the Devil and Satan, and bound him for 1,000 years. He threw him into the abyss, closed it, and put a seal on it so that he would no longer deceive the nations until the 1,000 years were completed. After that, he must be released for a short time" (Revelation 20:1–3).

Where is Satan today? First Peter 5:8 says, "Be sober! Be on the alert! Your adversary the Devil is *prowling around* like a roaring lion, looking for anyone he can devour" (KJV). Today Satan is roaming the earth to find people he can deceive and destroy. How are you living, knowing he is on the loose? Hopefully, you are living in a sober and vigilant spirit—just like you would be living if a real lion were on the loose in your neighborhood!

According to God's Word in Revelation 20, there is coming a time when this roaring lion will be chained and cast into prison. The court will meet. The final gavel will fall. And the arch criminal, Satan, will be pronounced guilty for murder and every other conceivable evil committed in this world. And he will receive the longest prison sentence in history—one thousand years.

How do I know the judgment of the court? Because God's Word tells us that "the dragon, that old serpent, which is the Devil, and Satan" is evil incarnate. First, he will be sentenced for murder. He brings spiritual, physical, and eternal death to youth, happiness, purity, and holiness. When talking to unbelievers, Jesus said, "You are of your father the Devil, and you want to carry out your father's desires. He was a *murderer from the beginning* and has not stood in the truth, because there is no truth in him. When he tells a lie, he speaks from his own nature, because he is a liar and the father of liars" (John 8:44).

He will also be sentenced for being a thief. Since his fall from heaven, he has robbed men and women, boys and girls of joy, contentment, and peace in his mission to bring despair and discouragement. Jesus said, "A thief comes only to steal and to kill and to destroy" (John 10:10).

The judge will also hand down a thousand-year sentence for the crime of extortion. He has deceived the minds of millions with his false advertising of fulfillment and prosperity. Why do you think the Bible refers to him as a serpent? The word *serpent* in the Bible speaks of deception. Revelation 12:9 says, "So the great dragon was thrown out—the ancient serpent, who is called the Devil and Satan, *the one who deceives the whole world*. He was thrown to earth, and his angels with him."

Can there be any more crimes with which to charge the devil? Yes! Slander. Libel. Defamation of character. Blasphemy. The word *devil* means "accuser." God's Word calls him the "accuser of our brothers": "Then I heard a loud voice in heaven say: 'The salvation and the power and the kingdom of our God and the authority of His Messiah have now come, because *the accuser of our brothers* has been thrown out: the one who accuses them before our God day and night'" (Revelation 12:10).

The final charge (if there can be just one final indictment) would be for high treason. Revelation 20:2 calls him Satan, and the word *Satan* means "adversary." Satan is charged with high treason against heaven's King. Behind every child molestation, rape, pillage, arson, hatefulness, and hellishness is Satan. He is an accomplice to every crime against God, and he is now judged guilty and cast into prison.

Actually, God's Word calls this prison a bottomless pit. That will not be Satan's final destination; it will be a holding tank until he is finally cast into the liquid lake of fire. In chapter 4, we learned that Satan was the original holder of that key. Do you remember that? In Revelation 9, we learned that Satan will open the bottomless pit and loose a demon horde upon the earth.

Isaiah 14:12–17 gives us a brief overview of Satan's biography and a prophecy of his end in the bottomless pit:

> How art thou fallen from heaven, O Lucifer, son of the
> morning! how art thou cut down to the ground, which didst

weaken the nations! For thou hast said in thine heart, I will ascend into heaven, I will exalt my throne above the stars of God: I will sit also upon the mount of the congregation, in the sides of the north: I will ascend above the heights of the clouds: I will be like the most High. Yet thou shalt be brought down to *hell, to the sides of the pit.* They that see thee shall narrowly look upon thee, and consider thee, saying, Is this the man that made the earth to tremble, that did shake kingdoms; That made the world as a wilderness, and destroyed the cities thereof; that opened not the house of his prisoners? (KJV).

I love the phrase Isaiah uses—that people will "narrowly look upon" Satan. They will have to squint to see him. Satan's arrogant desire to rise to the heavens to be like God will ultimately cause him to descend to the lowest part of creation. People will squint their eyes and say, "You mean that is Satan? That worm? That is the one who wanted to exalt himself above God?" Yes, Satan may be loose on the earth today, but one day we will see his forceful restraint.

The Future Reign of the Savior

Revelation 20:4–6 says:

Then I saw thrones, and people seated on them who were given authority to judge. I also saw the souls of those who had been beheaded because of their testimony about Jesus and because of God's word, who had not worshiped the beast or his image, and who had not accepted the mark on their foreheads or their hands. They came to life and reigned with the Messiah for 1,000 years. The rest of the dead did not come to life until the 1,000 years were completed. This is the first resurrection. Blessed and holy is the one who shares in the first resurrection! The second death has no power over these, but they will be priests of God and the Messiah, and they will reign with Him for 1,000 years.

After the Great Tribulation and the battle of Armageddon, Jesus Christ will literally reign on earth for a thousand years and the saints will reign and rule with Him. How do I know that? Because Jesus taught us to pray: "Thy kingdom come. Thy will be done in earth, as it is in heaven"

(Matthew 6:10 KJV). Has His will been done on earth as it is in heaven? No. Will it be? Yes, when He returns for His millennial reign.

The Changes That Will Take Place

And when Jesus returns to rule and reign, many glorious, global, miraculous changes will take place.

The human kingdoms will change. Isaiah, the prince of the prophets, prophesied: "And it shall come to pass in the last days, that the mountain of the Lord's house shall be established in the top of the mountains, and shall be exalted above the hills; and all nations shall flow unto it. And many people shall go and say, Come ye, and let us go up to the mountain of the LORD, to the house of the God of Jacob; and he will teach us of his ways, and we will walk in his paths: for out of Zion shall go forth the law, and the word of the LORD from Jerusalem. And He shall judge among the nations, and shall rebuke many people: and they shall beat their swords into plowshares, and their spears into pruninghooks: nation shall not lift up sword against nation, neither shall they learn war any more" (Isaiah 2:2–4 KJV).

The animal kingdom will change. Once again Isaiah prophesied: "The wolf also shall dwell with the lamb, and the leopard shall lie down with the kid; and the calf and the young lion and the fatling together; and a little child shall lead them. And the cow and the bear shall feed; their young ones shall lie down together: and the lion shall eat straw like the ox. And the sucking child shall play on the hole of the asp, and the weaned child shall put his hand on the cockatrice' den. They shall not hurt nor destroy in all my holy mountain: for the earth shall be full of the knowledge of the LORD, as the waters cover the sea" (Isaiah 11:6–9 KJV).

The plant and mineral kingdoms will change. About the King's reign, Isaiah said, "The wilderness and the solitary place shall be glad for them; and the desert shall rejoice, and blossom as the rose" (Isaiah 35:1 KJV). The Sahara Desert will be a veritable garden abloom with every imaginable flowering plant.

The First Resurrection

Revelation 20 tells us that there will be a first resurrection. This is not a general resurrection, as some believe. "Blessed and holy are those who have part in the first resurrection." What is the first resurrection? The Bible gives us the analogy that the first resurrection is like a harvest, which has three general aspects.

The firstfruits. In the Old Testament, when the harvest ripened the priest went into the field and gathered a sheaf of first-ripened grain. Then he took that sheaf into the temple and waved it before the Lord. It was called a wave offering. He would say something like: "Thank you, Lord, for this sheaf of wheat, for we believe it is a promise of the harvest to come."

In the New Testament, Christ is called the firstfruits. First Corinthians 15:20–23 says, "But now Christ has been raised from the dead, the first-fruits of those who have fallen asleep. For since death came through a man, the resurrection of the dead also comes through a man. For just as in Adam all die, so also in Christ all will be made alive. But each in his own order: Christ, the firstfruits; afterward, at His coming, the people of Christ."

When Jesus arose from the grave, He became the firstfruits. His resurrection demonstrated that a harvest would come. As a matter of fact, Matthew tells us that when Jesus breathed His last on the cross and the veil of the temple was torn from top to bottom, "the tombs also were opened and many bodies of the saints who had gone to their rest were raised. And they came out of the tombs after His resurrection, entered the holy city, and appeared to many" (Matthew 27:52–53). These saints were also considered part of the firstfruits in the first resurrection.

The general harvest. When Christ comes again, He will rapture the church. This is considered the general ingathering of the harvest. First Thessalonians tells us: "For the Lord Himself will descend from heaven with a shout, with the archangel's voice, and with the trumpet of God, and the dead in Christ will rise first. Then we who are still alive will be caught up together with them in the clouds to meet the Lord in the air; and so we will always be with the Lord" (1 Thessalonians 4:16–17).

The gleanings. The third phase of the harvest is the gleaning, which will be the resurrection of the tribulation saints—many of whom will be beheaded for Christ. These are the ones referred to in Revelation 20:4: "Then I saw thrones, and people seated on them who were given authority to judge. I also saw the souls of those who had been beheaded because of their testimony about Jesus and because of God's word, who had not worshiped the beast or his image, and who had not accepted the mark on their foreheads or their hands. They came to life and reigned with the Messiah for 1,000 years."

The Rulers with Christ

Other than the Lord Jesus, who will rule during the millennium? Not angels. There is a world to come, but the angels are not in charge of it. Hebrews 2:5 tells us, "He has not subjected to angels the world to come that we are talking about."

Paul said, "Do you not know that the saints will judge the world? And if the world is judged by you, are you unworthy to judge the smallest cases? Do you not know that we will judge angels—not to speak of things pertaining to this life?" (1 Corinthians 6:2–3). This passage not only has application in the reign and rule of Christ and His saints during the Golden Age, but it also has application for us today. If the church will have the future responsibility of judging angels, doesn't it make sense that we can resolve problems in the church today?

Romans 16:20 promises: "The God of peace will soon crush Satan under your feet." Won't it be a wonderful day when the criminal is in prison, Israel is back in her land, the bride is with the bridegroom, and the King is on His throne? That will indeed be the Golden Age.

The Final Rebellion of Sinners

Just when we think we have it made with Satan bound in the bottomless pit, he comes forth again. But it is not a jailbreak. He is released. God, who is always sovereign, allows Satan to have one final fling. Why? It is God's final test of mankind. Revelation 20:7–9 says: "When the 1,000 years are completed, Satan will be released from his prison and will go out to deceive the nations at the four corners of the earth, Gog and Magog, to gather them for battle. Their number is like the sand of the sea. They came up over the surface of the earth and surrounded the encampment of the saints, the beloved city [Jerusalem]. Then fire came down from heaven and consumed them" (explanatory note added by the author).

You may ask at this point, "Won't everyone be saved during the millennium?" No. During the Golden Age, Jesus will rule the nations with a rod of iron, but something will happen. Hearts will turn, but it will not be because Satan will lead a rebellious uprising. But latent in the human heart, men will covet sin that has not been washed by the precious blood of the Lord.

People will have children during the millennium. And when they have children, many of these children will not repent and believe upon Jesus Christ as their Savior and Lord. God has millions of children, but He has no *grand*children. Just because one generation is Christian doesn't mean the next generation will be.

When God lets Satan out of the bottomless pit, He is demonstrating to the world two great principles.

Man's Solution Is Not the Final Answer

Punishment is not the answer. When God releases him, Satan will have been in the prison doing hard time for one thousand years. In His divine wisdom, God knows that punishment is not the answer. And I agree—prisons are necessary, but they are not the final answer.

Changing the environment is not the answer. Many people think if you can change the environment, you can change the nature of man. Do you really believe that? If you do, let me tell you something. It was in the Garden of Eden that man got into trouble in the first place, was it not? Where will you find a more perfect environment than the Garden of Eden? Make your environment as good as you can, but after one thousand years of peace and righteousness, there will always be sin in the human heart.

The criminologist and his prisons are not the answer. The sociologist and his programs are not the answer. The educator and his philosophies will not solve the problem of sin. The statesman and his politics are not our hope either. Only Jesus is the answer.

Only Jesus Is the Answer

I read years ago that excavators opened the tomb of one of the Egyptian pharaohs who had been dead for thousands of years. Inside the tomb, they found some wheat and decided to conduct an experiment.

They put those grains of wheat into the right environment with moisture and warm sun, and those grains of wheat that had laid there for thousands of years began to sprout! Isn't that amazing? Thousands of years.

That is the way it is with sin in the human heart. Our salvation is never from within us, because we have only the seeds of sin in our hearts. Our salvation can come only from without. "For God, who said, 'Light shall shine out of darkness'—He has shone in our hearts to give the light of the knowledge of God's glory in the face of Jesus Christ. Now we have this treasure in clay jars, so that this extraordinary power may be from God and not from us" (2 Corinthians 4:6–7).

There is only one answer to sin—and it is the precious blood of the Lord Jesus Christ. John 14:6 says, "Jesus told him, 'I am the way, the truth, and the life. No one comes to the Father except through Me.'"

The Fixed Resolution of Sin

Many people may be asking at this point: "Can we ever say good-bye to sin?" Here is the answer: "They came up over the surface of the earth and surrounded the encampment of the saints, the beloved city. Then fire came down from heaven and consumed them. The Devil who deceived them was thrown into the lake of fire and sulfur where the beast and the false prophet are, and they will be tormented day and night forever and ever" (Revelation 20:9–10).

God lets Satan loose *only for a season.* Then God will end Satan's reign of terror by ultimately casting him and his demonic rebels into an eternal lake of fire. Jesus said that the everlasting fire is prepared for "the Devil and his angels" (Matthew 25:41). With compassion in my heart for your eternal destiny, let me say that if you reject Christ and follow Satan, the eternal lake of fire waits for you. Why follow a loser?

First Corinthians 15:24–25 says, "Then comes the end, when He hands over the kingdom to God the Father, when He abolishes all rule and all authority and power. For He must reign until He puts all His enemies under His feet." What application can we make from this truth for our lives?

First, it should provide *encouragement.* The gospel has not failed. We are not postmillennialists who are trying to make the world better so Jesus can come. We are not rearranging the deck chairs on the *Titanic.* We are telling people about the lifeboat, whose name is Jesus.

Second, this truth brings *anticipation.* Jesus Christ can come at any moment. Jesus said, "This is why you also should get ready, because the Son of Man is coming at an hour you do not expect" (Matthew 24:44). Over and over again the Bible tells us about the imminent return of the Lord Jesus Christ.

Third, this truth puts our focus on *evangelism.* The great proof that you believe what I have written is not that you highlighted any text or wrote notes in the margins of this book, but that God's truth has taken root deep within your heart. Is there a passion in your heart to bring people to Jesus Christ so they might be saved? Do you have the heart of a soul winner? If not, ask God to give you one.

Finally, this truth challenges us to do an *examination* of our lives. Do you *know* that you *know* that you are saved? Are you sure you are saved? Your soul is too precious for you to play loosely with it. If you are not sure, I have good news for you—Jesus can save you today. There is nothing to buy; it is a gift. There is nothing to earn; it is a gift. Ephesians 2:8–9 says, "For by grace you are saved through faith, and this is not from yourselves; it is God's gift—not from works, so that no one can boast."

Grace is God reaching down to you and saying, "I love you. I sent My Son to die for you. I want to save you. Here is My hand of grace reaching down to you." Faith is your hand reaching back up to God. When you put your hand of faith in God's hand of grace, that is when you are saved.

Revelation 20 tells us that there will be a forceful restraint of Satan, a future reign of the Savior, a final rebellion of sinners, and a fixed resolution of sin. Are you ready for the future?

A Guided Tour through Heaven

◄◌►

CHAPTER 27

◄◌►

Heaven is so much more than we can imagine. It is more than can be described in human terms—and certainly more than can be covered in one short chapter. It's like what happened when a woman visited Yosemite and asked one of the guides, "If you only had one hour to see Yosemite, what would you do?" The guide said, "Madam, if I had only one hour to see Yosemite, I would sit down on that rock and cry for an hour."

Has anyone ever made fun of you for believing in heaven? Perhaps they have said it is just "pie in the sky when you die." Well, I like pie. I am enjoying the main course down here, but I am looking forward to the pie in the sky called "heaven." Some people sneer and say Christians are so heavenly minded that they are no earthly good. May I suggest that it is just the opposite more times than not? Many Christians are so earthly minded they are no good to heaven or earth.

We have much to learn about being heavenly minded. Colossians 3:1–2 says, "So if you have been raised with the Messiah, seek what is above, where the Messiah is, seated at the right hand of God. Set your minds on what is above, not on what is on the earth." Jesus said, "Collect for yourselves treasures in heaven, where neither moth nor rust destroys, and where thieves don't break in and steal. For where your treasure is, there your heart will be also" (Matthew 6:20–21). It is not your treasure that God wants. God doesn't need anything. Instead, it is your heart that God wants.

John learned about that treasure in heaven when he received a guided tour from an angel. Let's eavesdrop on what he discovered: "Then one of the seven angels, who had held the seven bowls filled with the seven last plagues, came and spoke with me: 'Come, I will show you the bride, the wife of the Lamb.' He then carried me away in the Spirit to a great and high mountain and showed me the holy city, Jerusalem, coming down out of heaven from God" (Revelation 21:9–10).

The Geography of Heaven

Heaven is a real place. Heaven is not some mysterious, atmospheric realm of smoke and mirrors. Jesus said, "In My Father's house are many dwelling places; if not, I would have told you. I am going away to prepare a *place* for you. If I go away and prepare a *place* for you, I will come back and receive you to Myself, so that where I am you may be also" (John 14:2–3). Jesus did not say he was going to prepare a "state of mind."

Speaking of Abraham, the writer of Hebrews said, "By faith he stayed as a foreigner in the land of promise, living in tents with Isaac and Jacob, co-heirs of the same promise. For he was looking forward to the city that has foundations, whose architect and builder is God" (Hebrews 11:9–10). Abraham never built a house out of stone, brick, or mortar. He lived in tents because "he was looking forward to the city that has foundations, whose architect and builder is God" (Hebrews 11:10).

In addition to these things, we know heaven is a real place because the apostle Paul sojourned in heaven while he was still alive. This is the way he described it: "I knew a man in Christ above fourteen years ago, (whether in the body, I cannot tell; or whether out of the body, I cannot tell: God knoweth;) such an one caught up to the third heaven. And I knew such a man, (whether in the body, or out of the body, I cannot tell: God knoweth)" (2 Corinthians 12:2–3 KJV).

Paul said he was caught up to a third heaven, and he didn't know if he was in his body or his spirit. What does that tell me? You can go to heaven in your spirit or you can go to heaven with a body. Jesus is in heaven right now in His resurrected body. And one day every child of God will also have a resurrected body. So there must be a place where our literal bodies will dwell for eternity in the presence of God. It is called heaven. And it is a real place. Actually, it is *more real* than the town where you live. And if you have loved ones who have gone before you into glory, you can expect to see them in a real place called heaven.

John said, "I saw a new heaven and a new earth, for the first heaven and the first earth had passed away, and the sea existed no longer. I also saw the Holy City, new Jerusalem, coming down out of heaven from God, prepared like a bride adorned for her husband" (Revelation 21:1–2).

Why did John see a "new" heaven and a "new" earth? Because this present earth and its atmosphere will be burned. Second Peter 3:10–13 says:

> But the Day of the Lord will come like a thief; on that day the heavens will pass away with a loud noise, the elements will burn and be dissolved, and the earth and the works on it will be disclosed. Since all these things are to be destroyed in this way, it is clear what sort of people you should be in holy conduct and godliness as you wait for and earnestly desire the coming of the day of God, because of which the heavens will be on fire and be dissolved, and the elements will melt with the heat. But based on His promise, we wait for new heavens and a new earth, where righteousness will dwell.

God says that the earth is stored with fire. If you know much about the atomic nature of the universe, you know that everything has molecular fire in it. The atmosphere is stored with fire. Paper is stored with fire. Clothes are stored with fire. Carpets are stored with fire. The seat that you sit on in church is stored with fire. Everything is packed with fire. Earth has a molten core very much like the shell of an egg, packed with fire.

One of these days God will unleash the energy of the atom that He holds together by His mighty power, and the atmospheric heavens and the earth will dissolve under great heat. But they will still remain. How can that be? When God made the earth, He gave it an eternality. What will happen is this: God will melt the heavens and earth and take that material to create a new heaven and a new earth.

Think of this process as that which happens to an old automobile when it goes to the junkyard. They compact it and put it in a furnace. Then from this recycled material comes a new automobile. Did you know that the new automobile you are driving could be part of an old automobile that has gone through the furnace?

In 2 Peter and Revelation, the Greek word for "new" is *kainos*. It is the same word that is used when Paul said, "Therefore if anyone is in Christ, there is a *new* creation; old things have passed away, and look, *new* things have come" (2 Corinthians 5:17). I am the old Adrian made new. The old man did not evaporate and disappear, but I am transformed. My old nature has been purged by the blood of Jesus Christ, just as the old world and old heaven will be purged by fire and made new.

John says, "I also saw the Holy City, *new* Jerusalem, coming down out of heaven from God, prepared like a bride adorned for her husband" (Revelation 21:2). Is the Lord married to a city? No, allow me to illustrate. Normally when you talk of a city, you speak of the place or the people. But I might also say, "Memphis is a beautiful city." But I might also say, "Memphis is a friendly city." One time I am talking about the place, another time I am talking about the people. That is what God is doing here in the Book of Revelation.

The Government of Heaven

Heaven will be a majestic place because the King will rule there in majesty. In the Old Testament, God dwelt in a tabernacle, but now His dwelling place is with men. No longer do we pray, "Our Father, which art in heaven" (Matthew 6:9 KJV). Instead, He is right here with us. Revelation 21:3–8 says:

> Then I heard a loud voice from the throne: "Look! God's dwelling is with men, and He will live with them. They will be His people, and God Himself will be with them and be their God. He will wipe away every tear from their eyes. Death will exist no longer; grief, crying, and pain will exist no longer, because the previous things have passed away." Then the One seated on the throne said, "Look! I am making everything new." He also said, "Write, because these words are faithful and true." And He said to me, "It is done! I am the Alpha and the Omega, the Beginning and the End. I will give to the thirsty from the spring of living water as a gift. The victor will inherit these things, and I will be his God, and he will be My son. But the cowards, unbelievers, vile, murderers, sexually immoral, sorcerers, idolaters, and all liars—their share will be in the lake that burns with fire and sulfur, which is the second death."

When the Lord rules in majesty, there will be no more sorrow. I am looking forward to that. I have shed many tears and witnessed many tears.

My heart has been broken more times than I can count as I have stood by open graves, watched people in pain, and held the hands of parents who have wept over wayward children. In the ministry you see the best and the worst over and over again. Day after day, week after week the heart-wrenching news is heard and the tears flow.

A philosopher once said, "Man is the only creature that when he is born he can do nothing for himself except cry. It seems like we are born crying, we live crying, we die crying." But there is a time coming when God will turn every tear to a telescope, every hurt to a hallelujah, every Calvary to an Easter. There will be no more crying and no more dying. There will be no more funerals and no more disease. These things will be gone. And I am looking forward to it.

Have you ever wondered why there will be no more sorrow? Because there will be no more sin. Revelaton 21:27 says, "Nothing profane will ever enter it *[the heavenly city]:* no one who does what is vile or false, but only those written in the Lamb's book of life." Sin is ultimately behind every sorrow, sickness, or pain. Don't misquote me here. I am *not* saying that if you are sick, then you have unconfessed sin in your life. It may be true, or it may *not* be true. I am saying that we live in a world that has the curse of sin on it.

When our little boy Philip went to glory, Joyce and I turned to the Lord and renewed our devotion to Him, because we needed Him so much in our sorrow. Before that tragedy in our lives, I had regularly gone to the hospital to witness to patients. During one of my rounds, I met an elderly man who was very cynical toward God. Day after day, I witnessed to this man and tried to win him to Christ.

After Philip's funeral, I went to the hospital to witness once again to this elderly man. Somehow he had learned about Philip's death, and he asked me, "What are you doing here?"

"I came to see you," I replied.

"Are you still serving God after what He did to you?"

"I am not bitter at God," I told him, "but do you know who I am bitter at? I am bitter at Satan. He has a greater enemy in me today than ever, because I know behind all the sickness, sorrow, pain, suffering, and death is sin."

The Glory of Heaven

Revelation 21:9–21 says:

> Then one of the seven angels, who had held the seven bowls filled with the seven last plagues, came and spoke with me: "Come, I will show you the bride, the wife of the Lamb. "He then carried me away in the Spirit to a great and high mountain and showed me the holy city, Jerusalem, coming down out of heaven from God, arrayed with God's glory. Her radiance was like a very precious stone, like a jasper stone, bright as crystal. The city had a massive high wall, with 12 gates. Twelve angels were at the gates; on the gates, names were inscribed, the names of the 12 tribes of the sons of Israel. There were three gates on the east, three gates on the north, three gates on the south, and three gates on the west. The city wall had 12 foundations, and on them were the 12 names of the Lamb's 12 apostles. The one who spoke with me had a gold measuring rod to measure the city, its gates, and its wall. The city is laid out in a square; its length and width are the same. He measured the city with the rod at 12,000 stadia. Its length, width, and height are equal. Then he measured its wall, 144 cubits according to human measurement, which the angel used. The building material of its wall was jasper, and the city was pure gold like clear glass. The foundations of the city wall were adorned with every kind of precious stone: the first foundation jasper, the second sapphire, the third chalcedony, the fourth emerald, the fifth sardonyx, the sixth carnelian, the seventh chrysolite, the eighth beryl, the ninth topaz, the tenth chrysoprase, the eleventh jacinth, the twelfth amethyst. The 12 gates are 12 pearls; each individual gate was made of a single pearl. The broad street of the city was pure gold, like transparent glass.

How does one describe the glory of heaven? It's impossible to do because of our limited understanding, but God goes through the lexicons of the world and takes the things that we say are indescribably beautiful and uses them as symbolic prophecy of the greater glories of heaven.

The Source of the City

The city will come down from God (see Revelation 21:9–10). If it is going to come down from God, the city is already in heaven. It is a place where, for example, the firstfruits of the resurrected dead are already present. Jesus said in John 14:2 that when He returned to the Father, He would prepare a place for His children. That place is now prepared in heaven.

The Sights of the City

There is no need for the sun, moon, and stars in the heavenly city, because it shines with the glory of God. Imagine the brilliance and glow of the colored jewels of vibrant green, sky blue, crimson red, shining gold, deep violet, and more. The gold is so pure that it is translucent.

The walls and gates in this city of gold are breathtakingly beautiful. "But why are there walls in the heavenly city?" you may ask. They are not there to keep us in, because the gates are open. The walls are not there to keep the wicked out, because they are in hell. The walls are for the glory of God. In a sense, they are monumental walls engraved with the names of the twelve tribes of Israel and the twelve apostles (see Revelation 21:12–14). There is coming a time when Jew and Gentile will be together. There is coming a time when we will be one in the Lord Jesus Christ in a wonderful way.

The Sounds of the City

If Jew and Gentile are together, what will be our song? Revelation 15:3 says, "They sang the song of God's servant Moses, and the song of the Lamb: 'Great and awe-inspiring are Your works, Lord God, the Almighty; righteous and true are Your ways, King of the Nations.'" Our Jewish friends look to Moses, while Christians look to Jesus. But in heaven we will sing the song of redemption together.

I heard Dr. R. G. Lee, former pastor of Bellevue Baptist Church, say, "Our best music here on earth will sound like a bumble bee in a bottle compared to the music that will be there." Won't it be wonderful to praise the Lord forever and ever?

The Size of the City

In Revelation 21:15–16 we learn that the city is foursquare and measures twelve thousand furlongs. Do you know how far that is? Each furlong equals one-eighth of a mile, so the perimeter of New Jerusalem is 1,500 miles. Since Revelation tells us that the new Jerusalem is laid out like a square, then each side is approximately 375 miles long. So the new Jerusalem will have an area of about 140,625 square miles, or 90 million acres.

Another possibility is that each side of the city is approximately fifteen hundred miles long. You can be certain there will be sufficient space for all of the redeemed.

The foursquare reminds me of the Holy of Holies in the temple, which measured twenty cubits square. The high priest did not need any more than that, because when he went inside to worship the Lord and put the blood on the mercy seat, he was in there alone with God.

Have you ever heard someone say that there won't be room in heaven for all the people who have ever lived? Now that you have a better picture of the area of new Jerusalem, you can see that the ground floor in heaven will have room for a hundred billion, and everybody will have his own ranch. Heaven will be a magnificently glorious place.

The Sanctuary of the City

The Old Testament temple was a prophetic picture of the Lord Jesus Christ. It had a gate; Jesus is the door (see John 10:7–9). It had an altar; Jesus shed His blood for us. It had a laver; we are now cleansed by His Word (see Revelation 1:5). It had a table with bread on it; Jesus is the Bread of Life (see John 6:35). It had a golden candelabra; Jesus is the light of the world (see John 8:12). Incense was burned; Jesus is our high priest (see Hebrews 4:14–15). He is the temple. Remember, this book is about the revelation of Jesus Christ.

What will we do when we reach those gates of gold? The same thing I do when I come home from a long trip and walk through the front door. I run over and hug the television and kiss the lamp. No, I don't do that. I head for my bride. She is the one I want to see. I am grateful for the streets of gold and walls of jasper, but it is Jesus who makes heaven the place for which I long. It will be worth it all when we see Jesus!

The Godliness of Heaven

Revelation 21:24–27 says, "The nations will walk in its light, and the kings of the earth will bring their glory into it. Each day its gates will never close because it will never be night there. They will bring the glory and honor of the nations into it. Nothing profane will ever enter it: no one who does what is vile or false, but only those written in the Lamb's book of life."

Who is going to populate heaven? Every little aborted baby, the saints of all the ages, and believers from every nation in the world. But no one is going to be there above the age of accountability who has not received Jesus Christ as his or her personal Savior and Lord. The old song says, "Everybody who's talking about heaven ain't going there." Heaven is a "made-new" prepared place for a "made-new" prepared people. Second Corinthians 5:17 says, "Therefore if anyone is in Christ, there is a new creation; old things have passed away, and look, new things have come."

A man dreamed that he stood outside the gates of heaven and saw people trying to get inside. One man knocked at the gate, and a voice within asked, "Who seeks entrance into heaven?" And the man said, "I am a humanitarian." And the voice asked, "What is the password?" He replied, "The password is *charity*." The voice within said, "Depart from me, ye that work iniquity; I never knew you."

Another man knocked. "Who seeks entrance into heaven?" He said, "I am a moral man." The voice asked, "What is the password?" He replied, "It is *honesty*." The voice said, "Depart from me, ye that work iniquity; I never knew you."

Another knock, and the voice asked, "Who seeks entrance into heaven?" He said, "I am a religious man." And the voice asked again, "What is the password?" The man answered, *"Ritual."* The voice within said, "Depart from me, ye that work iniquity; I never knew you."

The last man stepped up to the gate and knocked. The voice within asked, "Who seeks entrance into heaven and what is the password?" And the man said, *"In my hand no price I bring, simply to Thy cross I cling."* And the voice within said, "Open wide the gate and let him in, for of such is the kingdom of heaven."

Have you ever honestly trusted Jesus? Have you come to Him all alone—not trusting in your humanitarianism, charity, religion, or church membership, but trusting only in His shed blood?

The Gladness of Heaven

Revelation 22:1–5 says:

Then he showed me the river of living water, sparkling like crystal, flowing from the throne of God and of the Lamb down the middle of the broad street of the city. On both sides of the river was the tree of life bearing 12 kinds of fruit, producing its fruit every month. The leaves of the tree are for healing the nations, and there will no longer be any curse. The throne of God and of the Lamb will be in the city, and His servants will serve Him. They will see His face, and His name will be on their foreheads. Night will no longer exist, and people will not need lamplight or sunlight, because the Lord God will give them light. And they will reign forever and ever.

A Place of Satisfaction

What are we going to see when we go down the main street of heaven? Satisfied people—because they are drinking from the crystal river symbolizing where our deepest needs will be met. Revelation 22:17 says, "Both the Spirit and the bride say, 'Come!' Anyone who hears should say, 'Come!' And the one who is thirsty should come. Whoever desires should take the living water as a gift." Every God-given thirst will be satisfied in heaven.

A Place of Sufficiency

There are trees in heaven with ever-ripening fruit "for healing the nations." The Greek word for "healing" is *therapeia,* which is the word from which we get our English word *therapeutic.* The glow of health will be on everyone in heaven.

A Place of Service

Revelation 22:3 reminds us that "His servants will serve Him." You will serve God like you have never served Him before. Who knows what God has for us to do when we get to heaven?

A Place of Sight

Revelation 22:4 tells us that we will see the face of Jesus. Our Lord prayed, "Father, I desire those You have given Me to be with Me where I am. Then they may see My glory, which You have given Me because You loved Me before the world's foundation" (John 17:24).

I received the following letter from one of the viewers of our television ministry:

Dear Adrian Rogers:

I hope you are doing very well. I just wanted to write you a few lines for the first time to tell you how much I enjoy your sermons. Your presentations are so plain and easy to understand.

I accepted Christ as my Savior about two years ago. Since then I have read the entire Bible three times, taken eight Bible study courses, mostly through mail. I have not been watching your program very long, but ever since I first listened to you on Sunday morning, I sit waiting for your program with my Bible and pen and paper.

You see, I can't do much anymore. God is my strength and salvation every day. Praise the Lord. I am an inmate in the state penitentiary on death row. I look forward to that great and glorious day when Christ comes to take His saints up into heaven. I got my dad listening to your show also. He even records them. I just wanted to give my thanks to you for all your wonderful preaching. With all my heart I say thank you.

I wrote him back and said, "Friend, you are not on death row. You are on life row, because Jesus said, 'Everyone who lives and believes in Me will never die'" (John 11:26).

Aren't you glad for a gospel that could take a poor, lost sinner who deserves hell and save him by His glorious grace and take him to heaven? What God has done for this man on death row, He will do for you.

The Lamb Has Overcome

◄o►

CHAPTER 28

◄o►

L ast words are very important. And the last words of the Bible are no exception. God's words are crisp and concise as He sums up this prophetic book that deals with the doom of the devil, the destiny of the dead, the mystery of history, and the triumph of the Lamb, the Lord Jesus Christ.

The Bible's Last Prophecy
Predicts the Savior's Sudden Return

Revelation 22:6 says, "Then he said to me, 'These words are faithful and true. And the Lord, the God of the spirits of the prophets, has sent His angel to show His servants what must quickly take place.'" Then the Lord Jesus said, "Look, I am coming quickly! Blessed is the one who keeps the prophetic words of this book" (Revelation 22:7). In essence, Jesus said, "Look! Listen! I am coming quickly, and I will bless all those who believe in the prophecies of Revelation." That is an ironclad promise from the Lord Jesus Christ.

John was overcome with emotion over what he had seen and heard. Revelation 22:8–9 tells us: "I, John, am the one who heard and saw these things. When I heard and saw them, I fell down to worship at the feet of the angel who had shown them to me. But he said to me, 'Don't do that! I am a fellow slave with you, your brothers the prophets, and those who keep the words of this book. Worship God.'" The angel made it very clear to John that God is the only one who can be worshiped.

Then the angel said to John, "Don't seal the prophetic words of this book, because the time is near. Let the unrighteous go on in unrighteousness; let the filthy go on being made filthy; let the righteous go on in right-eousness; and let the holy go on being made holy" (Revelation 22:10–11).

Then Jesus answered, "Look! I am coming quickly, and My reward is with Me to repay each person according to what he has done. I am the Alpha and the Omega, the First and the Last, the Beginning and the End" (Revelation 22:12–13).

The Greek word *tachu* for our English translation "quickly" does not mean that Jesus is coming immediately, though it could be immediate. A better translation is that He is coming back *suddenly*. First Corinthians 15:52 says that He is coming "in a moment, in the twinkling of an eye." And from what I have read in biology books, the twinkling of the eye occurs in one-trillionth of a second! Matthew 24:27 tells us, "For as the lightning comes from the east and flashes as far as the west, so will be the coming of the Son of Man." Light travels at 186,000 miles per second!

It is a fact. Jesus is coming back. Are you ready for His return? Revelation 22:10–12 tells us that our destiny is determined by what we've done with Him before He comes. How foolish not to be ready for His coming! The writer of Hebrews gives us this exhortation: "Today if you hear His voice, do not harden your hearts" (Hebrews 4:7). And, "Look, now is the acceptable time; look, now is the day of salvation" (2 Corinthians 6:2).

Let's look at three words in that last verse: *now, time,* and *day.* We are living in the space of time. The word *now* speaks of the present time. When your eternity begins after death, you will not have another chance to be saved. Now is the time. Then Paul mentions the day. One of these days there will be no more days. If you want to be saved, you can be saved, but you must remember your hope is made secure *today*—not *tomorrow* because tomorrow may never come.

Jesus said: "I am the Alpha and the Omega, the First and the Last, the Beginning and the End" (Revelation 22:13). As I mentioned in chapter 3 of this book, alpha and omega are the first and last letters of the Greek alphabet. Jesus is the first ray of hope in the Book of Genesis, and He is the last warning in the Book of Revelation. It is all about Jesus. Every page of Revelation is filled with prophecies about the second coming of Jesus Christ. Don't get the idea that I'm talking about something incidental. I'm talking about the major message of this book. Jesus has come, and He is coming again!

The Bible's Last Proposal Is For
The Sinner's Sure Redemption

Jesus proposes to you so that you can choose Him. Revelation 22:14–17 says:

> Blessed are those who wash their robes, so that they may have the right to the tree of life and may enter the city by the gates. Outside are the dogs, the sorcerers, the sexually immoral, the murderers, the idolaters, and everyone who loves and practices lying. "I, Jesus, have sent My angel to attest these things to you for the churches. I am the Root and the Offspring of David, the Bright Morning Star." Both the Spirit and the bride say, "Come!" Anyone who hears should say, "Come!" And the one who is thirsty should come. Whoever desires should take the living water as a gift.

This Is a Saving Word

Jesus is saying, "I am David's descendant and yet at the same time, I am the One who created David. I am the Messiah about whom David spoke. I am the Bright and Morning Star. Do you want to be saved? My word says, 'Whoever desires.'"

Revelation 22:14 presupposes that truth: "Blessed are they that do his commandments, that they may have right to the tree of life, and may enter in through the gates into the city" (KJV). The HCSB translates that text to read: "Blessed are those who wash their robes." The reason is that when you obey His commandments, you wash your robes and vice versa. He is talking here about being washed clean of your sin in the blood of the Lamb.

I've heard people say, "I'm a dyed-in-the-wool Baptist [or Methodist, Presbyterian, Church of Christ]." I have only one response to that: You had better be a washed-in-the-blood Baptist, Methodist, Presbyterian, or whatever. There is only one way to be saved—and that is through the shed blood of the Lord Jesus Christ. Had there been any other way to be saved, God would have taken it. He would never have allowed His Son to die in agony on the cross if there had been another way.

This Is a Seeking Word

Revelation 22:17 contains one of the most appealing invitations in the Bible: "Both the Spirit and the bride say, 'Come!' Anyone who hears should say, 'Come!' And the one who is thirsty should come. Whoever desires should take the living water as a gift."

Who cares if a sinner goes to hell? The Lord Jesus cares. Jesus said, "I sent a message to an angel, and I told that angel to go to the churches and give them this message. I want them saved." The Lord Jesus cares. That is why Jesus stepped out of the glories of heaven and walked the dusty shores of Galilee. That is why Jesus left heaven's love for earth's abuse. That is why Jesus was nailed to that hellish instrument called a cross and died in agony. Why? With every drop of His blood He was saying, "I love you, and I want to save you." If you die and go to hell, you will have to climb over the battered, bruised body of Jesus to get there while He shouts, "Stop! Don't go to hell."

This verse tells us that not only God the Son seeks, but God the Spirit seeks as well. Who is the Spirit? The apostles said, "We are witnesses of these things, and so is the Holy Spirit whom God has given to those who obey Him" (Acts 5:32). I would rather die than preach without the conscious anointing and assurance of the Holy Spirit speaking through me. I am nothing without God's Spirit.

As you are reading this book, another voice is speaking to you. It is the Holy Spirit of God. Speaking of the Holy Spirit, Jesus said, "When He comes, He will convict the world about sin, righteousness, and judgment: about sin, because they do not believe in Me; about righteousness, because I am going to the Father and you will no longer see Me; and about judgment, because the ruler of this world has been judged" (John 16:8–11). Who cares if you go to hell? Jesus cares. Who also cares if you go to hell? The Holy Spirit. And there is yet someone else who cares—the church of the Lord Jesus Christ.

Revelation 22:17 tells us that the bride of Christ also invites us to come. And this bride is not only here on earth, but also in heaven. Those in heaven are looking down and saying, "Come up here and be with us." Hebrews 12:1 says, "Therefore since we also have such a large cloud of witnesses surrounding us, let us lay aside every weight and the sin that so easily ensnares us, and run with endurance the race that lies before us."

Life is like a relay race. Saints in heaven are those who have run before us, and now they have placed the baton in our hand. I received it from Peter, James, Paul, and Andrew. The baton is in my hand, and I am running with it. What a thrill to think that we are one with the saints, the bride in heaven and earth!

What is the purpose of this church? It is evangelism. While I like a worship service, I never worship more than when souls are being saved. That is what church is all about. Why did Jesus come? Luke 19:10 says, "The Son of Man has come to seek and to save the lost." What is the Great Commission of the church? We are to make disciples. And a church that is not winning souls, making disciples, and serving in missions is not worthy of the ground upon which the building sits. A church exists by evangelism like a fire exists by burning.

The Lord Jesus cares if a sinner goes to hell. God the Spirit cares if a sinner goes to hell. And this church cares. Do you know who else should care? Everyone who hears this message. Revelation 22:17 says, "Anyone who hears should say, 'Come.'" When you hear the gospel of the Lord Jesus Christ, you have a solemn obligation to share that message.

There are two words in the Bible that summarize this message. The first word is "come" and the second word is "go." Come to Jesus, and go tell! How dare we be silent! How dare we say that we have the message of eternal life and not share that message with others. If you have heard it (and you have in this book), then you ought to invite someone else. People are waiting for you to invite them to hear about the Lord Jesus. Not everyone will come. Some will harden their hearts. But if you tell me that everyone is not interested, do you know what that tells me? You are not sharing. There are a lot of hungry people out there waiting to hear the message of the Lord Jesus Christ. Every person who loves Jesus and is filled with the Holy Spirit cares if a sinner goes to hell. This is the Bible's last proposal. It is to come to the Lord Jesus Christ.

The gospel is so simple. It is like drinking a glass of water. And we all know that you don't need a Ph.D. to do that. And it's free! You don't have to pay one cent for it. Take and drink. That is the reason I call this point "a satisfying choice." Your heart's deepest thirst will never be satisfied until it is satisfied with Jesus. I promise you, on the authority of this Word of God, that Jesus will save and satisfy you.

Some people ask me, "What if I am not one of the elect?" Let me answer that question this way. God says, "Whosoever." Instead, what if God said, "Come, Adrian Rogers, take and drink"? I still might not be sure if I were one of the elect, for there could be more than one Adrian Rogers in the world. What if God said, "Come, Adrian Pierce Rogers, take and drink"? Again, there might be another Adrian Pierce Rogers. What if God said, "Adrian Pierce Rogers, born in West Palm Beach, Florida, come, take and drink"? Well, there could be another Adrian Pierce Rogers born in West Palm Beach, Florida. What if God said, "Adrian Pierce Rogers, born in West Palm Beach, Florida, who now lives in Shelby County, Tennessee, come, take and drink"? Well, I think you can see where I am going with this kind of rationale.

Let me answer the question about the elect right now with God's Word. The elect are "whoever desires." Do you want to be saved? Come and drink! Jesus is reaching out His nail-pierced hands to you and saying, "Come." Jesus says come. The Spirit says come. The bride says come. The individual says come.

The Bible's Last Proclamation
Declares the Scripture's Settled Revelation

The Bible prohibits anyone from revising the Holy Scriptures. Jesus said, "I testify to everyone who hears the prophetic words of this book: If anyone adds to them, God will add to him the plagues that are written in this book. And if anyone takes away from the words of this prophetic book, God will take away his share of the tree of life and the holy city, written in this book" (Revelation 22:18–19).

The urge to revise the Bible is as old as the Garden of Eden when the serpent came to Eve and said, "Hath God said?" (see Genesis 3). Anybody who puts a question mark after the Word of God is doing the work of the devil. We play so loosely with the Bible. I heard of a man who was presiding over a business meeting, and someone closed the meeting with a word from the Bible. When the man finished, the leader absentmindedly said, "Now if there are no additions or corrections, the Scriptures stand approved as read." The Scriptures always stand approved as read because they are the very Word of God.

"These words are faithful and true" (Revelation 22:6). Where have you heard the phrase "faithful and true" before? Jesus said, "And unto the angel of the church of the Laodiceans write; These things saith the Amen, the *faithful and true* witness, the beginning of the creation of God" (Revelation 3:14 KJV). Who is the faithful and true witness, the beginning of the creation of God? Jesus. In Revelation 22, Jesus called the Bible faithful and true. Jesus applied to Himself the same words that He applied to the Word. A man and his word may be different, but God and His Word are always the same.

There are sixty-six individual books in the Bible—thirty-nine in the Old Testament and twenty-seven in the New Testament. God's Word is eternal and immutable. Jesus said, "It is easier for heaven and earth to pass away than for one stroke of a letter in the law to drop out" (Luke 16:17). God's Word is our sustenance. Jesus said, "Man must not live on bread alone, but on every word that comes from the mouth of God" (Matthew 4:4). God's Word serves as our guide and teacher. "All Scripture is inspired by God and is profitable for teaching, for rebuking, for correcting, for training in righteousness, so that the man of God may be complete, equipped for every good work" (2 Timothy 3:16–17).

God's Word is settled and sealed. Don't add to it. Don't dilute it. Don't try to revise the Bible by making it politically correct. I had sooner take forked lightning in my hand than to revise the Word of God as some so-called scholars are doing today. How can these men tell us which part is inspired and which part is not inspired? It is *all* inspired! Every word of God is pure. The Bible is very clear. Be careful what you do with the Word of God. Don't fool with it. Proverbs 30:5–6 says, "Every word of God is pure: he is a shield unto them that put their trust in him. Add thou not unto his words, lest he reprove thee, and thou be found a liar" (KJV).

The Bible's Last Prayer
Voices the Saints' Supreme Request

Revelation 22:20–21 says, "He who testifies about these things says, 'Yes, I am coming quickly.' Amen! Come, Lord Jesus! The grace of the Lord Jesus be with all the saints. Amen." *Amen* means "let it be." I want you to imagine the scene in which John wrote Revelation so you can get the full impact of the Bible's last prayer.

He was working in the rock quarries on the Isle of Patmos. He had been persecuted and abused. He was all alone. The Lord Jesus appeared to John and said, "John, sit down and listen. I am going to reveal the future to you." Then all of the glories, warnings, and intrigue of the great Book of Revelation unfolded before his eyes and ears. The Spirit of God moved in his heart as he learned of a new heaven and a new earth. Then Jesus gave John one final warning: "Tell people not to change one iota or scintilla of this Revelation. And John, I am coming soon." John clapped his hands and said, "Amen! Come, Lord Jesus!"

A Blessed Hope

Do you long for Jesus to come? You ought to if you know what will happen in the future with Christ's second coming and His eventual reign over a new heaven and a new earth. This is the "blessed hope" to which Paul referred when he wrote: "Looking for that blessed hope, and the glorious appearing of the great God and our Savior Jesus Christ; who gave himself for us, that he might redeem us from all iniquity, and purify unto himself a peculiar people, zealous of good works" (Titus 2:13–14 KJV).

Many people in this world have no hope. Their medicine is getting more expensive as their body weakens from the venom of bitterness and resentment they have harbored for years. And the only thing they are looking forward to is dying! They are *hopeless*. Some people have a *false hope* because they hope in things that are not true. They don't believe in the precious Word of God, and they don't have the witness of the Holy Spirit. Others have an *uncertain hope*. They say, "What you're saying sounds good. I hope it is true." Did you know that the word *hope* in the Bible doesn't mean "maybe" or "perhaps." Instead, God's Word defines "hope" as rock-ribbed assurance and anticipation on the surety of the Word of God.

Let me illustrate what that means to me. When I was a little boy, my parents took Sunday afternoon drives with the family. My brother and I would sit in the back seat, and sometimes we would say, "Daddy, he touched me," or, "Mama, he did so and so." Before you knew it, we'd be in a squabble in the back seat. Have you ever done that? My dad, being a very resolute man, would say, "Boys, when we get home you're going to get a whipping."

My father's word was like the law of the Medes and the Persians—there was no argument. A whipping was to commence when we returned home. That was assurance, but it wasn't hope. I'm talking about the blessed hope of Christ's long-awaited return. Sometimes I ask myself if I really want Jesus to come. And I can honestly say that I do with all of my heart. Is Christ's return the desire of your heart?

A Unifying Hope

Some people who read the Book of Revelation get hung up on symbolism. Maybe you think I may have missed a symbolism or perhaps misinterpreted some minute details. I probably have, but I am not going to argue with you about it. Because the Lord's return is not only a blessed hope, it ought to be a unifying hope.

Johnny goes away to war, and the family waits for his return. One day they receive a message that he is safe and coming home. They are over-joyed with excitement! But on the day of his long-awaited arrival, you walk by the house and hear voices raised and see shaking fists. What are they arguing about? Someone thinks that Johnny is coming on a bus. Another thinks Johnny is coming on the train. Another says Johnny is coming on a plane. And still another thinks Johnny is renting a car. They are at one another's throats, and about that time the doorbell rings—and there stands Johnny. Does this sound familiar? As I have already told you, I don't want to be on the program committee; I want to be on the wel-coming committee. Maybe I cannot explain every detail in the Book of Revelation, but I can tell you that Jesus has gone up into glory and is com-ing again.

Dr. Robert G. Lee told the following story about his childhood on a farm. He said their farm was so poor that you couldn't raise an umbrella on it, much less a mortgage. One day, he and his mother were on the front porch of their farmhouse. She was sitting in a rocking chair, and he was on the floor with his head in his hands. He noticed his mother's hands were calloused and worn.

He said, "Mama, tell me about the happiest moment in your life." He thought she would tell him about the moment when his daddy, a tall six-footer with dark eyes, expressed his love to her. But she didn't tell him that. Perhaps she would tell him about the time when the moon spread over the little farm and there by the fence gate his daddy asked her to be his bride. But she didn't tell him that. Would she tell him about the day in that cabin in the corner of their little farm where they expressed their vows to each other and how they had kept those vows for more than fifty years until he went to heaven? But she didn't tell him that.

Finally, she said, "Son, you've asked a hard question. When all the men went off to the War Between the States, times got hard. We got our salt from the smokehouse floor and our tea from sassafras leaves. We made a substitute coffee from corn. And the women did the work. One day our family received word that my daddy had been killed in the war. Before his death, my mama didn't cry much, but after that I could hear her sob-bing in her pillow at night.

"One day, my mama was sitting on a porch, very much like this, and I was sitting at her feet, very much like you're sitting at my feet right now. She had a bowl of beans in her lap that she was stringing and snapping.

Suddenly, a figure appeared across the field. My mama turned to me and said, 'Elizabeth, I declare that man walks just like your daddy.' And she kept on snapping those beans. After a while, she said, 'Elizabeth, honey, that man looks like your daddy.' I said, 'Now, Mama, don't get all excited. You know Daddy's dead. Don't get all excited.'

"By that time the figure had started across the cotton field. My mother exclaimed, 'Elizabeth, that is your daddy!' She threw those beans in the air, gathered up her skirt, and ran across the field. My daddy had lost an arm in the war, but he was alive. My mother met him, and he put his other arm around her. They kissed and hugged and laughed. I ran my finger up his sleeve and felt that funny little knob where his arm used to be. Son, I believe that was the happiest day of my life."

Dr. Lee concluded this story with these words, "That day will pale into insignificance when the Lord Jesus Christ comes."

This great song by Jack Hayford and Steve Stone perfectly sums up this chapter and this book:

The storehouse is full beyond measure,
The presses burst forth with new wine,.
Your blessing is on us,
Your word filled with promise,
But one prayer fills this heart of mine:

Come on down, Lord Jesus, and take us away.
Come on down, Lord Jesus. could this be the day?
Even so, come quickly, Lord Jesus, we pray;
Come on down, Lord Jesus, come soon!

He said, "Let not your hearts be troubled,
Though hearts all around fail with fear.
I'm coming to take you,
I'll never forsake you;
Look up! for my coming is near!"

Come on down, Lord Jesus, and take us away.
Come on down, Lord Jesus. could this be the day?
Even so, come quickly, Lord Jesus, we pray.
Come on down, Lord Jesus, come soon.

Take us home, Lord Jesus, Your church upward bring
"Maranatha" the word that our lips gladly sing;
For we long to assemble before our great King;
Come on down, Lord Jesus, come soon!
Come on down, Lord Jesus, come soon!

Notes

1. Associated Press, January 6, 2002.
2. "Rescue the Perishing," Fanny Crosby, 1869.
3. Alcatraz is a thirteen-acre island off the coast of San Francisco. It served as a maximum-security, minimum-privilege penitentiary from 1934 to 1963. Devil's Island is an eight-square-mile outcropping of rock off the coast of French Guiana. It was a penal colony from 1852 to 1945 and home to France's worst criminals and political prisoners.
4. Peter Stoner, *Science Speaks* (Chicago: Moody Press, 1969), 106–107.
5. Copyright 1989, John W. Peterson Music Company. Unknown author. Arranged by Jan Willard.
6. All quotes are taken from Share International's Web site http://www.shareintl.org.
7. Information derived from the Digital Angel Web site http://www.digitalangel.net.
8. Information derived from the Applied Digital Solutions Web site http://www.adsx.com.
9. *Business Week Online,* March 21, 2002, correspondent Jane Black.
10. Information derived from http://www.marinelab.sarasota.fl.us/~mhenry/WREDTIDE.phtml.
11. http://www.utm.edu/research/iep/m/monism.htm.
12. Information derived from http://www.infoniagara.com/gateway.html.

228 Rog

Unveiling the End Times
In Our Time.

Rogers, Adrian